International Political Economy Series

General Editor: **Timothy M. Shaw**, Professor of Commonwealth Governance and Development, and Director of the Institute of Commonwealth Studies, School of Advanced Study, University of London

Titles include:

Hans Abrahamsson
UNDERSTANDING WORLD ORDER AND STRUCTURAL CHANGE
Poverty, Conflict and the Global Arena

Morten Bøås, Marianne H. Marchand and Timothy Shaw (*editors*)
THE POLITICAL ECONOMY OF REGIONS AND REGIONALISM

Sandra Braman (*editor*)
THE EMERGENT GLOBAL INFORMATION POLICY REGIME

James Busumtwi-Sam and Laurent Dobuzinskis
TURBULENCE AND NEW DIRECTION IN GLOBAL POLITICAL ECONOMY

Martin Doornbos
GLOBAL FORCES AND STATE RESTRUCTURING
Dynamics of State Formation and Collapse

INSTITUTIONALIZING DEVELOPMENT POLICIES AND RESOURCE STRATEGIES IN EASTERN AFRICA AND INDIA
Developing Winners and Losers

Bill Dunn
GLOBAL RESTRUCTURING AND THE POWER OF LABOUR

Myron J. Frankman
WORLD DEMOCRATIC FEDERALISM
Peace and Justice Indivisible

Barry K. Gills (*editor*)
GLOBALIZATION AND THE POLITICS OF RESISTANCE

Richard Grant and John Rennie Short (*editors*)
GLOBALIZATION AND THE MARGINS

Graham Harrison (*editor*)
GLOBAL ENCOUNTERS
International Political Economy, Development and Globalization

Patrick Hayden and Chamsy el-Ojeili (*editors*)
CONFRONTING GLOBALIZATION
Humanity, Justice and the Renewal of Politics

Axel Hülsemeyer (*editor*)
GLOBALIZATION IN THE TWENTY-FIRST CENTURY
Convergence or Divergence?

Helge Hveem and Kristen Nordhaug (*editors*)
PUBLIC POLICY IN THE AGE OF GLOBALIZATION
Responses to Environmental and Economic Crises

Takashi Inoguchi
GLOBAL CHANGE
A Japanese Perspective

Dominic Kelly and Wyn Grant (editors)
THE POLITICS OF INTERNATIONAL TRADE IN THE 21st CENTURY
Actors, Issues and Regional Dynamics

Mathias Koenig-Archibugi and Michael Zürn (editors)
NEW MODES OF GOVERNANCE IN THE GLOBAL SYSTEM
Exploring Publicness, Delegation and Inclusiveness

Craig N. Murphy (editor)
EGALITARIAN POLITICS IN THE AGE OF GLOBALIZATION

George Myconos
THE GLOBALIZATION OF ORGANIZED LABOUR
1945–2004

John Nauright and Kimberly S. Schimmel (editors)
THE POLITICAL ECONOMY OF SPORT

Morten Ougaard
THE GLOBALIZATION OF POLITICS
Power, Social Forces and Governance

Richard Robison (editor)
THE NEO-LIBERAL REVOLUTION
Forging the Market State

Leonard Seabrooke
US POWER IN INTERNATIONAL FINANCE
The Victory of Dividends

Timothy J. Sinclair and Kenneth P. Thomas (editors)
STRUCTURE AND AGENCY IN INTERNATIONAL CAPITAL MOBILITY

Fredrik Söderbaum and Timothy M. Shaw (editors)
THEORIES OF NEW REGIONALISM

Susanne Soederberg, Georg Menz and Philip G. Cerny (editors)
INTERNALIZING GLOBALIZATION

International Political Economy Series
Series Standing Order ISBN 0–333–71708–2 hardcover
Series Standing Order ISBN 0–333–71110–6 paperback
(*outside North America only*)

You can receive future titles in this series as they are published by placing a standing
order. Please contact your bookseller or, in case of difficulty, write to us at the address
below with your name and address, the title of the series and one of the ISBNs quoted
above.

Customer Services Department, Macmillan Distribution Ltd, Houndmills, Basingstoke,
Hampshire RG21 6XS, England

Global Forces and State Restructuring

Dynamics of State Formation and Collapse

Martin Doornbos

© Martin Doornbos 2006

All rights reserved. No reproduction, copy or transmission of this publication may be made without written permission.

No paragraph of this publication may be reproduced, copied or transmitted save with written permission or in accordance with the provisions of the Copyright, Designs and Patents Act 1988, or under the terms of any licence permitting limited copying issued by the Copyright Licensing Agency, 90 Tottenham Court Road, London W1T 4LP.

Any person who does any unauthorized act in relation to this publication may be liable to criminal prosecution and civil claims for damages.

The author has asserted his right to be identified as the author of this work in accordance with the Copyright, Designs and Patents Act 1988.

First published in 2006 by
PALGRAVE MACMILLAN
Houndmills, Basingstoke, Hampshire RG21 6XS and
175 Fifth Avenue, New York, N.Y. 10010
Companies and representatives throughout the world.

PALGRAVE MACMILLAN is the global academic imprint of the Palgrave Macmillan division of St. Martin's Press, LLC and of Palgrave Macmillan Ltd. Macmillan® is a registered trademark in the United States, United Kingdom and other countries. Palgrave is a registered trademark in the European Union and other countries.

ISBN-13: 978-1-4039-9682-4 hardback
ISBN-10: 1-4039-9682-2 hardback

This book is printed on paper suitable for recycling and made from fully managed and sustained forest sources.

A catalogue record for this book is available from the British Library.

Library of Congress Cataloging-in-Publication Data

Doornbos, Martin R.
    Global forces and state restructuring : dynamics of state formation and collapse / Martin Doornbos.
        p. cm.—(International political economy series)
    Includes bibliographical references and index.
    ISBN 1-4039-9682-2 (cloth : alk. paper)
        1. State, The. 2. Globalization. I. Title. II. International political economy series (Palgrave Macmillan (Firm)).
JC11.D667 2006
320.1—dc22   2005055278

10 9 8 7 6 5 4 3 2
15 14 13 12 11 10 09 08 07

Printed and bound in Great Britain by
Antony Rowe Ltd, Chippenham and Eastbourne

Contents

Preface

This book's coverage may appear broad and wide-ranging, yet its focus is actually quite specific. Its central objective and interest is to explore and better understand the dynamics of state restructuring, state collapse and state formation in the contemporary global and globalizing context. I have sought to do this on the basis not only of conceptual and policy discussion but of experiences from widely different situations and where possible by juxtaposing these with historical parallels. Themes addressed include strategies of state construction and trajectories of state decline, collapse and re-start, as well as the politics of statelessness and the dynamics of identity and power. Particular attention has been given to externally orchestrated state restructuring and the varying capacities of state systems in the South to cope with the impact of global forces.

The study has drawn its stimulation from a highly diverse range of engagements, though basic to them all has been an ongoing interest in the phenomenon of state power and its variable manifestations over time and in different contexts. One source has been everyday current world events and the manifold interpretations and debates these give rise to, prompting a continuous interplay with one's own reading of the changing global context. At another level, teaching and researching for many years at the Institute of Social Studies in The Hague, devoted to global development studies, has constituted a highly conducive environment for pursuing the kinds of interests explored here. In particular the involvement it offered in developing its MA programme on the *Politics of Alternative Development* and engaging with PhD students on related themes, provided a stimulating and critical sounding board from students as well as colleague. Participating in the Netherlands' CERES Research School in Development Studies has also been rewarding. In recent years these opportunities have been extended through a visiting chair in Uganda at the Faculty of Development Studies of Mbarara University of Science and Technology, and a guest professorship at the Graduate School of International Development Studies, Roskilde University, Denmark.

Beyond this, the study bears traces of various other kinds of involvements. One has been that of participating for a good number of years in a 'club' of scholars from anthropology, ancient history and archeology concentrated at Leiden University, interested in the emergence and evolution of 'early', that is, generally ancient states, to which I had been invited in view of the possible relevance of comparisons with the formation of pre-colonial African chiefdoms and states. In a very different way the book also builds on several years of association with the action-research oriented UNRISD *War-torn Societies Project*, focused on the scope for rehabilitation and development in contemporary post-conflict societies, for me with particular engagements in Somalia and Eritrea. Involvement in an advisory capacity in the Institute of Development Studies/University of Sussex ESCOR Commissioned Research Programme on *Strengthening Democratic Governance in Conflict-torn Societies*, and the Consortium for Political Emergencies (COPE), Centre for Development Studies, University of Leeds, has been similarly relevant to the present work.

Prior to that, coincidence and chance had once made me choose at the time reasonably stable post-colonial countries like Uganda and Somalia as sites for more extensive academic research on post-colonial political developments and state–society dynamics. Nobody could then have anticipated that these two settings in due course would come to rank among the gravest examples of state failure, state-sponsored terror and state collapse of recent times. As it happened, these contexts over the years would offer many sobering learning experiences as regards evolving state–society relations. As a result of a continuing association with universities and institutions in these and other countries in the region and getting a fairly close glimpse of the ups and downs in the spirals of post-colonial state formation and collapse, one enters into academic and policy-oriented networks focused on 'state collapse' and 'post-conflict development'. Add to this a prolonged role as observer of 'the African state' – and, incidentally, the Indian state and the nascent European state framework – and one's reputation may, rightly or wrongly, get extended to the realm of 'good governance'.

For all these varied and deeply instructive exposures, it nevertheless remains one's own responsibility to lay the connections and demonstrate the relevance of different experiences and inputs. In this regard, one fundamental assumption on my part has been that processes of organizing state forms will reveal certain basic and recurrent similarities, whether they occur in widely different times, contexts, or at different scales. If this assumption is correct, then contemporary state builders, constitutionalists and others might have much to learn from comparative history or from different contexts. Today's designers of the European Union project, for example, could learn something from the Indian experience in managing a multi-cultural continental state framework, or from African experiences and failures in 'nation-building', while present-day American interventionists might draw some instructive lessons from the fate of precursor imperialist designs and operations. Most chapters in this volume have benefited from earlier exposures as seminar or conference presentations. In the Netherlands these have been at the Institute of Social Studies in The Hague, the Centre for Development Studies at the University of Groningen and at the Universities of Leiden, Amsterdam and Utrecht, in Denmark at the Graduate School of International Development Studies of Roskilde University and the Centre of African Studies at Copenhagen University, in Estonia at a conference organized by PRAXIS, in Geneva at a seminar organized under the auspices of the International Committee of the Red Cross (ICRC) and the Programme for Strategic and International Security Studies (PSIS), and in India during a 2004 lecture tour to several universities in South India as well as the Madras Institute of Development Studies and the Centre for Development Studies in Trivandrum, sponsored by the Indo-Dutch Programme on Alternatives in Development.

Most chapters have built on materials which have had a prior existence as journal articles or as contributions to edited volumes, emanating from conferences or workshops. All have nonetheless constituted continuing 'work in progress' and have been thoroughly revised, reworked or extended as the case may be to make them contribute to and highlight the orientation of the present volume. Thus Chapter 1 of this book has drawn, in strongly revised and expanded form, from 'State Formation and Collapse: Reflections on Identity and Power', in Martin van Bakel, Renée Hagesteijn and Pieter van der Velde, eds, *Pivot Politics: Changing Cultural Identities in Early State Formation Processes*, Amsterdam: Het Spinhuis (1994). Chapter 2 is new, though part of it was presented in preliminary fashion as 'Globalization, State Restructuring and Governance: Reflections on State Formation and Collapse' at the conference on *Coping with Globalization* organized by the Centre for Public Policy and Governance, Institute of Applied Manpower Research, Delhi, November 2004. Chapter 3 is based on 'The African State in Academic Debate: Retrospect and Prospect', *Journal of Modern African Studies*, vol. 28, no. 2 (1990), combined with sections from 'Globalization and the State: What happened to "Relative Autonomy"?', published in the *Indian Journal of Political Science*, vol. 62, no. 2 (2001) and as 'Globalisation, the State and other Actors: Revisiting "Relative Autonomy" ', in John Degnbol-Martinussen, ed., *External and Internal Constraints on Policy-Making: How Autonomous are the States?*, Occasional Paper No. 20, International Development Studies, Roskilde University (1999). Chapter 4 appeared in earlier incarnations as 'Good Governance: The Rise and Fall of a Policy

Metaphor?', *Journal of Development Studies*, vol. 37, no. 6 (2001) and 'Good Governance: The Metamorphosis of a Policy Metaphor', *Journal of International Affairs* (vol. 57, no. 1, 2003). Chapter 5 is based on 'State Collapse and Fresh Starts: Some Critical Reflections', *Development and Change*, vol. 33 no. 5 (2002) and Chapter 6 on 'Linking the Future to the Past: Ethnicity and Pluralism', in M.A. Mohamed Salih and John Markakis, eds, *Ethnicity and the State in Eastern Africa*, Nordiska Afrikainstitutet, Uppsala (1998), of which an earlier version was published in *Review of African Political Economy*, no. 52 (1991). Chapter 7 has built further, with substantially new sections, on 'Identity and Power in Europe and India: Some Comparative Dynamics', in Martin Doornbos and Sudipta Kaviraj, eds, *Dynamics of State Formation: India and Europe Compared*, New Delhi/Thousands Oaks/London: Sage Publications (1997), while Chapter 8 started off from 'When is a State a State?: Exploring Puntland', in Piet Konings, Wim van Binsbergen and Gerti Hesseling, *Trajectoires de libération en Afrique contemporaine*, Paris: Karthala (2000). Permission to re-use the materials concerned by the editors and publishers involved is gratefully acknowledged.

Over the past several years various friends and colleagues have influenced this work more than they may have realized, through kindly reading and commenting on a particular paper or chapter, through collaboration in other work to which the present study is related, or through pertinent interventions at seminar presentations or in other discussions. Trying to acknowledge these debts is bound to leave some important gaps due to oversight, yet my listing must at any rate include the late John Degnbol-Martinussen, Wim van Binsbergen, Pieter Boele van Hensbroek, Paula Bownas, Richard Boyd, Peter Burnell, Ray Bush, Henri Claessen, Lionel Cliffe, Wolfgang Drechsler, Dennis Dijkzeul, Ananta Giri, Helen Hintjens, Markus Höhne, Wil Hout, Sudipta Kaviraj, Christian Lund, Robin Luckham, John Markakis, Pamela Mbabazi, Robbie Robertson, Ashwani Saith, Mohamed Salih, Sharada Srinivasan, Peter Waterman, Fiona Wilson, an anonymous reviewer and last but not least, of course, Wicky Meynen, my most critical reader and constant support. The usual disclaimers apply.

1
Dynamics of State Formation and Collapse, Past and Present

Introduction

While in recent years crises in and about states have seemed to multiply across the globe, governance crises are essentially of all times. In ancient as well as in more recent history, misgivings about the manner of wielding political power have frequently caused a decline of trust in prevailing political arrangements, inviting conflict and searches for alternative ways of organizing politics. At least in this respect, history will never end. But the very recurrence of such issues appears to call for some historical–comparative reflection on processes of state formation, crisis and collapse and on the connections between power and identity that so often play a role within these dynamics. As times change, the way the issues present themselves may illuminate different aspects, open up new perspectives and allow novel connections and comparisons to be explored.

Thus, in political anthropology in recent years one area of research has been stimulated by intellectual curiosity in the conditions of early state formation – early in the sense of 'first-ever', usually ancient (Carneiro 1987, Claessen 2000, Harris 1978, Service 1975). Numerous aspects of political and social organization, economic resource bases, cultural attributes and others have in this connection been examined on their possible causal effects on the emergence of the first forms of statehood. Naturally, one has also discovered that in many if not most of such contexts, state formation was not anything like a linear process but came with numerous set-backs, prolonged stalemates, occasional breakthroughs and yet, perhaps, a gradual building up of a social and economic basis conducive to or calling for the emergence of a kind of state form (Claessen 2000).

This interest coincides at the present time with growing concerns about the proliferation and prospects of contemporary war-torn societies, in some instances the actual collapse of state systems and questions about subsequent fresh starts (*Disasters* 2000, Milliken 2003, Schaeffer 1999). Obviously these two kinds of situations are vastly separated in time and direction and differ fundamentally with respect to their wider contexts. Nonetheless, there are points of contact. At one end the dynamic presumably is from a situation of 'statelessness' to some form of 'state' or statehood, however embryonic; at the other, it is potentially from some form of statehood to a situation of 'statelessness'.[1] 'Statelessness' thus figures at or as the beginning and end of things. In regard to either of these settings, questions about the organization of power, like what makes for cohesiveness and what causes fragmentation, may be raised. Consideration may be given to the optimal balance of forces or how one might arrive at justice and equity, though experience shows that such balances finally depend on what prevailing power constellations will allow.

Further parallels may be envisaged as well. In some such different situations there may have been questions concerning the political relevance of cultural identities, as in states that are not nations or nations that are not states. There may also be some 'shared' domino effects in state formation as well as, possibly, in disintegration processes. Can any parallel insights thus be drawn from situations far apart in time and space? Can the present learn from the past in this respect, or the past from the present for that matter, at least in our understanding of it? A wide-ranging reflection on these questions appears to be invited, particularly with regard to the connections between the dynamics of state construction and collapse vis-à-vis those of identity and power. After a brief glimpse at contemporary conflict situations, this introduction thus looks at shifting connections between state and non-state in the past and present, taking note of conceptions of state formation and the role of 'push' and 'pull' factors that have arisen in this regard, and paying special attention to the interplay of power and identity within this overall complex of factors.

Conflict and disintegration

At the end of the second millennium, one newly emerging theme in social and political analysis found itself addressing 'the challenge

---

[1] Cf. the title of Maria Brons' dissertation: *Society, Security, Sovereignty and the State: Somalia, From Statelessness to Statelessness?*, 2001.

of rebuilding war-torn societies' (Bastian and Luckham 2003, *Journal of Peace Research* 2002). The challenge referred to the increasing number of countries, in Europe as well as in Africa, Asia and Latin America, where the very fabric of society and institutional structures had been torn apart as a result of civil war and prolonged violent conflict, or in some cases due to external interventions. In a number of these situations, the continued existence as somehow distinct political entities, let alone as 'national' states of the systems concerned, has become precarious, uncertain, or outright impossible. Recent examples include Afghanistan, Iraq, Somalia, Liberia, Sierra Leone, Congo, Rwanda, Cambodia, Bosnia and El Salvador, but the category may well come to embrace countries like Sudan, Burundi, Tadzjikistan, Saudi-Arabia and others within the foreseeable future. Increasingly, international agencies, somehow representing a new type of 'staying' element in a rapidly changing global context, find themselves called upon to restore law and order and to initiate peacebuilding processes in these internal conflict situations. In recent years, several dozen such active UN operations have been started across the globe, a number which may be expected to increase almost exponentially in the years to come. Uncertain futures, marked in various instances by queries about the premises, direction and viability of state forms or alternative political formulae, seem to present increasingly familiar yet agonizing questions with respect to the global political landscape.

Quite central among the queries concerned are questions about political identity, political futures and possible trajectories of state restructuring. What are, or could be, the social and cultural bases for fresh efforts at political structuring and what visions for a collective future are likely to be offered, and to be found acceptable? Somalia vividly illustrates a dilemma shared by other (ex-)states. Will it be conceivable for Somali clans that have been fighting each other to death to once again join forces in some common cause for 'Somalia'? What are the alternatives? What can happen in this regard and what *will* happen in the end? Offhand a return to any pre-state past is just impossible and can hardly present an alternative. But the experience with the state system, even if it had taken root much less in Somali society than in various other African states, was harsh and traumatic, and propositions to restore it as it stood are also problematic. Yet *something* is likely to happen, if only in response to growing *international* concerns that there should be *some* accountable body to which one can address matters, and also because in increasing numbers of areas Somalis, too, have come to be dependent on structures that at least can mediate relations with the external world.

Though Somalia is unique in not having had any meaningful central government since 1991, conditions in several other countries are actually not too dissimilar. Both Afghanistan, with a central government with a very limited reach into its various regions (Rubin 2002), and Iraq with a continuing if not deepening political stalemate in the wake of the American intervention (Tripp 2002), still confront agonizing and unresolved questions as to whether any common future will be possible in their situations, and at what price. Similarly, what viable political identity and state framework could there be with which Bosnians, especially Muslim Bosnians, could possibly associate themselves? Or what future can realistically be expected for Sudan and the social and cultural fragments that theoretically form part of it? The questions can be readily multiplied and would not but underscore the earnest, at times desperate, though often vain, searches for sensible political formulae pursued by communities in different corners of the world.

For a perspective on processes of state formation and state restructuring, and on the idea and phenomenon of the state itself, these growing uncertainties and dilemmas raise significant conceptual questions. Several of these concern the boundaries between the notions of 'state' and 'statelessness': these have not only often been fuzzy in reality, but conceptually have been subject to notable shifts over time. Conceivably, the distinction may come to embrace new dimensions in the wake of current developments. At least, a fresh exploration of the dimensions and characteristics of 'stateless' societies and politics seems to be called for.

State and non-state, past and present

In recent years, there has been a good deal of discussion of the ways in which the modern state as a form of political organization is increasingly losing its pre-eminence as the ultimate framework of collective action (Castells 1996). The pervasive impact of trans-national economic forces, the revolution in communications technologies, processes of cultural globalization and related tendencies are all drastically transforming the role of state structures across the globe, qualifying the normative centrality of the nation-state. Added to this – and partly influenced by it – comes now the increasing incidence of cases of disintegration and collapse of state systems, alerting us to the ultimate possibility of disappearance of some state systems from the world's maps.

Although these different tendencies are evidently on the increase, it would be erroneous to categorically hypothesize that the modern state as a form of political organization is on its way out, to be eclipsed by larger global structures, by fragmented localized entities, or by both. As a general proposition such an idea would seem premature and as yet unfounded (Hirst and Thompson 1999). Nonetheless, the increasing incidence of war-torn societies and dislocated states with their highly uncertain futures presents us with a significant caveat, conceptually speaking. We can no longer take the modern state for granted, as either a construct that exists or must exist as part of a seemingly 'natural' order of things, or as one that will necessarily be realized as the end-product of integrative processes of modernization. Instead, the distinction between 'states' and 'stateless societies', implicit to all discussions of early state formation (Claessen and Skalnik 1978) and first explicitly advanced as a tool of analysis by Fortes and Evans-Pritchard in their classical text on *African Political Systems* (1940), might well acquire a renewed significance with the proliferation of problematic political futures emanating from war-torn societies. In that event, the focus may need to be placed more than hitherto on the dynamics and constructs that limit or nullify potential options in state formation, blocking the development of common institutional 'state' structures and often making the search for alternatives an arduous one indeed.

Not unconnected to any possible rethinking of 'state' and 'non-state' spheres is another conceptual implication of some of the new situations that may be looming up. Taking a larger than usual intellectual jump we might ask whether some of the conditions concerned in these situations may have been applicable to the contexts in which some of the earliest state formation processes occurred, some x-number of millennia ago, or elsewhere more recently. For all their prevalence and centrality in the history of mankind, states have not existed at all times, and not everywhere. The only thing certain is that in the course of the twentieth century they have come to exist virtually everywhere, that is, in a particular form of configuration, and that within the contemporary system of international relations, they are *expected* to exist everywhere. Within that system, based on the Westphalian model which links state sovereignty to an exclusive control over territory, states have become 'normal' and the international system in principle has no more place for 'non-states': it cannot itself operate without them and in the event of states falling apart the system is prone to intervene in order to uphold the 'norm'.

But the 'normalcy' of states is likely to have influenced our thinking about *state formation*: if states are *normal*, it is also *normal* that they should (have) come into being. By implication, the non-state spheres from which they arose may then no longer be viewed as *normal*; at best, they are 'pre-normal' but they might also be regarded as 'abnormal'.[2] Accordingly, while in the theorizing about early state formation there has been a good deal of debate as to which kind of factors and pre-conditions should be held primarily responsible for triggering off the processes concerned, the end result, namely, 'the state', was beyond question, that is, 'normal' (Carneiro 1987, Krader 1968). It is this particular assumption which conceivably may itself come up for review. Pre-state and post-state situations in some cases, Somalia for instance, may in fact come to be viewed as having more in common than would earlier have been accepted (Brons 2001).

From a premise of the 'normalcy' of states, theorizing naturally became oriented towards explaining how the first state forms came about. The relevant processes thus became represented as marked by a seemingly self-evident unfolding of a given destiny, once certain objective pre-conditions are present: population growth, social differentiation, resource utilization patterns, trade routes, conquest, or some particular combination of these and other factors (Claessen 1993). It goes without saying, as also Claessen points out, that the premise of normalcy of state formation forms part of the perspective of contemporary scholarship, not necessarily of the practitioner/state-builders of the time. But with any increased frequency and relative 'normalcy' of the *collapse* and possible eclipse of state frameworks, state formation theory may eventually need to seek a less teleological point of departure. It might then not only allow for recognition that early state formation processes are likely to have been fraught with painful and enduring uncertainties, conflicts and innumerable failures to take off, but also leave room for the alternative insight that in a range of contexts there may not have been a particularly compelling need or logic to adopt state forms to begin with.

While the absence of original state forms in various contexts (admittedly largely peripheral and micro ones) should thus not necessarily be viewed as 'abnormal', at the other end of the spectrum questions have at times also been raised about the 'normalcy' of existing states. Notably, it has been observed how remarkable and surprising it has been that various precarious state systems have lasted and survived as long as they did, and that the 'normal' functioning of the state is by no means so normal

---

[2] Incidentally, the fact that, until quite recently at least, various societies in different parts of the world appeared to manage quite well without the benefit of state forms does not seem to have received the attention it deserves, not at any rate from the proponents of non-state initiatives and civil society oriented new social movements.

(Cowgill 1988: 251–258). This paradox was already noted in earlier times. When turning to his 'general observations on the Fall of the Roman Empire in the West', for example, Edward Gibbon in 1788 commented that:

> the decline of Rome was the natural and inevitable effect of immoderate greatness. Prosperity ripened the principle of decay; the causes of destruction multiplied with the extent of conquest; and as soon as time or accident had removed the artificial supports, the stupendous fabric yielded to the pressure of its own weight. The story of its ruin is simple and obvious; and *instead of inquiring why the Roman empire was destroyed, we should rather be surprised that it had subsisted so long.* (Gibbon 1952: 621, italics added)

Today, similar observations might conceivably be made in regard to some contemporary problematic situations. In regard to Sudan, for example, if somehow the Sudanese state framework were to collapse and fragment as a state following the belligerent way its 'national' government had been dealing for decades with the South and subsequently with the rebellion in Darfur, it might well be observed how remarkable it was that it had lasted so long, even though the artificiality of Sudan's construction as a state had seemed so apparent.

However, while a turn of events leading to state fragmentation and collapse should in no way be surprising with respect to Sudan, one should also anticipate immediate external efforts to keep a façade of state sovereignty standing in this case. Notably, Egypt with its obsessive concern to keep a control over the Nile waters would be most unlikely to idly stand by if Sudan were to collapse and fragment as a state (El Zain 2006, Waterbury 2002). Significantly, this may illustrate an important difference with Somalia and at the same time point to a broader factor at work. While Somalia's disappearance from the international map as of 1991 may have caused some unease and concern to the international community for the precedent it signified, its disintegration hardly posed a source of worry to its neighbours. Its main adversary over the years, Ethiopia, had little reason or motivation to help resurrect a united Somali state framework except on terms favourable to its own strategic goals, thus providing one ground among others for Somalia's continued 'statelessness'. Whether a trajectory of state collapse will run its full course to the point of disintegration and dissolution of the state structure thus also depends on potentially decisive external determinants. This has also been at stake in the case of Afghanistan and in a way in Iraq, though there the complexity of interventions may yet strike out into new directions.

Twilight zones

Numerous societies in Africa and Asia had never reached state forms before they became colonized by European powers, some as late – or as recent – as the early twentieth century. And if they had, they were generally not territorially defined sovereign states. Instead, in pre-colonial and per definition pre-Westphalian times in Southeast Asia and other regions, kingdoms or states did not base their rule on territorial sovereignty but, in James Scott's terms, on being able to 'attract and hold a substantial, productive population within a reasonable radius of the court' (Scott 1998: 185). In that respect, '[a] growing, productive population settled in the orbit of a monarch's capital was a more reliable indicator of a kingdom's power than its physical extent' (ibid). Outside these domains one entered 'non-state spaces', some of them with a loose tribute-paying relationship to the state centre, others usually with scattered, peripheral populations and often serving 'as refuges for fleeing peasants, rebels, bandits, and the pretenders who have often threatened kingdoms'. Therefore, Scott argues, 'these stateless zones have always played a potentially subversive role, both symbolically and practically' (ibid.: 187). Similar patterns had prevailed in many parts of medieval Europe.

In many contexts the state–non-state distinction acquired a very specific, territorially defined, meaning upon colonization. In this connection, Edmund Leach could comment in 1960: '[in] the ideology of modern international politics all states are sovereign and every piece of the earth's surface must, by logical necessity, be the rightful legal possession of one and only one such state. There are no longer any blank spaces on the map and, in theory at least, there can be no overlap between the territories of two adjacent states' (Leach 1960). In not a few cases the colonial state might still only have a nominal presence in various large areas, especially if these were peripheral either in a literal sense or in the light of the key production or trading objectives of the colonial enterprise. In many such instances no particular reversals occurred in this regard with decolonization either. As a result, at the present time there are not a few enduring 'twilight' situations, of formal state authority at one (distant) level together with various other wielders of power at other levels who might claim 'real' legitimacy (Lund 2001 and Lund 2006). Again, the state is not always as normal as at times one might presume.

In this light, any exploration of state and non-state spheres in the past and present must address questions about their shifting though often fuzzy boundaries, their interconnections and confrontations and their relative potential for structural innovation and effective leadership, all with pertinent implications for subsequent trajectories. 'State' and 'non-state' may translate themselves into a 'state' and 'stateless' dichotomy, but also into state–civil society distinctions. Both sets of distinctions have left vast grey areas which over time have experienced fluctuating 'encroachments' from both sides. It is within these parameters, for example, that one now needs to appreciate the reality and relativity of the post-colonial African state, with its powerful aspirations and its limited reach, its uneasy relationship to the non-state sphere and its uncertain future. In these situations, also, new forms of authority, including 'guerilla government' (Rolandsen 2005), have been emerging. But it is this context also which sets the background for a reflection on the future of state forms, a future which perhaps will be less preoccupied with the completion of territorial systems of command and more with the search for alternative and multilayered political forms. Lessons from the past, with its vast depository of experiences, may have something to offer here.

With these provisos, what themes suggest themselves when considering state and non-state options in the past and present? First, it needs to be remembered that state formation trajectories do not constitute a linear process, but will come with numerous ups and downs. Second, just as much as we need theories that can explain alternative routes of state formation, we need to better understand trajectories of state decline – current rethinking on the past and future of states demands that we raise questions such as why do states collapse, why do some states seem to collapse more readily than others and why and how are some states subject to pervasive degeneration while others retain greater resilience and integration? This calls for distinctions between different types of 'collapse' – including different 'routes' to state collapse as is discussed in Chapter 5 – but also distinctions between the disintegration of state structures and the collapse of an entire civilization (Tainter 1988, Yoffee 1988). Related to this are questions about the relative survival capacity of communities with different modes of encapsulation and integration into wider state structures (Simonse 1992). And last, there is the basic and intriguing question as to what lies 'beyond collapse' (Eisenstadt 1988).

Paradoxically, as noted, the dividing line between state collapse and state formation, or between disintegration and reconstruction, is an extremely thin one. There are virtually always new political relations and structures emerging after 'collapse', even though they may be radically different from the previous arrangements. Indeed, '[c]ollapse, far from being an anomaly, both in the real world and in social evolutionary theory, presents in dramatic form not the end of social institutions, but almost always the beginning of new ones' (Eisenstadt 1988: 293). It is in these dramatic conjunctures of collapse and rebirth of political systems, therefore, characterized by continuities and discontinuities at different levels as the case may be, that some of the most fundamental questions about the nature and functions of state systems tend to be posed, retrospectively and prospectively: what basic purposes do they seek to fulfil and what interests are they expected to serve? What is the resource base of the political organization that is evolving and what are its prospects of sustainability over time? What are the system's mechanisms to cope with conflict, internal and external, and how effective will they be? How is political power articulated, organized and legitimated – if at all? And with reference to what collective identities have political institutions been developing – again, if at all?

Each of these questions refers to elementary issues that are crucial particularly during transitional phases between disintegration and attempts at any fresh starts. Of these issues, often the most far-reaching in periods of flux between the fragmentation of an old order and the rebirth of new collective systems refer to social and political identities: on what ethnic, religious or other perceived commonalities and self-definitions are collective political entities, state or non-state, developing? What if these are lacking? What are the role and implications of the never-ending interplay between power and identity in the genesis of new forms and their generation of political choice? Closer examination of the question of cultural identities seems called for.

Identity and power

One key aspect in all state formation and transformation must concern its cultural dynamics and dimensions, specifically the questions as to what kind of cultural affinities may underlie state-formation processes, and what kind of cultural–political identities they may give rise to. Naturally, the discussion on nationalism and the origins of nations, with its more specific and slightly narrower focus, is of substantial interest in this connection (Anderson 1983, Gellner 1983, Smith 1986). 'Identity is people's source of meaning and experience', in Castells' phrase (Castells 1997: 6). Political culture may thus be understood as comprising the amalgam of popular orientations about what constitutes the political community and the identification of collective selves. With respect to the questions involved, a few elementary postulates have often served as points of departure. One is, simply, that state formation without at least some semblance of collective identity in terms of which the process has been perceived or pursued, or some reference to shared visions and symbols in terms in which legitimacy is being sought, may seem fairly inconceivable, either in the past or in the present. Thus, in Anderson's view, 'nationalism has to be understood by aligning it ... with the large cultural systems that preceded it, out of which – as well as against which – it came into being' (Anderson 1983: 19). Some perception of collective identity, whether in terms of solidarity, common aspirations or external threats, in principle would seem basic and prior even to state formation itself (Smith 1986). Even if this were true, however, an elementary point to note is that we cannot reverse this and assume that state formation will necessarily follow the articulation of collective identities. Many non-state political communities have collective identities, including some very strong ones, but may never achieve or in some cases even aspire to create a state of their own.

Moreover, it will be much easier to identify common cultural or ideological markers for state formation in some contexts than others. They certainly cannot be assumed as givens. Nineteenth-century Italian unification has often stood as an example of nationalist-inspired state formation based on shared cultural heritages, yet even here discontinuities between the Southern regions once belonging to the kingdom of Naples and the North, as well as other regional variations, would qualify that image. In many contemporary situations, the limitations and shortcomings of 'national' state building projects are even more readily apparent. Emerging out of a (civil) war situation, for example, such as has been the case for Mozambique, Angola and Zimbabwe where different national liberation fronts were first fighting the colonial power and subsequently confronted each other, the process of determining the ideological contours and political identity of the 're-united' state system may itself become subject to complex and prolonged negotiation and confrontation at different levels between competitive political groups (Pohlianen 2001, Ruigrok 2004). The scope for smooth convergence in this regard is generally limited as in the prevailing conditions of the countries concerned there is not much likelihood of a new dynamic to energize processes of economic and communications linkages concentrated on and conceived in terms of the larger 'national' entity (cf. Gellner 1983). Iraq may in future come to benefit more from its relative wealth in this regard, yet it appears that Shiite, Sunnite and Kurdish identities have been increasingly replacing Iraqi identities. The idea that state formation would almost per definition be based on notions of common fate or destiny thus must be seriously qualified.

If and where a reverse kind of dynamics is at play, as with instances of the potential or actual break-up of post-colonial state frameworks perceived as artificial and constraining, identity variables almost certainly will come in again. With prospects of fragmentation looming up, inclinations to want to fall back on 'basic' constituent elements defined in cultural terms, such as shared ethnic or regional identities, are likely to play a role. Still, identity and other cultural dimensions, no matter how 'basic', should not necessarily be viewed as presenting alternative *explanatory* variables of either state formation or fragmentation, somehow on a par or competing with a range of conditioning factors that have generally received prime attention in discussions of the topic – power and domination, territorial expansion, class hegemony and so on. Each of the latter variables remains centrally important, but should primarily be seen as contributing to social and political processes which may seek cultural points of reference and recognition for their direction and legitimation, and for people's expression of their support or frustration with them.

Articulations of political identity are essentially fluid and determined largely by variables of power. Again, we should generally expect no essential difference in this regard between processes in the more distant past and in the present or the not too distant future. Still, in at least one sense one might argue that there will have been a basic difference between identity processes in situations of early state formation as against those in contemporary contexts: in some current thinking about political identity formations there is the idea that state identity should be based on old, preferably ancient and somehow 'primordial' roots. Clifford Geertz (1963) has been the godfather for this mode of thinking, which has been heavily criticized since but has nonetheless demonstrated a remarkable resilience (Smith 1986). The raison d'etre, identity and position on a prestige ladder of state frameworks have thus often been equated, it appears, with the extent to which historical claims of common existence and destiny could be validated for them. For example, there have been the claims of the British monarchy in this regard, or those of some other European royalties. But the same tendency has also been noted in the case of some less well-known African polities. The missionary Roscoe, for example, when visiting the kingdom of Nkore (in what was yet to become Uganda) for the second time at the end of the nineteenth century, was presented with a greatly deepened genealogy of Nkore kings as compared to the one he received during his first visit; the motive appeared to be to emulate neighbouring Buganda, which had been boasting much longer genealogies of kings (Roscoe 1923). This emulation factor in state formation and identity processes needs more attention than it has received, a point to which we shall return.

Following Hobsbawm and Ranger's key text on *The Invention of Tradition* of 1983, in recent years we have been able to witness a great outpouring of writings in the *'Invention of ...'* genre, often showing how various claims to historical depth have in fact been fabricated in response to the need of state building or reconstruction projects for a veneer of legitimizing traditionality. Thus, we have Mudimbe's *Invention of Africa* (1988), Arvind Das' *India Invented: A Nation in the Making* (1992), Corbridge and Harriss' *Reinventing India* (2001) as well as *The Invention of Argentina* (Shumway 1991),[3] echoed by several others elsewhere. A closely related genre, pioneered by Benedict Anderson in 1983 was (and still is) that on *'Imagining ...'* different political communities, though the 'community' aspect appears to have been taken too easily and too often for granted here. These literatures at any rate seem to underscore the point of how deeply felt (virtually 'primordial') needs for such historicization play a role in state and nation building, inducing re-readings of the past in terms of the preferred self-images of the present. Accordingly, we learn to read the myths of the past that are offered to us with a grain of salt. Conscious that the portrayed past is not the 'real' past, we feel more intent to try and recover the reality behind the 'myths' (Schech and Haggis 2000).

In the light of historicizing identity claims with a penchant for roots and tradition, the very first instances of state formation that have taken place in human history cannot but present a curious paradox. Whenever or wherever it was that the earliest cases of state formation occurred, there were per definition no historical precedents or traditional roots to point to, or no fixed or self-evident reference points on which to construct a state identity. Instead, state formation and the construction of state identity of such early times might be viewed as a matter of pure pioneering, constrained nor guided by parameters or precedents derived from the past, and having before it unlimited openness in time and space. With no prior state identities claimed or projected, so to speak, there could neither be any question of disputes over names, as today over Macedonia, Congo and some other political identities. Meanwhile, we may presume that the state formations concerned were probably not bestowed with too much awe or special attention, but viewed and experienced primarily in terms of their practical expediency. Of course, early instances of state formation are unlikely to

---

[3] *The Invention of America* (O'Gorman 1961) was one precursor to this genre.

have been a matter of deliberate construction but may rather have culminated through a slow and incremental genesis. But whatever the precise record, the pioneering conditions within which the most ancient state forms may have come about stand starkly contrasted with the contemporary idea that state identity should be grounded in very old, primordial, or 'ancient' roots.

Identity formation under stress

Any discussion of political identity must take cognizance of the fact that identity formation is a matter of continuous construction and reconstruction. This also pertains to our ideas about how the first states may have come about and what identities they had or sought to develop. However, the cultural and identity dimensions of early states pose some highly intractable problems. We tend to approach the questions concerned in 'our' language and from 'our' contexts, in an attempt to visualize the kind of contexts that may have been prevailing at the time. We realize this can hardly be adequate, but there is little choice. Nonetheless, one reasonable assumption is that there must have been some sense of 'we' also or especially in the earliest times, and that any such collective identities probably emerged, as they often still do, in contradistinction or actual opposition to some other 'they': other communities, rival collectivities, or 'they' as deities, the gods (Bowra 1967, Ellis and Ter Haar 2004). Alternatively, a sense of shared identity of humankind *with* their spiritual counterparts was also conceivable. In either such cases, one would imagine that such collective identities provided the basis for, and could be translated into, hegemonic powers that eventually were vested in state-like structures, most likely a form of kingship. But the institution of kingship itself could give rise to markedly changing notions and attributions in the context of people's changing relations with the supernatural. Old Testament scholar David Daube put forward an interesting hypothesis as to how this may have occurred in antiquity:

> The institution of kingship may be [noted], first growing up on earth: then God's rule is construed by analogy; and finally his kingship confers increased dignity and new meanings on the original institution. In the wide field of *imitatic Dei* (or herois) it has long been seen that there is a constant give and take of this sort. The start is from an

admired human quality, mercy, magnanimity; then God is clothed with it: and now the divine attribute becomes a high ideal and a fresh source of progress in human intercourse. (Daube 1963: 17)

Such processes may have strongly influenced the shaping of collective identities, conceptions of spiritual and worldly powers and the relations that were evolving between them.

But just as mass and energy are mutually convertible, something similar may be said for identity and power. Indirectly, collective identities can be transformed into power, like mass turns into energy. The institutionalization of state religion has been a notable strategy in state formation, state extension and state maintenance, as exemplified by the adoption of Christianity by the Roman Empire, its use to push the Northern frontiers of the successor Carolingian state, and its continued pre-eminence as official religion in Greece and various other European state systems. Again, the inception and spread of Islam signified as much the creation of Islamic state forms as of the Islamic faith, thus providing for mutually supportive structures.

However, not only is identity convertible into power, under particular, rarer, circumstances the opposite might also occur. In the past as well as present, institutionalized power in some instances has sought, and at times succeeded, to recreate itself in collective identity. Divine rulers in ancient Egypt, the Aztec and Inca empires, and not so ancient Japan, superimposed themselves on society, Louis XIV declared himself to be the state, and powerful emperors and kings in different epochs have similarly sought to put a lasting mark on the state framework they had created or ruled. To the extent that the rulers' claims to power could then count on support from below, their rule would be much lighter and eventually might be presented as an expression of collective identity. The same principle and mechanisms have been pursued in many other instances, though as we know the record of unfulfilled claims in this respect is impressive. In recent times, various despotic rulers, including Central African Republic's 'Emperor' Bokasa not so long ago, as well as President-for-Life Kim Jong Il of North Korea and Turkmenbashi President Saparmurad Niyazov of Turkmenistan still at present, engaged deeply in personality cults, though by and large with adverse results. Only few bids for power become actually institutionalized into enduring political identities.

Whatever the outcome of these dynamics may have been in different individual instances, power and identity evidently constitute closely related universal themes, both highly topical and very ancient. While assertions of collective political identity are not quite conceivable without a striving for power, or resulting from power, power in turn is hardly conceivable without some efforts being made to add a distinct identity to it. Embodiment of power almost certainly will claim a certain identity to begin with. Identity in these respects also relates closely to notions of legitimacy, but is in no way identical to it. Legitimacy generally pre-supposes some accepted political identity, but any particular regime's or state's identity is not necessarily legitimate to all segments of its population (Doornbos 2005).

Affinity and political convertibility of the dimensions of power and identity are also reflected in the assertion, either in parallel or in competitive fashion, of popular and official identities, as explored in Chapter 7. Popular identities are often expressive of social aspirations, demands or protests articulated in distinction or in opposition to the state or to other groups perceived as dominant or threatening. Official identities, on the other hand, are the concern of state authorities and refer to their efforts to present the state framework as the embodiment of collective aspirations and legitimating consensus. National museums and the way they represent or construct national histories are of particular interest in this connection (Horne 1986). Rather than 'the nation' constituting a single shared 'imagined community', in Benedict Anderson's (1983) term, debates on what are the 'true' state foundations may sharply divide proponents of contrasted portrayals of it. Official and popular identities tend to relate to one another in complex and dynamic ways, varying from close harmony to deepening tension and in the ultimate instance to a parting of ways.

State formation, but also state disintegration, is indeed profoundly influenced by, as much as giving shape to, processes of identity articulation. In times of crisis, which is usually the case when states emerge or collapse, political identities are likely to be under stress. Under duress identities may shrink, subject to distortion and simplification, and become stripped of nuances and broader commonalities. Subjects may feel compelled to see conflicts in terms of 'them' against 'us'. Outsiders may grope for the sort of simplification that appears to offer a handle to understand the complex dynamics. Political mobilizers in or out of power will seek to manipulate and influence either kind of orientations, potentially adding new twists to the identity labels entertained. All this will carry collective identities miles away from the kind of multilayered, emphatic and relativistic notions of self often sported in sections of the cosmopolitan world.

Emulation and 'pull' in state formation

While identity and power as noted are in complex interaction within particular political entities, their dynamics may also play a role within wider contexts, potentially serving as models for emulation. Emulation and borrowing of political institutions may indeed be closely connected to and grounded on assertions of power and identity. To better appreciate this, we might first recall that discussions of early state formation have largely focused on the conditions that may have promoted the development of the 'first' or 'original' state forms, that is, processes of state 'invention'. Fascinating as these are, such processes are per definition different from emulation: once the idea of state has emerged within a wider setting in which different communities coexist, compete, or are at least aware of each other's existence, state formation within that setting is henceforth more likely to occur through emulation. Instances of such emulation processes can again be found in the distant past and in the present, as can be illustrated by two examples. For ancient times, there is the case of the Hebrews, who in antiquity, according to the Biblical account, were ruled by prophets until the time of Saul. Again, as David Daube recounts the story, the prophets were seen as God's direct representatives, and they were in actual charge of temporal affairs. But then a far-reaching innovation took place:

> [A]bout 1000 BC the people asked the last such prophet-ruler, Samuel, to institute a kingship on the Canaanite model [Matthew 19.8, Mark 10.5] He took it very amiss and so, indeed, did God: the petitioners preferred henceforth not to be led by God's immediate messengers. Yet, though the request meant a rejection of the perfect order, it was acceded to and Samuel, at God's bidding, anointed Saul. (Daube 1972: 63)

Upon this fundamental change, prophets for some time continued to exercise considerable influence, but significant changes occurred in the respective roles of and relationships between kings and prophets. In the light of our discussion, however, it is the emulation aspect which is of particular interest here, and of at least equal significance as the profound internal transformations that it entailed. Presumably out of strategic considerations the Canaanite model of statehood was thought to be of superior value to the experiences with a prophet-led government and thus became a model for emulation to the Hebrews.

A more contemporary example is that of the Rwenzururu Kingdom, established in the early 1960s on the Rwenzori range in the Ugandan-Congo border area. The Rwenzururu movement began as a separatist movement from Toro Kingdom, which had been incorporated within colonial and post-colonial Uganda (Doornbos 1970). Within Toro, Batoro constituted a slight numerical majority, as against Bakonzo, Baamba and some smaller population groups living mainly in the Western parts. Toro kingship was basically a Batoro affair. Bakonzo and Baamba had felt neglected for decades, and felt they had been treated as second-class citizens. In 1961 they demanded a separate district for themselves. When this was refused by the Uganda government, the Rwenzururu movement erupted, which would remain active for several decades to come. After a short while, one (Bakonzo) wing of the movement, led by Isayah Mukirane, decided to secede altogether from Uganda. This was first done in republican fashion, with Mukirane as President, but soon it was decided to opt for monarchical status, again with Mukirane becoming the first king of the Rwenzururu kingdom. After his death in 1966, the titular kingship was passed on to his son, Charles Wesley, thus turning the new monarchy into a hereditary one on the model of European royalty.

The interesting aspect of the adoption of kingship in the Rwenzururu case, similar to that of the Hebrew kingship, was that of its emulation. The Bakonzo's socio-political structure had itself not had monarchical institutions, but following their incorporation into Toro kingdom they had come to feel acutely that the Toro kingship was not 'theirs'. They had aspired to equal social status with the Batoro and an unequivocal declaration by the King of Toro to the effect that Bakonzo and Baamba were equally dear to him as the Batoro possibly could have given them this desired sense of equal status and identity. As this was not done – the Toro kingship instead tended to reinforce all the lingering feelings of discrimination – separatism followed, but for Mukirane's radical wing the process was not complete until they themselves could boast equal status with the Batoro by installing their own kingship. The case, therefore, not unlike that of the Hebrews and Canaanites, provides another illustration of the idea of state formation, specifically the introduction of kingship, by emulation. What should also be observed is that in both these cases emulation concerned the adoption of an institution of a *rival* people, though not necessarily with the same expectations. The ancient Hebrews' motivations presumably were primarily strategic, in the sense of wanting an institution offering greater scope for collective deliberation of possible courses of action. In the Bakonzo/Rwenzururu case, it signified the assertion of their own political identity and distinctiveness through adoption of the symbols of power of their main adversaries. Kingship in this regard carried an important symbolic meaning for them.[4]

The two cases illustrate how closely interrelated can be the emulation and adoption of worldly state institutions, the assertion of political power and the articulation of identity. Rwenzururu, as it happened, was pretty much a 'war-torn' society by the time it sought to develop its own monarchy. In the Hebrew case, one could probably validly speak of a 'crisis' when they decided they wanted to opt for 'direct' rule. Both instances illustrate how the search for alternative political arrangements may receive an important impetus amidst very adverse conditions.

For the Rwenzururu case, a further manifestation of the emulation factor has been occurring more recently. In 1993, proposals were launched in Uganda for the reinstatement of kingship in the four former monarchies of Buganda, Ankole, Toro and Bunyoro. These kingships had been abolished in 1967 by the Obote government, a move which at the time had been received enthusiastically in the Bakonjo/Baamba areas of Toro. In Toro, like in Buganda and Bunyoro – but not in Ankole[5] – symbolic kingship (called 'cultural leadership') was indeed restored in 1993. Following this, the Bakonzo too have wanted to restore their own, newly created monarchy and have since been pleading with the Uganda government for its recognition (*The Monitor*, August 1993, Stacey 2003).

There is another dimension to consider in this connection, potentially of far-reaching significance in state formation theorizing. In discussions of state formation it is usually 'push' factors of one kind or another which have been receiving most attention: population growth, conquest, expansion in social differentiation, trade, or a mix of these and other

---

[4] This orientation appears underscored by a further example from yet another context: at the final revision of this chapter, my newspaper recounts how in the context of Rumanian-Hungarian rivalries in Transylvania, the Rumanians are proposing to have their national hero Stefan the Great, whose 500th day of death was commemorated in July, 2004, canonized, a move intended to achieve symbolic parity with the Hungarians whose King István (St. Stefan) introduced Christianity into Hungary in the year 1000 and became canonized (NRC-Handelsblad, 3 August 2004, p. 4).

[5] In Ankole, the pro-monarchy Nkore Cultural Trust had been pleading for restoration on historical grounds. Fierce opposition however was mounted by the rival Banyankore Cultural Foundation, which perceived possible restoration as the reinstatement of the symbol of past oppression. Historically Ankole's kingship had functioned within a context of ethnic subordination, with a relative minority of Bahima of pastoralist derivation ruling over a majority of Bairu peasants. See further my *The Ankole Kingship Controversy: Regalia Galore Revisited*, 2001.

variables (Claessen 1993). While there is no reason to underrate the relevance of these long-term factors, it seems that in certain periods or at particular moments the example of an alternative model to emulate may have had such an appeal that it may well be recognized as a powerful factor in state formation in its own right. If it had not been the case that the Canaanite or Toro kingship had somehow seemed a superior political institution to the Hebrews or Bakonzo, there would evidently have been little incentive for them to try to emulate it. The same goes for other groups which at one time or another may have found themselves in similar circumstances. Presumably, they would have continued without kings, kingship and whatever else it implied institutionally, and might have practised their own type of political organization just as they had done for ages. After all, a time honoured, prophet-based system of governance is no minor thing to put aside. When searching for the determinants of state formation processes, therefore, these examples suggest that we should give some consideration to what may be called 'pull' factors involved. The exact attraction and nature of such 'pull' factors is likely to vary in specific instances. As noted, the Rwenzururians almost certainly had different reasons to aspire to having a kingship than ancient Hebrews. But in both cases there apparently was a feeling that without an institutional instrument such as the one which their rivals possessed, they would stand to lose out in the inevitable ongoing competitiveness, whether for prestige, power, or strategic institutional alertness.

There is yet a further point to note. Rwenzururu was a late arrival on the political scene, as a movement as well as in its symbolic claims to kingship. A cluster of kingships had already existed in pre-colonial times in the broader region and we do not know exactly which had emerged first. There are competing claims about that. However, in a discussion of factors of *emulation* it is particularly significant to recognize that certain types of state configurations historically existed and have possibly emerged in particular regions *as clusters*, such as the cluster of kingdoms in the pre-colonial African Great Lakes region, the city states in the Italian Po delta, Polynesian chieftainships, Javanese sultanates, or even the nineteenth-century idea of European nation-states. In any of these instances it appears that emulation may have been playing a major role, if not to borrow the whole idea of 'state', then at least for some basic structural features. By implication it suggests that in a variety of contexts we should not so much be looking at state formation in isolation but rather at the emergence and development of common state forms within certain larger regions.

But although various instances of historic state formation may be attributed to 'pull' factors, it does not necessarily follow that wherever there is an interest in state emulation it will work. The Karen people in Burma, whose peripheralized socio-political status resembled that of the Bakonzo in Uganda, are said to have often expressed their keen desire for a kingship of their own in recurrent millenarian movements, and to have had recurrent attempts of popular leaders taking the first moves towards establishing monarchical institutions on the model of the Burmese kingship (Hinton 1979: 90–93, Stern 1968). However, each time their attempts were frustrated either by the superior force of the Burmese army, or by their own lack of social cohesion and mobilization. Besides, a further difference was that in the Bakonzo/Rwenzururu case the Uganda central government in principle represented an over-arching layer for arbitration, as opposed to that of the Karen versus the Burmese state, which was one of direct confrontation. Evidently, therefore, successful state formation may also depend on key conditioning factors in the wider political context and the nature of social organization.

'Pull' factors and the factor of emulation in state formation processes may be likened to Galbraith's idea of *countervailing power* in institutional economics (Galbraith 1978) – they illustrate the strength and importance of organizational models in competitive processes, whether political or economic. The same factor can also be discerned in other kinds of institutional transformation: historically there was the rapid proliferation of European 'nation-states' following the development of its first model in France, and the race between European powers in the setting up of colonial governments once the first examples had been set for it in the late nineteenth century. In recent times, we have witnessed the efforts to come to the organization of globally operating trade blocs, like the EU, NAFTA, MERCOSUR, ECOWAS, APEC, COMESA free trade areas, and others. There has been some discussion as to whether this amounted to (intra-)regionalization or to another, inter-regional, dimension of globalization (Castells 1996: 110–112). What matters in the present context, however, is the borrowing of institutional models within a broader competitive setting. In each of these instances, an overriding factor appears to have been the fear that without engaging in similar organizational forms as the ones possessed by rival powers, one might lose out in the un-abating race for hegemony.

In a more innocuous but deceptive way, similar kinds of mechanisms might appear to have been at work in the way in which post-colonial African states seemed to be imitating and trying to improve upon each other's constitutions, flags, anthems and the like, often with only minor variations in the phrasing or colour schemes used. At first glance the extent of borrowing here appears to have been impressive, underscoring once more the role of emulation in patterns of state construction and institutional development. However, in reality this amounted to emulation of an altogether different kind and level. At independence, in the early 1960s, most of the designs of African flags and constitutions concerned were imported, usually from just a few designers and legal firms in metropolitan centres specializing in these matters. As such their symbolism tended to reflect notions entertained in key global centres at the time rather than reflecting any tendency to 'peep over the wall'. The same goes for various new policy approaches that more recently have been pervading different world regions, like the promotion of decentralization, or of 'good governance'. Each of these represented new waves of policy thinking at centres like the World Bank rather than constituting new, experience-based propositions being emulated from one context to the next.

If state formation processes in some instances must be explained by 'pull' rather than – or in addition to – 'push' factors through the urge to emulate what appears to be a rival power's superior form of organization, could this also tell us something about instances of state deformation and the collapse of state structures? Obviously this is a different story. *Prima facie* it would seem uncertain whether or to what extent fragmentation processes leading to the decline and erosion of state institutions could be prompted by 'example'. Still, a potential argument could be explored here. For instance, it appears that the elaborate and ingenious constitutional structure of the former Yugoslavian federation lost its cohesive power once the fear for being overrun by the larger Soviet system had disappeared. Thus states' disintegration and their possible collapse in some cases might well be explained by their increasing redundancy due to the slackening of the appeal of common structures once developed to offset perceived threats by rival powers. In a broader sense it could be argued that the lifting of support structures that had come with superpower hegemony in the post Cold War period was a key factor bringing various vulnerable economies and political frameworks to the brink of collapse.

In some such cases it is possibly the lack or discontinuity of 'pull' factors which enhances the vulnerability of political frameworks and the prospects of their disintegration. For theorizing state formation processes, in any event, it does seem that 'pull' factors inherent in the drive to emulate 'rival' models may not have received the attention they deserve. More generally, a wider reconsideration of the contribution of 'pull' and 'push' factors in both integrative and disintegrative directions may be a useful undertaking in the analysis of state formation and indirectly in state deformation processes. This may be so in particular during a time characterized by the increasing incidence of the collapse of state institutions and, by implication, of their lessened 'normalcy'.

Looking ahead

The third millennium started off with some seemingly highly contradictory signals. On one side we can note growing confusion and political conflict in different corners of the globe, punctuated by increasing incidence of the collapse and questioning of state structures. At the same time the break-up of states may also give rise to the birth of new political forms, in Africa and in parts of Asia and Europe, carrying with them new focal points, rationales and sources of support. At the present juncture, we may in fact be witnessing the emergence of a whole range of new political formations without fully appreciating it. Patterns of collapse and creation, emulation and invention, prompted by 'push' and 'pull' factors generating and degenerating political institutions, all tend to mix and make up the current general context and crisis. Issues and images of power and identity stand central amidst this interplay of forces and counter forces. Not surprisingly, in times of crisis questions of power and identity may become matters of wide and overriding concern, or indeed of life and death. In crisis, power reveals itself in unmediated form, brutal and harsh as some of the warlords illustrate. In crisis, too, identities are peeled off to hard cores, becoming the test for 'go' or 'no-go', for ethnic cleansing, 'liberation' and chauvinism. Kingship in some such situations may enjoy renewed popularity: among the expectations it engenders are those for a 'strong' saviour of the 'nation', for a locus of stability in a flux that appears to run out of control.

Political conjunctures at which states break down or from which new political systems may emerge are almost inevitably indicative of deep crisis. Paradoxically, state formation and state disintegration may both occur under duress. Today's examples include war-torn societies providing the focus for peacebuilding operations and other challenges. The post '9/11' era offers a rapidly changing context for the emergence and handling of these dynamics, including the possibility of unpredictable as well as unprecedented superpower interventions, or their absence precisely where they might have been called for. Recurrent admonitions in terms of 'good governance', decentralization and state restructuring in other respects add a further layer of complexity to the relations at stake. New and complex interactions between global power constellations and local forces will then further unfold, engendering the interplay with dynamics of identity and protest from below. Questions of identity and power may become of prime importance and sensitivity precisely in contexts of state deformation and reformation. In the context of the transformative processes concerned, identity and power may come to fuse, mix, coalesce or contradict each other to give birth to various novel experimental forms. The overall record is not very encouraging but occasionally an inspiring new political project may take off.

This volume

Taken together, these different dynamics of state formation, state restructuring and state collapse comprise a vast field of different yet related tendencies, which is worth examining more closely and within a single perspective. Opposite though they are in terms of their direction, dynamics of state formation and state failure culminating in state collapse belong to the same field of analysis, conceptually speaking. State failure may manifest itself through incapacity of the state to prevent or curb pervasive violence and insecurity, mitigate ethnic or religious conflicts, or to contain arbitrary and oppressive action by its army or other state agencies. State collapse constitutes the ultimate phase in any such spiral of deteriorating political dynamics, characterized by the wholesale disintegration and falling apart of a state's institutional fabric. Conversely, state formation, which almost invariably is a long-term process, may be said to be taking place wherever a state system establishes, extends or enhances its capacity to overcome these problems and succeeds in playing a pivotal coordinating role in initiating integrative economic and social policies. State restructuring meanwhile may be taken to refer to the manifold ways in which a state's institutional infrastructure is adjusted and amended to meet changing priorities and roles of the state.

There have been significant connections between these opposite tendencies, historically as well as at present. In recent times the two tendencies have often been brought to coincide more closely as a result of various key factors. Globalization in several of its key aspects impacts significantly on processes generating state restructuring, state collapse and state formation. Globalization must not be reified into a single massive force or movement. Nonetheless, in the contemporary context a powerful ensemble of economic mega powers and global institutions constitute active global forces setting critical constraints, conditionalities and demands to the scope for manoeuvre for state systems at the receiving end of the line. Global forces may encourage state formative processes at particular levels, while in other respects they induce or accelerate dynamics of state destruction and collapse. Also, pervasive institutionalization of new jurisdictions at global or regional levels tends to create organizational structures increasingly with functions like those of a state, while simultaneously usurping powers held earlier by formerly autonomous state systems. The eclipse of state powers may thus be directly related to the emergence of new over-arching structures which curb or take over some of their jurisdiction. A case in point is the European Union (EU) in its evolution towards becoming a regional state framework of sorts, though various other transnational bodies might similarly illustrate the trend.

In the light of these trends, this volume aims to highlight current inroads of global forces on the state, paying particular attention to processes of state restructuring and collapse affecting countries in the South and to the latter's varying capacity to maintain themselves amidst new risks and uncertainties. In thus looking at globalization, state restructuring and collapse from a unified perspective, the book explores a field of political transformation and analysis which is key to an understanding of factors and forces at play in the contemporary context. Among the main themes in this volume are therefore the dynamics of globalization and their political and institutional repercussions, patterns of externally engineered state formation and state restructuring, the role of the 'good governance' discourse, and trajectories of state collapse and re-starts. Within this context attention is also devoted to the politics of statelessness, to manifestations of identity and power and to ethnic conflict triggered or fanned by these impacts.

The study approaches these questions from a deliberately eclectic perspective, and builds on arguments borrowed from anthropology and classical studies as much as from contemporary development studies, international relations and international political economy. The aim is to foster a broader critical understanding of how key global forces are impacting, with pervasive and often devastating effects, on the role of state structures and on societies' capacities to organize themselves within the contemporary context. The book first pursues this theme, in Chapter 2, with a general reconnaissance of the connections between the contemporary dynamics of globalization and the changing role and position of the state, paying special attention to the varying capacities of state systems to withstand or adjust to forces of globalization. This chapter, on *Globalization and the State*, therefore engages in a preliminary exploration of the connections between global forces and the role of the state, highlighting patterns of institutionalizing power at the global level and the debates around global civil society as well as the resultant thinking on state restructuring, state capacity and collapse.

In Chapter 3 the perspective from which these dynamics are viewed is reversed, that is, the way external forces impinge upon different states and state structures are here considered from the receiving end. Shifting appreciations of the role of the state within their broader and changing context are illustrated by a look at the fortunes of the post-colonial African state, which after independence first enjoyed the (externally sanctioned and encouraged) status of 'prime mover' in virtually all development efforts and designs, but later came to be regarded as a major obstacle to 'development', relegated to an increasingly marginalized role and existence. Chapter 3 illustrates the impacts of global forces on the changing thinking and practice of the role of the African state. It first reviews some major debates that illustrated the shifting perspectives on the role and nature of the state in Africa and the patterns of state formation lying at its basis. The chapter then utilizes the notion of relative state autonomy to consider the implications of the far-reaching 'de-statification', that is, the dramatic decline and change of state functions that have been occurring in recent decades in Africa and in other parts of the South. Against this background, the chapter also takes a closer look at the changing connections, and appreciations of them, between the state and 'non-state' spheres.

In Chapter 4 this is followed up with a discussion of the 'good governance' notion, which has become exemplary for the thinking underlying a whole range of external interventions impinging upon state systems and structures in the South. The chapter recounts how the 'good governance' notion was first introduced to offer a normative umbrella for the launching of political conditionalities, focused on the restructuring of state systems of aid recipient countries, though later became restyled as a selection principle of aid 'deserving' countries. The chapter thus looks into the origins and ambitions associated with this 'good governance' doctrine, tracing back the idea to the geo-political opportunity context of its launch at the end of the Cold War. It then examines the metamorphoses the concept has subsequently undergone as a policy metaphor, due in part to unanticipated complexities at the level of implementation. As a dominant policy discourse the 'good governance' notion has conceptually shortened the road to the more radical proposition of externally engineered 'regime change' *à la* Iraq.

Irrespective of its practical or operational results, which do not appear to have been momentous, its influence on global policy thinking thus should not be underestimated.

Chapter 5 then examines dynamics of state collapse and attempts at state re-formation, with special reference to the intervening role of international actors. The chapter, on *State Collapse and Fresh Starts*, is concerned with the anatomy of state collapse and its determinants, conceptually and comparatively, and with various contrasted trajectories of state collapse that may be engendered. In examining the incidence of state collapse, it focuses on two central themes, one concerned with the search for causalities and the other concerned with appropriate responses. In regard to these, there is often a misplaced tendency to look for single causes and explanations of state collapse, and similarly to propose single, preferably 'quick-fix' solutions. As the chapter highlights, these actions on the donor front are generally guided by prevailing neo-liberal ideas as to how state systems ought to be structured and functioning in the modern world, and by 'good governance' inspired recipes as to how that should be achieved.

The changing realities of the role of the state in the context of state restructuring also call for discussion of the shifting dynamics of identity and the politics of pluralism. Thus Chapter 6, concerned with *Ethnicity, Reforms and Pluralism*, looks at the identity dimensions of state building exercises, though without losing sight of the central question of power and power relations. It examines several recurrent questions raised about the role of ethnicity in connection with political restructuring intended to promote multi-partyism and decentralization in Africa. The chapter provides an exploration of the relation between ethnicity and political reforms in the context of the broader 'good governance' agenda. While examining issues and tendencies in the context of changing state–society relationships in Africa, it also seeks to highlight their specificity in contrast to patterns elsewhere in the world.

The theme of power and identity is also central to Chapter 7, concerned with the dynamics of state and identity in Europe and India. This chapter is devoted to a broadly comparative analysis of state formation processes in Europe, focused particularly on the emergence of the European Union as a supra-national 'state', as against continued processes of conflict and integration characterizing India's state legacy. The chapter explores key dimensions of state formation processes with respect to these different contexts with an eye on illuminating relevant comparative dynamics of the processes concerned.

Chapter 8 returns to the question raised at the beginning of this enquiry about what lies beyond collapse. With a special focus on the case of Puntland State in Northern Somalia, the chapter seeks to explore some aspects of the ongoing Somali searches to regain statehood out of the situation of statelessness that followed total state collapse. This examination relates again to the discussion about state collapse and fresh starts, and raises fundamental questions as to when it is relevant to refer to a 'state' with respect to political formations emerging from amongst the debris of collapsed states, and when not. In the final analysis this is a matter of criteria for statehood and state-ness and may require exploring the 'twilight' zone between state and non-state, comprising different and potentially competing institutions of public authority whose popular recognition may wax and wane. It is here that we are likely to encounter instances of state formation 'at work' as well as instances of decline and prolonged intervals of stalemate and stagnation. It is in such terminal, yet at the same time embryonic, situations that we may find dynamics of state collapse linking up with those of state formation, and at times vice versa. Remote from the centres of global power shaping the broad contours and direction of state restructuring, there are important lessons to be gained from the deliberations and debates generated in these exceptional grassroots situations about the realities and limitations of efforts at state construction.

Finally, Chapter 9 summarizes and concludes the discussion, in retrospect and prospect drawing several common lines from it. Pointing to the dynamics of changing state forms as the common element in all instances of state formation, state restructuring and state decline, it emphasizes the distinction between processes generated and directed from within as opposed to externally directed processes of state restructuring. As the latter have become increasingly prevalent in recent times, it appears that the future of state forms and the role they are expected to play will strongly depend on global power configurations and the priorities they entail. By implication, studying state–society dynamics in the future is likely to start off from agendas that are vastly different from those pursued at present.

2
Globalization and the State: Reconfiguring the Connections

Introduction

There are many pertinent reasons today to explore the impacts globalization makes on the state, specifically the way political and institutional functions and structures associated with the state are being reoriented and reshaped through the demands and directives from contemporary global forces (Nordhaug 2002, Strange 1996, Weiss 1998). As a corollary, it is important to enquire what implications global forces have for the integrity and survival capacity of state frameworks, that is, what are the latters' prospects of sustaining and strengthening themselves vis-à-vis the challenges of globalization, or alternatively what are their chances of falling victim to erosion and collapse.

Though processes of state formation and state collapse have been of all times, within the current era of globalization the realities of state formation, state decline and state restructuring have come to be forefronted in a pronounced way in various regional contexts. Much of that has to do with the differential ways and degrees in which different state systems are undergoing the impacts of global forces, and with the varying extent to which they are equipped to 'cope with globalization'. In that light, a range of different contemporary dynamics in state–society relations is relevant, calling for better understanding of the kind of processes that may lead to the decline, fragmentation and collapse of state systems, or alternatively their reorientation and new forms of state structuring. In this connection, it will be useful to see political processes, and the continuities and discontinuities of interest and power from which they arise, as linking up to such seemingly opposite tendencies as decline and recovery, fragmentation and political formation, and to approach them as a single dynamic field.

In pursuing these questions, attention should particularly be given to externally directed or influenced state formation and state restructuring, and to changing state–(civil) society relationships that may result from them. Beyond this, it will be important to try and raise questions about the relative propensity of state systems to maintain themselves, as opposed to their chances to collapse under global pressures. In other words, we should enquire into the implications of global forces and state restructuring for the room and capacity for proper governance. Inevitably, this calls for exploration of a host of dimensions, ranging from the cultural to the economic, together determining the relative extent of social fragmentation or resilience with which states face the dynamics of globalization.

This chapter attempts an initial reconnaissance of this problem area. It starts off from a general discussion of the relations between globalization and the state and looks at different dimensions of the changing global context in which today's state systems function. This is followed by a discussion of globalization in its institutional aspects and the question of feasibility of global democracy. Last, the question of the future of the state is taken up, leading on to an exploration of regional variations in the relative propensity of state systems to 'cope with globalization' and survive.

Globalization and the state

Among the numerous implications of what we call globalization, some of the most far-reaching ones are its impacts on the role of the state (Strange 1996, Weiss 1998). More drastically than at any earlier times, it seems, state systems across the globe in recent years have been reshaped through global transformations, affecting both the inter-connections between states and their internal structuring. At the present time a discussion on questions of state restructuring and governance, more specifically on the dynamics of state formation and state collapse, thus must start off from a preliminary reconnaissance of the relations between globalization and the state.

Globalization of course has numerous facets, which cannot be detailed here. A vast and growing literature has explored many of its core dimensions (e.g. Robertson 2003, Stiglitz 2002), and there will be more to follow. For present purposes, though, we may provisionally refer to globalization as comprising a set of pervasive forces – economic, political and cultural – transforming relations between collectivities and individuals across the globe, including those among 'nation-states'.

This is roughly in line with Stiglitz's formulation, who describes globalization as 'the closer integration of the countries and peoples of the world which has been brought about by the enormous reduction of costs of transportation and communication, and the breaking down of artificial barriers to the flow of goods, services, capital, knowledge, and (to a lesser extent) people across borders' (p. 9). The 'artificiality' of barriers which Stiglitz alludes to, though, suggests something unwanted, out of place, and calling for removal. In a discussion of globalization and the state this view will call for some closer attention, as not everybody would agree that states should no longer play a role in this regard. Given its manifold dimensions, meanwhile, it will often make good sense to talk of different *kinds* of globalization, or of different globalizations, closely interacting with or confronting each other.

When zeroing in on the relation between globalization and the state, we must also unpack the 'state', a task which again is strictly undoable: the state is many things to many people, and has presented itself in many varieties and appearances in the past as well as present. Basic nonetheless remains the Weberian notion (though not always reality) of the state as a final, 'sovereign' authority and rule-making body with respect to the society and economy within a given territory. More narrowly, we can look at the state as a set of rules and structures as embodied in the state bureaucracy, or as the site or target of political power, implying ultimate control over the means of violence. Pragmatically, it is helpful at times to see the state as a set of institutions for the equation of different competing interests, which it supposedly translates into overall policy vis-à-vis (civil) society and the external context. With these various attributes and dispositions, states can be found pursuing different kinds of objectives, depending on the kind of impulses they receive and from which quarters: their agendas will be as varied as the enhancement of social welfare, economic growth, justice and the reconciliation of competing interests, but also of self-enrichment of the state elite, maintenance of power or even sheer plunder and oppression.

Globalization as a set of successive processes of transformation has been drawing its own history, and its relation to and impacts on the state have varied considerably in the course of this trajectory. Earlier waves of globalization had seen the expansion of the West, the industrial revolution and modern imperialism, establishing new but unequal economic inter-linkages with the rest of the world (Wallerstein 1974, Robertson 2003). Significantly, globalization then was spurred through competition of rival European powers for access to markets and resources. The European states involved actually derived additional strength through their engagement in this imperial globalization, and could further embellish their distinctiveness as 'nation-states'. The same could hardly be said for states being subjugated in the process elsewhere, even if at times efforts were made by the new powers to make the symbolic semblances of state continuity look very magnificent indeed, as in India. Other than that, however, the colonial enterprise featured many elements that people in the South today would regard as the essence of globalization – the resource capture, market incorporation and systems of remote control.

The present wave of globalization, especially in the post Cold War period since 1991, in some respects presents a qualitatively different picture. Here globalization seems prompted less by competitive state action, except at the level of mega powers like the United States, China and Japan in their quest for economic hegemony, but states across the globe are all subject to major inroads into their roles through globalization in different respects. Several dimensions of globalization in particular have been noted for their impacts, direct or indirect, on the role of the state. These include the communications revolution, cutting across state and other boundaries; the push towards market liberalization, deregulation and the like, no matter on how unequal terms; the unprecedented re-ordering of global manufacturing and service industries; the demands placed on many states for structural adjustment, decentralization and state restructuring in additional respects; and the spread of supra-national policy-making institutions and directives, paralleling the other dimensions while also constituting an autonomous trend in its own right.

Earlier, shifts in hegemonic regimes within the global orbit had also prompted formative as well as degenerative processes. Notably, superpower rivalry and hegemonies had their effect in creating or propping up state structures of client states in various parts of the world, amounting to a state formation dynamics of sorts. Once that protective hegemonic umbrella was lifted at the end of the Cold War, internal contradictions and conflicts of various kinds could more easily manifest themselves, in some cases leading to the break-up and eventual collapse of state entities. Global economic 'liberalization' has since then dictated the breaking up of national protective measures meant to support autonomous economic spheres, not without consequences for the resilience of state frameworks in various cases. The lifting of the Cold War was also followed by the spelling out of new directives as to how various state systems in the South should go about their 'governance', inaugurating a fresh spell of state restructuring initiatives under external supervision (as discussed in Chapter 4). The recently launched policy discourse, and action, of 'regime change' – triggering the Iraq quagmire – constitutes a provisional culminating point of these tendencies, extremely narrow as its chances of engendering any meaningful transitions are. Evidently, globalization is bringing processes of state collapse and state formation more closely together in several interlocking ways.

The current wave of globalization is strongly pushed by global capital and by organizations like the World Trade Organization (WTO), the World Bank and the International Monetary Fund (IMF), all working in close partnership with the US government. Pressures are put on virtually all states to bring down protective barriers in the name of economic liberalization and free trade, and to adopt matching principles of 'good governance' selectively derived from the Western experience. These pressures are also largely supported by various donor consortia for aid recipient countries, which represent a key factor in pre-determining the development options and paths of the countries concerned.

There is ongoing debate about the extent to which globalization impacts on the powers and capacities of the state (e.g. Hirst and Thompson 1999, Weiss 1998). While the various positions put forward cannot be reduced to simple dichotomies, one position has been to argue that state systems have basically lost their pre-eminent role as generators of economic wealth and well-being (e.g. Ohmae 1995, Strange 1996). Closely related, it has often been advanced that there is a weakening of state structures in various ways, and that the state is rather in a 'dis-aggregation' (Slaughter 2005). Another position holds that the state continues to play an essential role, though shifting to other modes of intervention (Dengbold-Martinussen 2001, Wade 1996, Weiss 1998). While specifics vary from case to case, it would appear that the two sides can broadly agree that globalization causes reduced distinctiveness of 'national' contexts, such as for the organization of production, the setting of norms and regulations, or as a venue for political debate. In cultural respects, not many states still figure as a point of gravity or enabling context, though globalization may sometimes provoke a pronounced nationalist or religion-based stance. This need not always be true, or not in every respect: shifting priorities and functions of the state may cause it to shed certain policy structures while putting its weight on others, possibly in line with shifts in its resource and support basis. In many countries, especially in the African and other Third World states, there has been a notable re-statification of violence, and a 'securitization' of civil society (taking the 'civil' out of society) (Gregory 2004: 261). A key factor all over is that in many instances the state no longer figures as the final nerve centre for policy-making and coordination, as many policies are increasingly being developed elsewhere – for European states at the level of the European Union in Brussels, for aid-dependent countries in Washington with the IMF and World Bank. In not a few cases, the role of the state has thus been changing from one that supposedly serves as a centre of policy initiatives to that of an implementing agent of policies designed elsewhere. Many states have surrendered several layers of their 'sovereignty' in the process, and a severance of the links between territory and sovereignty has followed in several respects.

Many of these transformations should be understood as signifying shifts in the priorities and functions of state systems, reflective of shifting resource and support bases in which the sources of finance play a critical role. States on all continents are now expected to act as facilitators of economic growth, and, bringing down their welfare functions, in most cases have had to renounce any earlier claims of giving primacy to social equity. Also, in the wake of far-reaching state restructuring taking place in terms of decentralization and other respects, over-arching state agencies often are no longer available or capable to carry out traditional functions such as interest reconciliation or protection of the weaker sections (Meynen and Doornbos 2004). Instead, in an increasingly volatile global economic environment, not a few state-systems have themselves become more vulnerable, at times running the risk of collapse. Nonetheless, states are not so much on their way out (except in incidences of total collapse), if only because they will be 'needed' at least to safeguard the operations of monopoly capital, or to convey and implement the ever changing set of donor policy priorities. Hence, we may well expect a strengthening of states and state functions in certain respects, and a weakening or withdrawal in others. In terms of social support for the state and the nature of identity politics, moreover, these shifts may well lead to the forging of new kinds of alliances. These may entail moving away from government programmes and client relationships based on social categorizations like 'the poor' or 'the backward classes', searching instead for modes of cultural legitimation that are reflective of the hegemony of new dominant coalitions, as in India or Mexico.

A changing global context

Against a general background of the impacts of globalization on the role of state systems, particular attention is warranted for contemporary dynamics of state restructuring and collapse. As a sign of changing times and global conditions, phenomena of state collapse and state restructuring of late have come to draw as much attention – or even more – as notions of state formation with which we have been familiar for much longer. In recent times, these tendencies have often coincided due to several crucial factors in the global context. Globalization in several of its key aspects may promote state formative processes at particular levels, while in other respects it induces or accelerates dynamics of state destruction and collapse. Pervasive institutionalization of new jurisdictions at global or regional levels tends to create organizational structures with functions like those of a state, while simultaneously usurping powers earlier held by formerly autonomous states. Evidently, the future of the state as a territorially demarcated jurisdiction and the centre for policy coordination is itself seriously affected by these trends.

In the light of this it will be useful to have a closer look at some of the dynamics of globalization. Globalization dynamics are important for an understanding of processes of state formation and state collapse in three major ways. First, processes of state formation and state collapse may often be triggered by key forces from within the global context, as these may prompt the growth of more encompassing political entities but also undermine weak state frameworks insufficiently equipped to safeguard themselves. Second, the global context strongly determines the scope for manoeuvre and survival of individual state systems and their development patterns, as well as the room for the emergence of new states, as a result of increasingly tightening webs of inter-state interdependency. And third, the global context is itself subject to pervasive forms of inter-state and state-related institutionalization, impinging upon and to an extent absorbing the role of existing states and proto-states. These impacts are closely related, each sharing grey areas with each of the others. All three call for some closer attention.

With regard to the first aspect, from the commanding heights of the global economy it can be easy to view instances of failing states and violent conflict in the South as aberrations from the model of the neo-liberal state, caused by tribal or ethnic enmities and the like. A variant of this view would add an emphasis on the greed motive being at work in applicable resource-rich locations (Berdal and Malone 2000). By implication, such assumptions can comfortably ignore the manifold ways in which global economic dynamics and policies impact on the economic and in turn political survival chances of many vulnerable Third World economies and societies. At times indeed there have been denials that there are any such connections. Yet, to mention but one factor, the distortions arising from heavy subsidies given to American and European farmers for products like grains, meats, cotton and dairy products on the domestic as well as potential export markets of many countries in the South, impact very negatively on the scope for sustainable agriculture in these countries. Indirectly, the global impact of such policies is to accelerate the successive erosion of environmental, livelihood and in the end food securities, in turn making many situations ripe for complex emergencies and potential state collapse. In addition, the debt crisis that many countries find themselves in can only amplify these implications.

Aside from ultimately bringing fragile polities to the brink of collapse, at a different level today's global dynamics also induce processes of state formation. Notably, the current EU project is inconceivable without the strong impetus it receives to compete with other major economic and political players like the United States, China and Japan within the global context. Here global economic competition is evidently leading to enlargements of scale, which in the case of the European Union has begun to assume state-like dimensions. Bloc formation elsewhere in the world may in time follow similar kinds of patterns.

In either of these cases, the dynamics of state formation not only result in the institutionalization of power relations, but entail important and sensitive options in identity re-structuring and political mobilization. Political identity, focused on either national, supra-national, ethnic/regional or other collective symbols, is never static, as it is invariably subject to influences generated by dynamic power relations. Thus, processes of political identity formation in different situations may well move in opposite directions. Contemporary situations include some where territorial disputes are still seen as involving a struggle in terms of officially upheld national integrity and identity, such as in the recent, as yet unresolved Ethiopian–Eritrean dispute (Jacquin-Berdal and Plaut 2005), or in that over Kashmir. In other contexts meanwhile the whole idea of 'national identity' appears to be on the way out or is getting seriously qualified. Thus, one may find the *de-territorialization of sovereignty* being discussed as a characteristic transformation of modern statehood at cosmopolitan centres (LSE Seminar 2003), while at the same time old-style territorially focused state nationalism in parts of Africa, Asia or ex-Yugoslavia as yet allows extremely little flexibility to resolve inter- and intra-state conflicts of sovereignty. These kinds of transformations, too, need to be brought into focus.

As regards the second aspect, the scope for manoeuvre for individual state entities within the current global context and inter-state system has clearly become very limited and is rapidly shrinking further in the face of a multitude of demands for global conformity. By and large, states big and small have progressively become intertwined within the global inter-state system, and in some sense have come to increasingly resemble each other – through the adoption of similar kinds of government institutions, the introduction of parallel legislation, and the global orchestration of policy initiatives led by key global actors and inter-state institutions. As a matter of fact, there are today only two or three kinds of actors displaying an inclination or disposition to stand outside and defy the growing body of global statutory inter-linkages. One evidently is the sole remaining superpower, the United States, which in respect to several vital global concerns – Kyoto, the International Criminal Court, Guantanamo Bay and various UN Security Council and General Assembly resolutions – takes the position that it does not consider itself bound by the norms and procedures constituting the international system, but is standing 'above' them. From this position it has increasingly arrogated the power to impose its own terms on other actors within the system, thereby nonetheless adding significantly to the impacts of globalization through the repercussions it causes. In their otherwise perceptive analysis of the emerging corporate 'Empire', Hardt and Negri advance, rather apologetically, that 'the US world police acts not in imperialist interest but in imperial interest' (Hardt and Negri 2000: 180), a fine distinction to imply that it is just happens to be the case that the policemen's role has befallen the United States in the maintenance of global coherence in the present era, rather than the latter harbouring any new-style imperialist ambitions.

A second category comprises the 'semi-official' deviants like North-Korea, Cuba, and Libya until recently, though the extent to which they challenge or abide by the international system could be a matter of further debate. Other deviants constitute a very different category found at the bottom end of the international system, namely the array of failed and collapsed states comprising the system's dropouts, like Somalia or Sierra Leone. Without relevant institutional capacity, in some cases even without a mailbox, these have no way of taking part in this process of increasing institutional integration and globalization, thus underscoring the reality of these trends through their lack of involvement in them. No longer able to comply with global directives, the occurrence of these new non-conformist bodies raises important theoretical questions about the longer-term viability of the inter-state system as a whole and about how it should respond to blank spaces emerging on the world's map.

The limited scope available for autonomous departures by state and non-state actors in the global context also appears confirmed, albeit indirectly, by the international demands upon even a stateless entity such as the former Somali Republic to be seen to conform to the UN-sanctioned inter-state system. To uphold the system's overall integrity, the myth of continuity of the sovereignty of Somalia as a member-state is strenuously being upheld. This is illustrated, among other things, by the UN Security Council's refusal to recognize 'break-away' Somaliland, which has been effectively functioning as a state since 1991, though without international recognition. Out of fear for gaps appearing in the intricate global network of treaty obligations and reciprocities, it is thus currently virtually impossible to conceive of alternative state formation initiatives being given a chance of success. Nonetheless, dropouts from the system are more likely to be on the increase than not. If the global inter-state system proves unable to accommodate them, a prospect of a growing 'underclass' of opt-outs or failed states emerges.

Third and possibly most important, the growth of political and institutional linkages globally and the formulation of norms for the reorientation of state structures by dominant global centres, may themselves be viewed as processes of institution-building and 'state' formation, but now on a kind of mega-scale. There appear to be two major forms in which this manifests itself. One, formally sovereign state structures are progressively becoming integrated within larger regional and global supra-state frameworks, in the process shedding several layers and attributes of their erstwhile autonomy. Sometimes, as most visibly in the domain of the European Union, the effect tends to resemble a pattern towards federalization. In the process, the nature and role of the joining (member) states undergo drastic transformation, raising the question, in Habermas' words, whether 'any of our small or medium, *entangled and accommodating* nation-states [can] preserve a separate capacity to escape enforced assimilation to the social model now imposed by the predominant global economic regime?' (Habermas 2001: 5).

Second, there is an emphasis in various regards on arriving at common institutional norms and procedures, which often contains an element of tutelage especially vis-à-vis Third World governments. Trends towards globalization in this respect, with an increasing focus on the introduction of particular kinds of institutional norms and structures, most of them derived from Western models, are unmistakable. The 'good governance' agenda propagated by the World Bank and other global institutions, for example, has underlined the conformity that is expected of state actors across the globe to abide by the norms for conduct of government affairs advanced by these institutions – intrinsically non-specific and non-descript as these norms may be upon closer inspection (see Chapter 4). In the process, the role of Third World states shifts from searching to enhance their own internal policy coherence and autonomy, to being increasingly expected to act as the vehicle for transmission of externally determined policy objectives. Though reciprocal influences between states and emulation of organizational forms are of all ages, in recent decades these globalizing pressures towards increased institutional uniformity have been accelerating at an unprecedented scale.

In the extreme case, an insistence on the transplantation of 'acceptable' institutions takes the form of the US–UK invasion of Iraq to effect 'regime change'. It is astonishing of course that at the present time and age key global powers are advancing the proposition of 'democratization' from the barrel of the gun. The notion that the removal of an autocratic leader of government will have 'democracy' spontaneously spring up is not just utterly naïve, revealing an alarming degree of ignorance about socio-cultural realities elsewhere in the world. It is also a gross overrating of the global powers' own capacity to change things at their will. It evidently carries grave consequences for the way 'world order' is to be managed and human rights principles are being observed (Gregory 2004, Ch. 8) In this connection it must be recalled that earlier, softer efforts by the 'international community' to use a new generation of political conditionalities to bring about democracy have had but poor results, as is discussed further in Chapter 4. The record on this score boils down to the simple truth that there just are no convincing cases where democratization has been brought about by external engineering. As Bastian and Luckham (2003: 311) conclude after examining a vast array of comparative evidence, 'there are no universally valid institutional blueprints for broadening democracy or managing entrenched political and social conflicts'. Democratization, if it is to be viable and sustainable, must get its basic impetus from within. Notwithstanding these givens, the pressures to conform and abide by external agendas persist.

Institutional globalization and global democracy

Clearly, processes of institutional globalization deserve attention as a powerful force in their own right. As elaborated elsewhere (Doornbos 2000: 255–258), under their influence the role and nature of the state are progressively changing. It is not just that the state in most parts of the world has been forced to surrender a good deal of the space it occupied in favour of markets and civil society. Equally important is that states, markets and civil societies alike have all become highly dependent upon larger and more powerful forces at the regional and global level. These linkages and pressures are by no means uni-directional, but often pose contrasting demands on states and institutions at the receiving end. At times different agencies within the UN system, for example, have been known to confront member-states seeking assistance in post-conflict rehabilitation with entirely opposite conditionalities (Boyce 1996, Dijkzeul 2003). Still, from a broader perspective such collisions may also be taken to underscore how the web of global institutional connections is growing increasingly dense and complex.

When considering the role and performance of particular global agencies, the context is evidently no longer one defined by a simple state–society paradigm, but one in which external agencies and global processes play decisive roles. At the same time, international agencies should not only be looked at in terms of their relation to the state. One of the most revealing aspects of their current role concerns the manner in which they seek to extend their own institutional identities, sometimes competing for control over 'functional' territories and spheres of involvement amongst each other. Indeed, a shift in emphasis from the classical kind of state territoriality to functionally defined 'territories' claimed by global agencies, each with their characteristic claims and with different kinds of boundary demarcations, appears to be one key dimension in what goes on under 'globalization' today. The implications of these tendencies for understanding relevant political relationships and interactions, and indeed for spotting and locating the political element in the first place, are momentous but as yet appear to have been insufficiently recognized.

Generally, these trends towards global institutionalization should primarily be viewed as affirmations of newly emergent global power relations rather than as any evolution towards global unity or the emergence of a democratic political world order. A priori they imply neither cultural homogenization nor democratization at the level of global institutions, however desirable the latter may be held to be (Held 1992, 1995). Even if, in very incremental and basically imperceptible ways, some sort of global government were emerging, thus representing a kind of state formation at the global level (Hardt and Negri 2000), one should never expect this to signify the end of conflict within or among the constituent entities concerned. In many respects the trend indeed goes together with increased tension and a resurgence of diverse stakes and interests, comprising tendencies towards what might be termed global *de-democratization* as well as *democratization*. Democratization at a global level should refer to the strenuous efforts being undertaken in various instances to try and make institutions operating in the transnational orbit more responsive and answerable to representative bodies and the popular voices of global citizens. 'Global civil society' is the key phrase and focus for the relevant debates (Dower 2003, Keane 2003), which have recently come to be orientated largely on the World Social Forum (Waterman 2002, 2003). Global de-democratization in contrast comes with the rapid proliferation of new institutional constructs that assume or are given power and authority over vast areas of international public policy and concern, though often with surprisingly limited accountability to constituent national governments, let alone to civic representations (Scholte 1998). However, Mary Kaldor has also advanced the argument that, 'global civil society has contributed to the erosion of national democracy' (LSE Seminar 2003), suggesting that participatory energies directed at global targets may weaken engagement with nationally defined causes.

The debate on how these far-reaching transitions should be read touches on a range of dimensions – cultural, legal, political, socio-economic and others – and is of definite relevance to an interest in the prospects and processes of state building and decline. It is certainly true that internet and the global communications society that has been shaping up provide immense and unprecedented opportunities towards the linking up and creation of social movements and solidarity groups on a global scale (Castells 1996, Waterman 2002). In this respect 'global civil society' can be said to have become a force, albeit a 'soft-power' one, to be reckoned with. But the same advanced technologies for global communication and interaction are also available for less visible, less heard-of, yet highly influential networks – public, private, corporate and 'greyish' – exercising an increasingly powerful global institutional sway over many key areas of vital human concern. The potential scope for global social action in the internet era, therefore, must be weighed against the likelihood of a loss of democratic control in various spheres.

These trends parallel those exemplifying the creation as well as the destruction of 'social capital'. On the one hand we might consider the attainment of new and meaningful institutional structures with clearly laid out civic accountabilities as the creation of novel forms of social capital. On the other hand, there is an everyday destruction of social capital by way of the erosion of once relevant institutions into redundant entities. Such institutional decline often comes in the wake of the introduction of supra-level bodies of institutional command. Again, the decline and eclipse of once relevant institutions is of all ages, yet in the contemporary era it is likely to be the destiny of various institutions currently still held in high esteem by its constituents. Trends and efforts towards 'global' civic democratization and de-democratization may thus be seen to be in a continuous race and competition, with democratizing forces trying hard to neutralize or mitigate de-democratizing initiatives, but on balance so far, appearing more often to lose out than catch up in the process.

What future for the state?

In the light of these institutional globalizing processes, their overall impact on existing 'national' political autonomy and the role of democratic institutions can only be one of gradual decline rather than of a strengthening of the institutions concerned. With various layers of their substantive powers being progressively usurped by regional or global bodies, the role of national governments and parliaments increasingly becomes one of 'ratifying' international and global policy documents originating from the mega bureaucracies in Brussels, Washington and other key centres.

One question often raised in this respect, therefore, is what future, if any, is there for the modern state, specifically the nation-state. The question's import has been enhanced as a result of the worldwide wave of neo-liberal economic policies advocating privatization and public austerity, carried to fresh shores by highly influential international agencies, bringing pressure to bear on the state in favour of increased room for the market mechanism. Thus, highly diverse types of regimes have been seen withdrawing from direct control over vital aspects of their economies, and from offering a safety net to the weaker sections through the provision of welfare. The trend has reinforced, and been reinforced by, political pressures to curtail the public bureaucracy in various instances. Besides, shifts may be noted in the support basis of states, such as when the state moves away from the 'mass' support it enjoyed in exchange for public welfare provisions, to seeking strategic support from key industries and external backing up. Virtually no state, it should be remembered, is monolithic, as states usually are reflective of different interests and orientations competing with one another for dominance even within the state apparatus and trying to push the role of the state in different directions. Clearly, therefore, the state does not necessarily disappear but a different kind of state, or kinds of states, are likely to emerge in the process.

With respect to these issues, it seems useful to avoid premature teleological perspectives, either about the future of the state or its possible successor-bodies, or about the nature and destiny of the transformation processes to which it is being subjected. While the future of the state is uncertain and evidently deserves a question-mark, it would be unwise at this stage either to read the signs concerned as pointing to its demise (Hirst 2001, Hirst and Thompson 1999, Weiss 1998), or to underestimate their potential significance (LSE Seminar 2003). In a dynamic perspective, we may need to see the state as continuously reshaping itself as well as being reshaped. We could also see it expand or contract at different intervals, to be succeeded or superseded by other forms in due course and being subject to major reorientation as to what constitutes its 'core business'. It would thus be necessary to be alert to new institutional 'grey zones' opening up, which it will be important to try to map out, as well as to shifts regarding what states do and do not do. In short, the transitions around us invite re-examination, among other things, of what states are, what they are for, and of degrees or kinds of 'state-ness'. Such an approach might have some merits in examining current tendencies, provided we do not presuppose a kind of iron cyclical movement that would have the state temporarily recede and come back to resume its former role and position (Azarya 1988).

The pervasive processes of transition occurring in many parts of the world essentially amount to *changing forms of organization of collective activities*. The need to modify state-focussed theories invites further exploration of this largely uncharted territory defined by the unfolding of new state and non-state forms of political management and control. In that context, moreover, it will be important to examine the proliferation of new kinds of partnerships and/or patterns of competition between state and non-state agencies. In part, this involves an exploration of shifting boundaries of sorts: not of state boundaries in any conventional sense, but of the changing boundaries of state functions and the state's 'reach' in different respects.

Among the 'visible' sides of these transitions have been patterns of 'top-down' deregulation and de-institutionalization, the disintegration or fragmentation of political entities, the erosion of the state's monopoly over the means of violence and the proliferation of arms among non-state political actors. Other manifestations of these processes include 'everyday forms of state formation', referring to the micro-world of 'bottom-up' shifting allegiances to alternative power-holders – including state, anti-state and non-state forms as locally represented. At yet other levels, as noted, there is ample evidence of supra-state re-alignments, of pervasive integration and incorporation of trans-national institutional structures, and of a rapidly widening scope of novel organizational devices.

But questions about the future of the state or state systems do not only concern the changing nature of their 'core' business and related structuring. By implication they also relate to their relative capacity to 'adjust' and maintain themselves in an increasingly capricious global environment, or, in other words, to their propensity to collapse or survive. That, it could be argued, is also part of their core business. Ever since 'structural adjustment' was adopted as one of the strategies of intervention by the major global financial institutions, massive evidence has been accumulating to attest to the impacts of globalization in terms of the increasing social and economic vulnerabilities of numerous groups and individuals in countries of the South. In not a few instances, growing livelihood insecurities have led to widespread destitution, intensified rural–urban and trans-national migration and social conflicts, and increasing prospects of political failure to cope with these deteriorating conditions, in the end with a question as to whether state institutions will be able to survive. Nonetheless, while it is clear that there are these effects, their impacts have been differential. Not all countries of 'the South' have been equally vulnerable to state crisis and potential collapse. Some, particularly several of those that have been heavily dependent on agricultural production but have been fetching lower and lower prices on the world market, have been hit especially severely. Some others, which had the mixed blessing of being mineral-rich, or becoming the producers of profitable drugs, have also proven particularly vulnerable as governable state frameworks. Yet others, particularly those that managed to make their industrial entry into the global market, have instead proven remarkably resilient.

Regional variations

At the risk of over-generalization, there appears to be an important regional dimension to the patterns discussed here, with more instances of state systems in Africa having fallen victim to state failure and collapse than has been the case in Asia. Still, the evidence is not exactly overwhelming. Africa in recent years has gone on record with the cases of Somalia, Liberia, Sierra Leone and basically Congo, while there have been other 'near-collapse' cases on an almost continuous basis. Earlier Chad, Angola, Mozambique, Uganda and Rwanda would similarly have ranked as failed or collapsed states. As a generalization, an equation of African states with state collapse will need to be qualified, however. In Asia and the Pacific, at least, the cases of Afghanistan, Cambodia and earlier Lebanon, as well as 'potentials' like Papua New Guinea and the Solomon

Islands, suggest that though Africa has a stronger record of problem cases, it has no monopoly on state failure or state collapse.

Iraq incidentally does not fit these equations. No matter how one might have wanted to assess the Iraqi state in its earlier incarnation, in the absence of external intervention it would have had every chance of remaining a firm and stable state for quite some time to come – by no means 'free' by White House standards, though with possibly at least some 30,000 more Iraqi survivors. And while the former Iraqi state was very 'statist' indeed, that statism also reflected a compulsion to maintain a unity of sorts among quite differently oriented segments in the population (Tripp 2002). With that semblance of unity broken up, Iraq's fragmentation is evidently proving difficult to repair.

But if generalizing about the nature of the state in Africa is already hazardous, this appears true even more for Asia, where Afghanistan, Indonesia or Nepal have been constituting significantly different kinds of state systems compared to, say, China, Japan or India. And the latter, again, have as much to distinguish themselves from each other as they have in common. At any rate, asking whether there might be a stronger *propensity* for state collapse in Africa than in Asia or elsewhere may be a more relevant enquiry than just trying to count the respective numbers of state failure and collapse at either end. If one were to do this, and ask why that could be the case, then such features as the relative extent of cohesion, concentration of power and especially social mobilization within and through the state framework, may need to be recognized as being of special significance. Beyond the crucial question as to how countries have come to be inserted in the world market, it is in the end these kinds of factors which may make a difference as to the extent to which societies and states have remained either relatively insulated from or become vulnerable to the risks of collapse. 'Propensity to collapse', in other words, could possibly be conceived as an alternative yardstick for assessing the nature and relative robustness of the state in its relations with society and the environment. Conversely, some of the same features, like social and political cohesion and the extent of social mobilization, might possibly help to appreciate ongoing dynamics of state restructuring where they occur. The vast transformations in its economy, society and state structures which China is undergoing, for example, could be seen as a complex of restructuring processes building on the country's high degree of social cohesion and mobilization. This is not to underestimate the magnitude of internal contradictions and potential tensions within the country itself, such as between the coastal regions and the interior, North and South, the new business class and the peasantry. Far from having its state framework under threat as a result of globalization, however, China instead appears to be emerging as one of the main new engines of globalization.

Finally, a fuller scrutiny of the 'propensity' question will require us to look back into the respective historical records, including the differential ways in which Western imperialism has impacted on Asia, Africa and Latin America. By and large, Asian states, even if undergoing major structural transformations during colonialism like in India, have known much stronger continuities of political organization than has been the case in Africa (Kaviraj 1997). Asia has had a number of long-standing state entities, often largely inwardly focused and with sizeable internal markets allowing significant degrees of economic differentiation and integration. Culturally, broad civilizational continuities in some of the major countries have helped to sustain basic political and administrative cohesion and facilitate social mobilization on virtually a mega scale (Kumar 1997). None of this was to preclude major violence and political upheavals at critical historical intervals, but surely there was nonetheless a strong focus on continuity and preservation of the state system or systems. Mostly old and complex entities, they would often be so complex that they could not easily come to fall apart. Instead, they would feature a relatively strong interweaving of structures of state and society, and a shared engagement in mass culture. Colonial rule, though severely impacting, largely took the form of 'trickle-down' and (selective) absorption of Western elements. This stood in contrast to the African situation, which was characterized by fragmentation of the continent into arbitrary entities and the imposition of a wholly new and alien order. The resulting 'gap' in state and society relations in the African context has never really been closed since, and has been perpetuated through the lack of a political class which does *not* have its roots within one of the characteristic states' ethno-regional groups. Economic dynamics have not been able to counter these tendencies, but have, on the contrary, for a long time reinforced the presence and continuity of essentially vulnerable bureaucratic ruling classes. As contrasted to recurrent formative economic and political processes in several of the larger states of Asia, therefore, Africa's state systems indeed appear to have been bequeathed a stronger vulnerability and propensity for collapse. Latin America figures less distinctively in this equation. While most Latin American countries have been notably 'statist', in some like Argentine and Chile strong state systems were ruling over largely immigrant populations, whereas in others, such as in most of the Andes countries, states and urban classes alike have tended to confront an amalgam of indigenous rural communities. Neither of the two kinds of systems have been particularly known for their tendency to collapse, though the challenges to the state from different kinds of rival powerful movements in Colombia, Bolivia, Peru and Mexico, among others, have been clearly on the rise.

Concluding remarks

This chapter culminates in the thesis that globalization dynamics, beyond constituting a major challenge to all existing state systems and causing their transformation and re-orientation in significant respects, tends to prompt incidences of state collapse and novel forms of state formation in various situations. Such incidences underscore the relevance of the question about the relative capacity of state systems to 'cope with globalization', in other words their propensity to either withstand and 'absorb' globalization, allowing themselves to be transformed by it, or to collapse under its direct or indirect impacts.

Trying to ascertain such relative propensities opens up a wholly new research agenda for enquiry into the relative strength and robustness of state systems in a changing global context, probing into aspects in which they appear vulnerable and exposed to global impacts. While noting that any such agenda, or even part of it, by necessity is extraordinarily complex, one aspect in particular that will complicate analysis is the fluidity and lack of homogeneity of the constituting political bodies. As globalization in its manifestation of market and trade liberalization causes state bodies to make policy choices which entail differential effects on different social strata, chances are of ever-widening socio-economic rifts between new middle classes which benefit from the new openings and large sections of the population for whom there is hardly any more place or sustenance. For its own sake, as well as to be able to play a meaningful role in terms of protecting social cohesiveness, the way the state handles its capacity to cope with these challenges is crucial, determining in the end whether it will survive or submerge. Ultimately state systems can only neglect their role in this regard at their own peril. The 'state', after all, represents a much more concrete and visible target for confrontation, and arena for conflict, than 'globalization'. But to safeguard itself as well as to be able to play its role it needs a sufficient measure of that quality called 'relative autonomy'.

3

The African State in Academic Debate: Shifting Perspectives

Introduction

State systems across the globe in recent decades have been subject to pervasive transformation and restructuring in the wake of global waves of liberalization and external demands placed upon them. The nature of these changes and reorientations, however, has varied considerably from one world region to the other. While East and Southeast Asian states and more recently India have demonstrated remarkable resilience as state systems and a capacity to make their economies competitive and grow on the global market, adjusting their state structures to facilitate that while maintaining a certain measure of autonomy vis-à-vis the external world, African states in contrast have been doing less well on these scores. Not a few of the latter have instead undergone, or continue to be subject to, severe crises with respect to the role of the state, the economy and state–society relationships. Several state systems have in fact been at or beyond the point of crumbling down and falling victim to overall collapse. Others have been able to maintain themselves, but often at the price of assuming a rather threatening stance vis-à-vis their population or segments of it, rationalized as the case may be by the need to 'hold things together'. Indeed, the idea of 'state' as an authoritative institutional apparatus separate from yet intimately engaged with monitoring and regulating social processes has often appeared to match uncomfortably with underlying societal forces and dynamics within the African context.

As a result, while questions about the role and position of the African state are by no means new, in recent years they have come to be asked with increasing concern and emphasis. The specific reasons for this may vary with the position and perspective of the questioners, but they have often included a concern about capacity and performance, about the styles and orientations of leadership and about the measure of representativeness and legitimacy which African state governments enjoy within the society at large. In short, strong currents of academic and other opinion have posited serious problems with the African state, prompting a good deal of discussion as to what its role should be as well as fostering a variety of proposed and actual interventions by international organizations and consultants to help 'solve' the problem.

It would be futile to try and reverse the picture and argue that there is no 'problem' with the state in Africa. Nonetheless, it will be useful to try and place existing preoccupations in perspective by highlighting some aspects of the debates on the African state in the post-colonial period, which as will become clear have been as much subject to change and revision as the African state itself.

Key themes

Questions about state power and capacity, and about national identity and unity have largely defined the debate about the nature and role of post-colonial African states. These have also been basic to a better understanding of their predicaments and future options. In this connection, the concept of the state in Africa must refer to a territorial entity as well as to an institutionalized expression of political power, the political institutions and the state apparatus, the bureaucracy. Both dimensions are related and problematic.

Before developing these themes of state power and identity further, however, a few preliminary observations will be useful. One is just to note the relative ease with which one may generalize when talking about 'the' African state, in contrast to the way we might refer to its counterparts elsewhere in the world. With respect to Europe, for example, we are generally less likely to refer to 'the state' in the first place. But such differences already seem indicative of a particular image of the state in Africa, as well as of the occurrence of a more or less distinct species throughout most of the continent. The African state for long has been highly visible and has stood in rather marked distinction to the non-state sphere, except perhaps for the ways in which the latter was able to infiltrate the former in order to lay claims on its resources.

One has often generalized about the nature, role and position of the African state despite notable demographic and socio-economic differences, as well as for a long time marked variations in political and ideological orientation. From the late 1960s until the early 1990s these were African socialist, Marxist–Leninist, outright neo-colonial or middle of the road, though subsequently most states conformed to a capitalist oriented profile in the context of powerful external impulses. African states shared significant common characteristics pointing to a particular configuration, notably (i) their post-colonial status, with all the implications this had for the evolution of the non-state sphere or 'civil society', (ii) their a priori problematic relationship as regards their territorial jurisdiction, (iii) the heavy and continuing involvement in a restricted resource base (usually primarily agricultural, though in some, often turning out the most problematic, also the exploitation of minerals), (iv) their economically rather undifferentiated yet ethnically heterogeneous and volatile social infrastructure, (v) the salient processes of consolidation of power by new ruling classes and, last but not least, (vi) their pervasive external context and dependency. Each of these characteristics significantly conditioned the specific patterns of post-colonial state formation that have been taking place in Africa and the questions to which these have given rise. Nonetheless, these common features, important as they are, should not cause us to lose sight of significant and at times striking variations in the political trajectories of different post-colonial state systems in Africa (Doornbos 2005).

Second, when discussing patterns of state formation, one is basically concerned with a set of ongoing processes. Specifically in the African context these have evolved around the crystallization and the transformation of the role of the post-colonial state and the particular manifestations of its power. Theoretically therefore this has included the establishment, growth and differentiation of state structures and the redefinition of the position of various social and political formations, groups and organizational networks within wider state contexts. These processes lie at the heart of the dynamic of state–society relationships and raise fundamental questions about the manner in which the post-colonial state sets out to establish its linkages with constituent social units and categories and the extent of autonomy it has granted them. But as the state often first embarked upon an incorporating path on its way towards maximizing its power and control, these attempts at state formation and integration have also implied deformation and disintegration of pre-existing forms, giving rise to continuous processes of confrontation, adjustment and absorption. Earlier, through indirect rule and other devices the colonial state had also displaced and incorporated various pre-colonial formations.

The moment of independence, for most African countries shortly before or after 1960, is not always the most appropriate point in time from which to begin analysing state formation and performance. Taking independence as a break-off point for purposes of periodization, *prima facie* plausible as it may seem, has often led to distorted and unwarranted 'before and after' comparisons (Doornbos 1974: 557–564). A vast literature has identified basic structural determinants inherited from the colonial era setting definite limits to the actions of the post-colonial state and to a large extent predetermining the trajectories of its formation. Still, for a discussion of changing perspectives the post-colonial years do represent an appropriate time span, if only because it was with the beginning of this period that an academic interest in the African state beyond the purely anthropological began to manifest itself in any significant way.

In retrospect, two matters appear to have been grossly underrated at the time, with serious consequences for subsequent perspectives. One was the occurrence of a much wider differentiation and proliferation of social movements, reactions and interactions during the immediate pre-independence period than appears to have been recognized at the time, which in the long run would severely curtail the social basis for longer-term national reconstruction and reconciliation. In other words, the nationalist front in many instances was less pervasive and less unified than subsequent state ideology would make it out to be and the interventions and reactions during de-colonization were more varied and complex than was usually recognized (Twaddle 1985). The other blind spot, so striking in retrospect, was a profound lack of awareness of how uncertain and precarious would be the efforts of African states and their leaders to define and develop their role and position within and vis-à-vis the larger society. In comparison with Asia, for example, there was much less – or even less – by way of relevant historical precedent and experience from which inspiration and guidance could be derived. Besides, it was not as clear to observers within or outside Africa as it might become later on how distinctively the dominant leadership would be pursuing its own conception of what the 'nation' would look like, as opposed to some imaginary or yet to be negotiated identity that would give equal recognition to other groups included in the post-colonial inheritance.

Instead, there was at the time a strong belief, shared by many scholars and some practitioners alike, in the scope for engineering social processes, demonstrated by the relative ease with which new institutions and organizational experiments were set up (though often subsequently abrogated and reconstituted as the case might be), in the expectation that projected patterns of social interaction would soon follow as a matter of course. Quite fundamentally, this belief was not unrelated to the notion that one *knew* the direction in which state and society would develop in Africa: that of modern, secular frameworks with all the familiar functional checks-and-balances and appropriate administrative technologies. In the process, members of African communities were expected to develop new identities as modern, national citizens, shedding ethnic identities and relationships that were perceived as traditional and backward. Today such assumptions might be considered erroneous and misplaced, but at the time these destinies were seen as quite natural and self-evident: there was little awareness, academically or otherwise, that there might be something basically problematic about the perspective as such.

In terms of ensuing paradigms, the results of these notions were dramatic. There were very high initial expectations about the role the state would play as the prime mover in all development efforts. Whether in agriculture, industrialization, education or other sectors, the burden of formulating and implementing the policies that would transform society was laid squarely with the government. The state was to pull the whole society along in an all-out development drive on several fronts. One should note, though, that this perspective was not a monopoly of the liberal paradigm, or projected only onto capitalist-oriented states. In formulating an alternative to what soon became recognized as a 'neo-colonial' path, Marxist scholars assigned a similarly central role to the state in the projected 'transition to socialism' of African countries. These opposite yet parallel perspectives naturally led to a good deal of debate with respect to the *kind* of society that was to be engineered, capitalist or socialist. However, it should be noted that they were similarly 'statist' or state-oriented in their identification of the key variables. They also reflected the choices made in reality, which essentially amounted to state capitalism or state socialism. In either case, the state was to direct the economy and, through product marketing and other mechanisms, seek to extract a surplus, which it would redirect partly for the mainte-nance and expansion of its own apparatus and for redistribution to other sectors (Chabal 1986: 1–6, Doornbos 1977: 317–330, Saith 1985).

As was increasingly realized, however, the high expectations bestowed on the state could hardly be fulfilled under the prevailing conditions. They proved ill-founded, both vis-à-vis the state and the society it confronted. In case after case, high expectations were followed by profound disillusionment and the role attributed to the African state changed from one of prime mover of development to that of its main obstacle. By impli-cation this laid the ground for a prolonged dialogue on the structural position of the state highlighting a range of key problems and dilemmas.

Three debates

In the late 1960s, the concept of 'political penetration' helped to provoke an interesting controversy in East Africa (Cliffe *et al.* 1977). This was a time when many scholars were sympathetic towards the newly independent states and their aspirations and it was hoped that research itself might make a contribution to 'development' by indicating, for example, how government programmes could be implemented and replicated more effectively in different social contexts. Starting from this preoccupation, one of the first requirements of the state was seen to be its 'penetration' of society and the enhancement of its capacity to implement policies. In James Coleman's much quoted definition, 'political penetration' referred to

> that ensemble of processes by which the political-administrative-juridical centre of a new state (1) establishes an effective and authoritative central presence throughout its geographical and sectoral peripheries, and (2) acquires a capacity for the extraction and mobilization of resources to implement its policies and pursue its goals, however these may be determined. (Coleman 1977: 3)

This concept, it was thought, would be of value in providing an orientation on the mobilizing role of governments in bridging the macro–micro gap.

It soon became evident, however, that the same concept of penetration provided a suitable focus for other kinds of queries. Various researchers began to have apprehensions about the role of the state and its implications for the so-called target populations. The very notion of state or political penetration lent itself very well to voicing these concerns. Noting the emergence and class behaviour of new bureaucratic élites, questions were raised as to whose purposes and interests were being served by their penetrative efforts (Cliffe 1977: 19–50, Saul 1972: 118–126, Thoden van Velzen 1977: 223–250). By implication, question marks were placed on the priority of enhancing the state's reach and control over local social and political networks, on its dominant role in the relations of production and on the dislocating effects of its interventions. In the years to follow these concerns became increasingly and crucially important.

Many of the same conflicting premises were echoed somewhat later in the debates in Tanzania during the 1970s at the University of Dar es Salaam. Their importance lay partly in a historical conjunction of policy and research objectives and marked a significant period in the thinking on state–society relationships in Africa. The Arusha Declaration of 1967 had inaugurated a *prima facie* progressive state policy and the Tanzanian leadership appeared open to a kind of policy dialogue with concerned scholars. In a sympathetic climate which came to be known, in Ali Mazrui's terminology, as 'Tanzaphilia' (Mazrui 1967: 20–26), committed neo-Marxists, in particular, were attracted to the prospect of contributing to the clarification of policy choices in support of developing a state-led socialist strategy. Initially much attention was devoted to the identification and analysis of rural class formation and to the state's responsibility in restraining this. However, the policy discourse was soon extended to many other areas – to import substitution, taxation, and education, for example – out of concern for developing proper socialist strategies and instruments (Cliffe and Saul 1972).

But this policy-oriented search for appropriate interventions was seriously challenged, and in a sense disoriented, when Issa Shivji and others began to point to the dominant and exploitative role which was being manifested by the new bureaucratic bourgeoisie in post-Arusha Tanzanian development (Shivji 1975). Exponent and embodiment of the 'over-developed state' (Leys 1976: 39–48), this class was viewed to be syphoning off an increasing share of the surplus created by peasant agriculture, though not for productive re-investment. State and class formation came to be seen largely as twin processes reinforcing each other and in this new perspective the state lost its relatively autonomous and progressive image. Debates on the strengthening of its capacity and effectiveness were thus qualified and countered by questions as to which class interests were being served by government policy and whether those of the peasants were being subordinated rather than promoted in the process. Again, the theme of debate had essentially shifted to that of 'state *versus* society', in which the former had emerged as disproportionately powerful and central, while 'society' stood primarily for a largely undifferentiated and vulnerable peasantry.

A third instance of a debate on this theme was the discussion in *Development and Change* around the work of Göran Hyden in the late 1980s (Hyden 1986: 677–705). In the light of the new situation – the severe crisis in which Africa found itself in the 1980s – the nature of the questions had changed from a basically forward-oriented dialogue about 'transformations' and the overcoming of 'obstacles to change', to a more pessimistic and retrospective questioning of 'what went wrong?'. (One might wonder, however, whether that in itself was the right question, as it would seem to presume that the foundations for African development had been basically sound, but that some unanticipated variable caused the process to be detracted from its proper course.)

Some of the basic arguments advanced at this point could be linked to earlier positions with respect to the dichotomy between state and society. In two widely read books, Göran Hyden had pointed to the limits of socialist societal engineering (Hyden 1980, 1983), the core of his argument being that serious objective constraints militated against state efforts towards economic transformation. In Hyden's view, their relatively secure access to land gave African peasants an 'exit option' from market incorporation (a position epitomized by his phrase 'the uncaptured peasantry'), in turn creating a basic impediment for state-led (or any other) transformation. Under the prevailing circumstances the African state was too weak and too 'soft', in Hyden's analysis, to overcome this constraint. Hence, unless it would develop a capacity to 'capture' the peasantry and extract a surplus from it in order to strengthen its own position, stagnation would continue to prevail.

In their critiques, Nelson Kasfir, Lionel Cliffe and Gavin Williams pointed to the manifold ways in which the peasantry in Tanzania and other African countries had already been ensnared by national and international market forces (Kasfir 1986: 335–357, Cliffe 1987: 625–635, Williams 1987: 637–659). In their interpretation of the crisis confronting state–peasant relationships, they emphasized external determinants, especially the debt burden and the deteriorating terms of trade. These constraints severely restricted the scope for possible alternative interventions and had little to offer by way of positive inducements and recognition of popular interests. Put more plainly, their argument was that African peasants had been squeezed too much and certainly not too little, as in Hyden's analysis. In turn, the state's weakness and the developmental impasse could partly be attributed not to its inability to overcome the defences of the peasants, but to its own inroads into their agrarian resource basis. Still, as regards Hyden's question in his final rejoinder in *Development and Change* as to what, then, should be an alternative programme of action (Hyden 1987: 661–667), this particular debate, as others, remained basically unresolved.

For all their varying emphases and preoccupations, these three debates shared some important common ground: the prime-mover state meant to engineer development and the obstacle state actually obstructing its own ambitions, for a long time figured as two opposite poles, and as familiar landmarks, in the discourse on state and society in Africa. However, the focus each time was on the state, not on society, and notwithstanding different appreciations of its role, each position perceived the state as *central*. To a large extent, of course, these particular emphases were not restricted to the African context but followed directly from the nature of the whole development discourse. So much of development planning, for example, would be inconceivable without a central role for the state as object and rationale of analysis and intervention or, where external involvements would be concerned, as its chief linkage and counterpart. Still, the relative absence of big landowners and industrial interests in many African countries made this emphasis on the state even more pronounced than in other regions of the Third World.

Shifting perspectives

From the latter part of the 1980s onwards, reflecting a drastically changing global context, significant shifts began to manifest themselves into the positions concerned, and indeed into the discourse itself. Another debate was in the making. To appreciate this, a brief digression into the 'real world' at the time may be useful. Here, it should be noted that the crisis of the African state did not go unnoticed by the main global organizations and the international donor community, public and private. For many years, however, in the implied policy debate on giving priority to improving governmental capabilities versus responding to popular demands, the collective weight of the external variable had been biased squarely towards strengthening the interventionist powers of the state.

In the course of the 1980s, this picture began to change. From policy statements as well as actions, it appeared that the global organizations and the donor community began to embrace wholesale the critique of the 'overdeveloped state' which had earlier been espoused by radical scholars (often, no doubt, to the irritation of those same organizations). There had already been a heavy external involvement in African policy-making for many years, but since the mid-1980s a *qualitative* difference appeared to be manifesting itself in this area. In an age of structural adjustment, liberalization and privatization, the international community as led by the World Bank and the International Monetary Fund showed signs of a major reversal in its appreciation of the role of the African state and seemed to opt for what might, at first sight, appear an almost anarchistic route. Earlier the exclusive recipient, partner and rationale of international aid and attention, the African state's 'most favoured' status increasingly appeared to be getting eclipsed in the eyes of donors by a veil of assumed obsolescence. Aside from the chains of the debt burden, the autonomy of the African state was increasingly being bypassed and eroded by the international donor community in a whole range of critical ways such as: (i) advocacy of privatization and of increasing involvement of private enterprise in aid arrangements; (ii) significant diversion of aid funds via non-governmental organizations (NGOs) and channels; (iii) the formation of donor co-ordinating consortia, with corresponding national counterpart 'front' organizations, which began to assume major policy roles in, for example, the planning and disbursement of food aid; (iv) the rapidly growing donor specialization and involvement in selected sectors and/or regions within African countries, facilitating a gradual shift of policy-preparation activities to donor headquarters, away from national co-ordinating ministries or organizations for the sector concerned; (v) donor preferences to work with autonomous 'non-bureaucratic' corporate statutory bodies, believed to combine the advantages of public jurisdiction and private discretionary powers and considered attractive as external agencies could establish close working relationships with them, thereby gaining direct influence; (vi) detailed specification of external parameters and prescriptions in national budgetary and policy processes; and (vii) the introduction of highly advanced and sophisticated monitoring and evaluation methodologies, for which there was often insufficient national expertise available to constitute an effective counterpart in the policy discussion and implementation concerned (Morss 1984: 465–470; Smith and Wood 1984: 405–434; Wuyts 1989). Also, in decentralization policies, privatization and non-government initiatives were increasingly being encouraged, occasionally leaving questions as to which bodies are theoretically still responsible for guarding the 'common interest' (Meynen and Doornbos 2004).

No doubt many of the policy initiatives concerned were motivated by earnest desires to raise the effectiveness of aid programmes, to make use of insights gained through experience, including earlier mistakes and generally to improve performance and outputs. Still, the combined impact, magnitude and complexity of all these incremental contributions by the collective international community already began to constitute an overwhelming weight on the policy-making processes of individual African countries, for the totality of which nobody would take responsibility. Given the limited financial and staffing resources vis-à-vis the collective external expertise, the role of the national government often became necessarily limited to accepting – or possibly refusing to accept – ready-made policy packages prepared elsewhere, or already agreed upon by the main donors. For some time some governments had managed to give a fresh meaning to Hamza Alavi's concept of the 'relative autonomy of the state' by skilfully playing off one donor against another (Alavi 1972: 59–81), but increasing insistence on donor co-ordination was making this more difficult, closing off this limited room for manoeuvre.

Out of impatience with the poor formulation and implementation of plans by African states, various donor organizations and governments sought engagement in 'policy dialogue' – a process which was based less on equal status of discussion partners than the name might suggest. However, the question arose whether a critique on state *performance* justified the far-reaching interventions, verging on custodianship, which began to be made into the policy determination of African states (Ravenhill 1988: 179–210). In the final analysis, this involved questions of national sovereignty. In this connection, Robert Jackson and Carl Rosberg put forward the thesis, in their discussion of African statehood, that if it were not for the *de jure* recognition of their status by the international community, many states would have collapsed as a result of internal conflicts (Jackson and Rosberg 1982: 1–24). True as this might be for some cases, one could also wonder whether a point might not be reached where the state as the nerve centre for national policy-making might risk collapse under the collective weight of the international community's involvement and interventions, well-intentioned or otherwise. 'Policy dialogue', the international donor euphemism, ultimately appeared to turn the discussion about the African state into a very academic debate.

With such changing contextual conditions, an inevitable shift in the theoretical positions concerned could also become discerned (Ravenhill 1988). While some of the former international supporters of the African state began to turn into its chief fault finders, now arguing the case of broader societal interests, its earlier radical critics were more likely to come to its defence by maintaining that, notwithstanding all the problems involved, there was as yet no alternative to a key role for the state, and insisting on the state's legitimate right at least to be able to make its own policy judgements and misjudgements. Behind these shifts in position loomed larger questions of the choice between state-led and market-led development. In the polarized fashion in which these questions tended to be posed, meaningful answers were unlikely to be forthcoming, or even possible. While the complexities and failures of state-led development had been sobering and manifold, as Ali Mazrui remarked it remained to be seen whether privatization might not prove a greater impediment to the releasing of market forces than the state (Mazrui 1989).

On the 'relative autonomy of the state'

One alternative way of appreciating the changing role and position of the African state in the context of these various transformations is to look at it through the lens of the once much used concept of the 'relative autonomy of the state'. During the first post-colonial decades reference was frequently made to this notion with respect to countries in Asia, Africa and Latin America. Hamza Alavi's influential article of 1972 on the 'relative autonomy of the state' had first been developed to refer to the position of the state within broad power constellations in countries like Pakistan and Bangladesh, while subsequently his analysis was adopted and adjusted by others to throw light on conditions in Africa and Latin America.

'The state' was then fairly generally viewed as a central and powerful actor in most countries of Asia, Africa and Latin America: one dominant image as noted above was that of the post-colonial state enjoying a fair amount of latitude and indeed 'autonomy', embarking on major strategies of social and economic transformation. Accordingly, the leadership of many states saw themselves as indeed powerful and 'in command'. In various respects they appeared to pose as 'autonomous' from the large majority of their respective populations, on the untested assumption that through their vote 'the people' had bestowed upon them a historic mission to lead the nation into new and modern futures. It was this kind of vision, and mission, that would also give rise to the monuments of modern state planning described by James Scott in his *Seeing Like A State* (1998): mega dams, large collective agricultural and resettlement schemes, scientific forestry, grandiose urban planning and in some cases new capital cities.

'Strong state' notions abounded almost irrespective of whether they were factually correct or not. An important early qualification, for example, came from Gunnar Myrdal, who in his *Asian Drama* (1968) pointed to the existence of 'weak' or 'soft' states unable to implement what they aspired to or claimed they would do. Other such voices would follow, together constituting a broad stream of counter perspectives that have proliferated ever since, including the qualification that even if 'soft' states might not be 'strong', they could nevertheless be 'harsh', as Jan Breman (1977) once observed. Thus, while notions of the state as a strong, key player occurred in 'mainstream' perspectives, basically supportive to see the state take the lead in social and political transformation towards 'nation-building', critics would underscore the other side of the coin of the 'developmental' state: its frequent arbitrariness, its exploitative tendencies, and its lack of neutrality in discharging its roles – attributes which in due course would be more strongly highlighted. Basically, the 'autonomous' post-colonial state in not a few situations came to constitute a major target for critique from the 'left', while by and large enjoying support from the 'right'. Within both perspectives, nonetheless, the state for a long time tended to be seen as 'strong' and 'autonomous'.

Semantically, two aspects of 'autonomy' were relevant, namely, autonomy in the sense of an enabling *'autonomy of action'*, or *'autonomy to'*, and second, autonomy as *'autonomy from'* that is, without interference or constraints. Though closely connected, analysts might choose to emphasize one or another depending on what particular aspects they would want to highlight. Thus, 'modernizing' and developmentalist notions of the state might stress the 'autonomy of action' dimension, while neo-Marxists were more likely to focus on the extent of the state's 'autonomy from', that is, its capacity to act as a force in its own right vis-à-vis other powerful interests within the society and economy. In Alavi's original formulation, for example, this referred to the state's autonomy from – and room for manoeuvre vis-à-vis – powerful categories like landed classes, industrialists, or a metropolitan bourgeoisie (a postulated relationship, incidentally, which generally appeared more applicable to countries like India or Pakistan than to most African state systems). Both notions of autonomy were essentially state-focused, one viewing the state as the central initiator and instrument of development strategies, the other meant to explain the state's role and position vis-à-vis different class forces and class contradictions. In either case, though, the notions concerned essentially referred to *perceptions* of relative state autonomy, which did not always correspond with realities. In other words, relative autonomy is 'relative'. Not unrelated to this, Skocpol (1979) spoke of the *potential* of state autonomy: it is not a given, but it may emerge or be constructed within particular political and economic constellations. Variations in reality also called for the need to appreciate differences in complexity and context. Through reviewing contrasted taxation regimes – and tax bases – among different countries in the South, for example, Mick Moore (1999) highlighted substantial differences in terms of state autonomy which they implied. Nonetheless, both connotations of 'autonomy' have remained important when assessing the transformations the state has been subject to within the context of global forces in more recent years: in not a few instances autonomy in either sense has shrunk significantly.

Again, in the light of these parameters, many post-colonial states, especially in Africa but also elsewhere, in the course of time have run into severe problems. High expectations versus low performance, exalted promises versus low capacity, forcefully maintaining state power versus demands for 'voice' from below, preserving 'unity' versus 'diversity', as well as other discrepancies, became manifest. All these tended to restrict and tone down many state claims to *'autonomy of action'* as well as their *'autonomy from'*, the latter from external as well as internal organized interests. Global forces impinging upon African states' capability to act have had much to do with this.

But while the constraints on autonomous state performance and state action of the post-colonial 'developmental states' proved formidable, these discrepancies did not become immediately visible, largely due to the Cold War. In fact, the Cold War in a curious way propped up and prolonged the idea of state autonomy. As the post-Second World War world became divided into blocs of client states plus others that remained 'non-aligned' (which by itself was good for the idea of 'autonomy'), client governments could count on substantial support from one or the other of the major powers, often enabling them to maintain a very 'autonomous' position vis-à-vis their own populations, to the point in fact of notable arbitrariness and abject authoritarianism in a number of cases. It also seemed that this situation enabled some of the governments concerned to do a bit more in terms of public policies in the social sector (education, health, welfare) than might otherwise have been the case. Besides, except for the relationships with the key global powers, 'autonomy' vis-à-vis the external world was usually kept up with particular keenness: sovereignty was perceived as sacred. Ironically, though, for all the display of 'autonomy', the 'dependency' on global powers with which this came hand in hand was often insufficiently appreciated.

The eclipse of state autonomy

By and large, this constellation continued until the early 1990s. By that time this particular (Cold War) motivation for external support disappeared, making room for other – quite contrasted – forms of external attention. There were deliberate external efforts to push back the autonomy which the post-colonial state, especially in Africa, still retained, and to have it conform to the directives set for its role by external agencies, the International Financial Institutions (IFIs) in particular – all, of course, 'for its own good'. This became a matter of 'disciplining democracy' and trying to construct entirely different (aid) regimes as well as rationalizations for them (Abrahamsen 2000). In the pursuit of these strategies, the IFIs themselves tended to act in a remarkably 'autonomous' manner, for a long time with notably little sensitivity to 'civil society' (Scholte 1998). Besides, following the lifting of Cold War related support structures maintained by the superpowers, the room now became wide open for global forces of various kinds – financial, institutional, commercial – to claim direct access to the economies and societies of the post-colonial state systems, many of them quite vulnerable. In Africa in particular, the stipulating of political conditionalities for continued development aid, the 'good governance' agenda among them, came to play a key role in these transitions (Mkandawire 2004). What suffered most as a result of the withdrawals of external backing, however, was the 'public side' of state action – health, education, and social welfare programmes. The latter by necessity became candidates for 'privatization', in practice meaning: better quality, but accessible only to those who can afford.

When considering the ensemble of these transitions, all aimed at 'rolling back the state', several points are worth noting with respect to the idea of the relative autonomy of the state, especially in the African context. Basically, an altogether different discourse was introduced, structured around key terms like 'civil society', 'human rights', 'democracy', 'multi-partyism' and of course 'good governance', which left little room for concern with the 'autonomy' of the state; rather, its implication, if not intention, was to 'de-throne' the state from its dominant position in the thinking about development issues and strategizing. A related motive was to get political liberalism to match economic liberalism, the latter constituting one of the basic driving forces for global reforms. More specifically one of the objectives appears to have been to get dominant parties removed from the scene, perhaps not only, or primarily, because they were not 'democratic' (by conventional Western standards), but because they were seen as prime obstacles, still enjoying some political clout, to the kind of reforms demanded by the IFIs and major donors.[1] In the wake of this, as is discussed further in Chapter 4, came novel and almost unprecedented conditionalities prescribing for donor-dependent states how to (re-)structure their internal organization and management procedures – in a number of instances turning independent state status into little more than a formality. Clearly, the idea and practice of setting political conditionalities was directly antithetical to upholding the notion of 'state autonomy'.

---

[1] The process bears similarities to the way producer co-operative societies, once set up to enhance farmers' bargaining powers, have been sidelined in various countries to make room for the unbridled operation of market forces.

Most far-reaching of all, probably, has been the erosion of the ability of formally independent states to engage in their own policy thinking, planning and formulation: donor-dependency in many cases has implied becoming subject to numerous policy criteria and demands developed elsewhere (which amongst themselves could well be in contradiction), and having to accept (or to let go) many ready-made packages of policy and project proposals. Probably the most serious critique of the phenomenon of IFIs and donors running the show, as has become observable in different parts of Africa, is indeed that it stifles and takes away responsibility and initiative in policy formulation towards basic development strategies from where it belongs, namely with the relevant government and planning departments and authorities. The latest instruments introduced in this connection, namely the World Bank-initiated Poverty Reduction Strategy Papers (PRSPs), hardly seem a means to restore that responsibility to its proper place but rather appear a more refined way of deepening external monitoring and control (Campbell 2005). Besides, PRSPs again are based on the implicit assumption that the faults of mal-development lie within the countries of the South and their policy performance, leaving out of consideration the impacts of global forces and constraints on the chances of successful performance and development.[2] Surely, if sovereignty and 'autonomy' are in question in Africa today, this seems due as much to the massive external inroads into the policy-making realm as to the erosion of social and territorial integration as suffered by some states.

Outside Africa, meanwhile, a markedly different experience from that of the recurrent eclipse of relative autonomy of the state, has been that of the Asian 'developmental states', Malaysia, Singapore, Taiwan and Thailand in particular. With respect to these, Manuel Castells refers to the 'relative autonomy of the state' in a different vein. In these cases, the state 'has been able to retain an appreciable measure of autonomy both vis-à-vis the external context and particularly the international financial institutions, and vis-à-vis their own societies'. The two relevant dimensions, in Castell's view, are 'relative autonomy vis-à-vis the global economy, making the country's firms competitive in the international realm, but controlling trade and financial flows', and second, 'the state's relative autonomy vis-à-vis society, repressing or limiting democracy, and building legitimacy on the improvement of living standards rather than on citizen

---

[2] As observed by Dr. Enrique Iglesias, Director of the Inter American Development Bank, during a public lecture at the Institute of Social Studies, The Hague, 25 April 2005.

participation'. 'All this', Castells adds, 'under the banner of serving the nation, or even creating it, while serving the rulers themselves' (Castells 2000: 333–334). Castells also makes the point, however, that developmental states that feature these capacities in the end run the risk of falling victim to their own success.

Zeroing in on these East Asian 'developmental states' is helpful for the differences in state capacities it illuminates. If we look at the defining characteristics of a developmental state as exercising relative autonomy in the above respects, it is clearly on these two counts that so many other states are now lacking 'relative autonomy'. Numerous countries, many in Africa but also in the Pacific, the Caribbean, and elsewhere in Asia, have seen their state systems being captured 'from below' by various societal groups sapping their energies, and 'from above' as they have come under the tutelage of IFIs and donor fronts prescribing their policies.

Castells' rendering of the concept is echoed by Thandika Mkandawire, who writes of 'autonomy' in terms of the state's 'ability to make independent decisions such as policy choices around economic development', and distinguishes two meanings of state 'autonomy' used in the political analysis of African state capability:

> The first is autonomy of the national state from external pressure ... Poverty and the level of aid donations limit a state's capacity to provide universal access to primary health and good schooling ... The second meaning of autonomy looks inwards, to the state's relation to its own citizens. [This refers to] the need to establish the autonomy of the new states from particularistic social forces in order to allow the state to devise long term economic and social policies, unencumbered by short-term claims of myopic private interests. (Mkandawire 2004: 298–299)

In the light of these definitions we can note a certain evolution which the concept of relative state autonomy has undergone. At the time of Alavi's discussion, the emphasis lay largely on the role the state could or should play vis-à-vis different dominant interest groups: big landowners, an industrial bourgeoisie. Though Alavi also distinguished metropolitan interests and power, Castells and Mkandawire now place stronger emphasis on the idea of relative state autonomy with respect to the global economic and political context, in addition to that of the state's position vis-à-vis societal forces. In brief, if in the era of globalization the state is to regain a meaningful role, it will require a substantial measure of autonomy in both senses. African states, as Mkandawire argues, have suffered a severe setback in this regard from their earlier start, due to the IFIs' policies impinging on their capabilities in the 1980s and 1990s. Against this background, to regain the prospect of becoming developmental states has become all the more difficult.

The non-state sphere

The realities of state performance and 'policy dialogue' ultimately also had to lead to closer consideration of the 'non-state' sphere and of 'civil society'. What is meant here is not the withering away of the state in a fashion as yet neither foreseen nor intended by the main authors of the idea. What had been happening, rather, was almost the opposite, namely, the prolonged withering away of African civil society, real or imagined, from academic and policy attention. In retrospect the implications of this neglect appear to have been far-reaching. Over several decades, it was striking just how much the discussion on African state–society relations had been focused on the state per se, that is, the seat of power (and who occupied it), the state institutions and the nature of state interventions.

By the same token, socio-economic relationships and institutions at the 'grassroots', in both rural areas and urban centres, received attention mainly in their reaction to interventions from 'above', as it were. One important exception to this relative neglect of 'grassroots' organizations from a wider political perspective was the French 'articulation of modes of production' school of analysis, which sought to understand how West African village communities experienced 'development' from within (Meillassoux 1977, Geschiere 1982). Within the predominant vision, however, state formation essentially equalled formation of state institutions and hardly considered the formation of new kinds of interaction and new balances of power between state and civic institutions. What was lacking, by and large, was closer consideration and understanding, in this connection, of the non-state sphere as represented by potentially autonomous institutions such as the judiciary, professional bodies, mutual-aid societies, farmers' organizations, unions, religious and cultural bodies and many other informal and traditional groupings such as the Ghanaian *asafo* companies, fraternities and kinship associations.

It is quite conceivable that several of these institutions might have acquired more significant civic functions had it not been for the increasingly encompassing dominance of the state. Still, it is not enough to view civil society, as Chabal suggests, as what is *not* of the state:

> Civil society ... consists not just of what is obviously not part of the state but also of all who may have become powerless or disenfranchised ... Civil society is a vast ensemble of constantly changing groups and individuals whose only common ground is their being outside the state. (Chabal 1986: 15)

On closer inspection this equation of 'non-state' and 'civil society' may have been made too readily (cf. Eriksen 2001). For all the different connotations associated with the term (Keane 1998), one should expect a certain extent of organizational linkages and cohesion within some civil law framework, in interaction with the state, to be able to speak of 'civil society'. 'Civil society', as David Sogge observes, may also be understood 'as a realm or domain of different and even opposing camps. It is a social and political space for both consensus and conflict' (Sogge 2005: 21). Nonetheless, 'state' and 'non-state' or an incipient 'civil society', which in other contexts can be strongly interwoven and complementary, in deeply polarized situations can become each other's opposites and opponents, with shifting boundaries between them. Significantly, it is particularly in those instances where the state came to a virtual breakdown, such as in Uganda and Somalia at different intervals in recent decades, that attention was being drawn to a myriad of ways in which local and regional groups or networks tried to cope with their situation and develop novel, autonomous, 'non-state' forms of social organization (Brons 2001, Green 1981, Kasfir 1984, Lemarchand 1988: 149–170).

In recent times, also, important advances were made in historical sociological research, tracing continuities and discontinuities in non-state institutions and in the changing ways in which the state has been perceived, experienced and dealt with, from the side of the populace. Research linking the analysis of state–society relationships in the precolonial, colonial and post-colonial periods, such as in the work of John Lonsdale and Jean-François Bayart, have deepened our understanding of the evolution of social processes and of alternative organizational forms that developed over time (Bayart 1989, Lonsdale 1981: 139–225, 1986: 126–157). Ultimately, such studies might also provide support in the search for cultural revitalization of African forms of social organization. No less important was that throughout the continent local history societies emerged through which groups and individuals have sought to illuminate their own past and present.

A broader historical view may also provide a better perspective on the longer-term dynamics in African state–society relationships. Victor Azarya has sketched a picture recognizing a certain pulsating element in these dynamics, in the sense that phases of state ascendancy, aggrandizement and penetration into the society, marked by the progressive incorporation of different social groups and strata into the state's programmes, and their association with its ideological thrust, might be followed by periods of relative disengagement, retreat, and shrinkage of state functions, or vice versa (Azarya 1988: 3–21). Quite evidently, it can thus be argued, a tendency towards disengagement has been manifested in various countries under the influence of the general crisis within which the African state and economy increasingly found themselves.

It has been a matter of some debate whether in such instances it was societal forces which were seeking to disengage themselves from the state, or whether, as Kwame Ninsin argued on the basis of the Ghanaian experience, it rather was the state which was selectively disengaging itself from popular demands, thereby prompting the detachment of certain social categories as a result of its choice of actions (Ninsin 1988: 265–281). Similarly, in discussing phases of growing state involvement and ascendancy more generally in Africa, such as in the first years after independence, 'incorporation' and 'engagement' could be taken to refer to the extent to which various groups and interests sought association and involvement in the state's programmes and structures, or be taken to reflect the state's own incorporative designs and strategies.

In either case, it became increasingly evident that the processes concerned could not be perceived as operating in a vacuum but should be understood in the light of the pervasive external pressures and inducements, economic as well as political, that were being brought to bear on the African state and society. Indeed, this 'precarious balance' – as captured in the title of Donald Rothchild and Naomi Chazan's volume on evolving state–society relationships in Africa (Rothchild and Chazan 1988) – has become critically affected throughout by the external factor.

Changing identities

It was significant to see the implications of these trends on changing identities, both at the level of the state and of popular groups. Specifically, if there were a basic validity to the incorporation and disengagement thesis, then this might also help explain some of the changing manifestations of ethnicity and some of the new interpretations of it that one has seen occurring over time. In periods of expanding state involvement and high expectations about its mobilizing role and capacity, such as in the years immediately before and after independence in several African countries, various groups in the society could be found identifying more closely with the aims and objectives of the new national political centre and in the process to develop stronger self-identification as members of the new national state, or of the party in power. In times of relative disengagement, in contrast, growing popular disillusionment with the central state would cause various social groups to turn away from it, at least in terms of ideological identification, and lead to their emphasizing ethnic, regional, or other communal identities.

At the level of the state itself, national identity and unity was invariably given strong emphasis during most of the post-colonial period, often all the stronger as different social movements began to question the centrality of the state. State domination was initially reflected in a heavy stress on *nation-building* and from this perspective ethnic pluralism was almost by definition suspect. Promotion of non-state organizations or 'civil society', which might have allowed or encouraged recognition of the positive aspects of nationality, as well as of ethnic and cultural pluralism, was virtually nowhere on the agenda. The ideological claims made by the new ruling élites in support of national unity might allude to some very general universal values, such as in constitutional preambles (Doornbos *et al.* 1984), or be based on selective neo-traditionalization (Ranger 1983), but they tended to be remarkably silent on the question of the cultural basis of the new national society and thus usually carried more rhetoric than intrinsic weight.

Naturally, the search for identities on the part of states as well as popular movements generated its own share of academic interest and debate. Some of the discussion concerned boiled down to questions of understanding as to what kind of phenomena one was observing in the first place. Other questions were essentially normative, and were based on a priori notions as to the direction in which it was thought political identities *should* evolve. Clearly, any such expectations were closely related to the role and position one saw for the state. Postulating a primacy for the central state, for example, almost by necessity induced a special interest in ideologies and strategies of national unification and identity. Interestingly, however, some notable shifts emerged in the course of time in analytic perspectives on the questions of popular and national identity.

At the outset, differences in understanding of the ethnic phenomenon could hardly have been greater. Various liberal scholars, conceptually akin to Clifford Geertz, viewed ethnic identity as a primordial, that is, a deep-rooted existential given, infusing tradition with meaning and turning nation-building projects by definition into almost insurmountable, heroic challenges (Geertz 1963: 105–157). Most Marxist scholars, on the other hand, first considered ethnicity as no more than an epiphenomenon; in other words, either a misunderstood or false consciousness, or a purely surface reflection of more basic and important class variables. With such a priori distance in the theoretical positions involved, not much could be expected by way of any substantive dialogue. The debate then was more in the nature of a long-distance battle, with opposing arguments not too sharply targeted, while making a lot of noise. But subsequently both main perspectives began to shift, not least in response to changes in the actual situation, and more meaningful exchanges became possible thereafter.

On the liberal side, the primordial thesis was first criticized and qualified through recognition of much greater flexibility and variability of popular identities than was previously assumed to exist and through a growing understanding of identity as a kind of multi-layered, multifaceted phenomenon. Ethnic identities, first thought to be deep-rooted and immovable, began to be seen to acquire fresh meanings in response to new situations and challenges, while other studies reported also on new 'ethnic' identifications emerging where they had not existed before – for example, where migrants from different origins found themselves placed in common social situations and thus could develop new collective self-images (Robertson 1978). In critical analyses, the importance of contexts in fully appreciating the role of ethnicity began to be stressed – especially class and the competition for resources and positions controlled by the state (Doornbos 1972: 263–283, Leys 1975: 198–206). Accordingly, the expression of ethnicity was increasingly seen to follow rather than to determine social action and, consequently, it shifted from an independent to a dependent variable in the analysis.

On the Marxist side, a reverse process seemed to be taking place. Increasingly, neo-Marxist analysis recognized ethnic protest as an important form of class or peasant protest, voicing locally specific grievances against dominant and demanding states and ruling classes. Ethnicity also came to be viewed as offering an important protective shield, emotionally as well as in terms of basic social networks, in times of economic and political crisis (Shaw 1986: 587–605). Moreover, serious attention was given to the rediscovered position of nationalities within the post-colonial African states and the implications of this for a proper understanding of the national question (Alavi 1989: 1527–1534, Mamdani 1983: 36–54). As far as the analysis of ethnicity is concerned, this concept, with its implicit recognition of continuity and stable boundaries in nationality consciousness, seemed to come surprisingly close to the notion of primordial ties and could be seen as putting ethnicity back on the cards as a semi-independent variable. Basically, however, it was evident that consciousness of nationality/ethnicity and class could be related in several significant ways and that posing the question in simple either/or terms would only result in unproductive debate.

The increased attention given to the emergence and significance of ethnic, nationality-based, or religiously inspired protest and revitalization movements in various African countries could not but lead the discussion back to the role and position of the post-colonial state and the extent of its dominance at the time. How should these developments be understood and what could they tell us about the nature of the state? For example, should the Holy Spirit Movement initiated by Alice Lakwenya in Northern Uganda in the late 1980s (Behrend 1991) and continued to the present time as the Lord's Resistance Army led by Joseph Kony, or many of the ethnically or nationality-based liberation movements in the Horn of Africa (Markakis 1987), be taken as a sign of the prolonged 'weakness' of the state and of its incapability to handle dissent and keep law and order? Or should they instead be seen as an indication of the 'strength' and the threatening role of the state vis-à-vis groups who felt their position to be weak and vulnerable, with little defence but their ethnicity? The answer to begin with is probably both and the question might not have arisen in the first place if local non-state infrastructures had been allowed a chance to develop, instead of being eroded. But intervening variables of sorts, such as the manipulative and exhorting movement leaderships that have emerged in several of these instances, the Ugandan one in particular, may make the picture inordinately more complex and difficult to resolve. The question relates both to the 'greed versus grievance' debate discussed in Chapter 5 and to the distinction between 'liberation ethnicity' versus 'parochial ethnicity' taken up in Chapter 6.

With respect to the uncertain search for state identity that drew so much attention in the early days after independence, one may wonder in retrospect whether the stress on nation-building and national unity at the time reflected a genuine desire to create a new 'national' society, or whether it constituted the beginnings of an ideological defence of the colonial heritage which had become the state system. If that is what has been happening, then the notion of national identity may be said to have had a remarkable career: from 'nationalist' rationale for replacing the colonial presence, it seemed to have become the successor state's line of defence of that very inheritance, being used against the rising demands and protests of dissatisfied and dissenting nationalities and ethnic popular movements.

Concluding remarks

Looking back over the discussion on the post-colonial African state during the first decades after independence there appears to have been a kind of internal logic to its evolution and changing focus. It was virtually inevitable that the initial emphasis would be on the new state institutions and the performance of the political leaderships. Similarly, when the first contradictions became apparent, there was some logic to the search for socialist, though still state-centred, alternatives. Then again, as African states came under increasing internal and external stress, there somehow was a logic to the conceptual exploration of the non-state sphere for possible alternatives or supports. This search paralleled the rapid emergence and proliferation of numerous non-governmental organizations and donor dependent corporate bodies, but also of social and religious protest and revitalization movements and liberation fronts, all of them in their different ways intent on capturing some of the political space in the non-state sphere (Bratton 1989: 569–587, Mamdani *et al.* 1988). In turn these trends appeared to lead on to some of the key issues facing Africa in the decades ahead.

It did not seem too difficult to hazard a prediction as to where the focus of debate may lie in the years to come: on the predominant nature and role of new political formations, institutional arrangements and patterns of domination and participation emerging in the non-state sphere and on the quality of society–state relations that may result from them. In some instances, such as in Ghana and Uganda, the state itself sought to relate to this drift by initiating defence committees and resistance councils which theoretically were to provide for novel means of decentralization and local representation. Whether they would actually be able to do so remained to be seen, however, and for some time these various innovations have continued to be a matter of prime interest to observers of the African political scene (Brett 1991, Kasfir 1989, Konings 1986, Livingstone and Charlton 2001, Mamdani 1988, Ray 1986). In recent times, as is discussed in Chapter 6, decentralization policies adopted throughout the continent have give rise to a host of self-focused local groups and communities demanding their share from common resources, thus no longer expecting this to come their way through any equitable dispensations from the state.

With regard to these various actions, initiatives and demands, the important question became whether their collective impact would change the balance of power and the historically established relationships between the post-colonial state and the non-state civil society and in what direction. Would they open up new scope and channels for empowerment and democratization, culminating in autonomous organizations with effective popular participation? Or would they lead to novel forms of control by dominant classes at local and regional levels, or by the state, or both? Put differently, would they, through a surprising new consensus between grassroots social movements, NGOs and international corporate interests on the desirability of an 'autonomous' alternative, make the state less all-embracing and omnipresent? Or would they, by the same token, open the door for more direct external intervention and domination together with the dominance of parochial interests at the local level?

4
'Good Governance': The Metamorphoses of a Policy Metaphor

Introduction

In the ensemble of forces and strategies pushing for state restructuring in the contemporary global context, the idea of 'good governance' has come to be accorded a key role as a metaphor highlighting and justifying some of the envisaged transformations. For well over a decade, the notion of 'good governance' has served as a general guiding principle for donor agencies in demanding adherence from recipient governments to proper administrative processes in the handling of development assistance and expecting them to put in place effective policy instruments towards that end. At the present time, donor references to the 'good governance' notion aimed at inducing reforms in the institutional environment of recipient countries may have had their longest day due to the twin difficulties of defining and operationalizing the concept. Nonetheless, the infinitely repeated references made to 'good governance' principles the world over, no matter in what specific way these are understood, can themselves be seen to contribute markedly to 'globalization'. A closer look at its origins and conceptual life history is therefore relevant to a general discussion on globalization and state restructuring. This chapter seeks to accomplish this interest and to illuminate some of the contradictions it has entailed. It will explore the conditions under which the idea of 'good governance' first became adopted as a donor policy metaphor and how it was later reformulated to serve as an instrument of 'selectivity' (Hout 2004), though not without leaving increasing gaps between principle and practice. Particular attention will need to be given in this regard to successive shifts in the relevant policy thinking within the World Bank.

As a background, it should be recalled that around 1989–90, all of a sudden, the 'good governance' notion became prominent on the international aid front. First launched as a donor discourse, it came just as unexpectedly as the fall of the Berlin wall which happened only a little earlier, and in fact the two developments do not appear to have been entirely unconnected. Until that time, aid agencies and other development institutions had generally not been approaching their programme relations with counterparts in terms of criteria of 'good governance'. Nor had, for that matter, the term 'governance' constituted a significant part of the vocabularies used in, say, political science courses at European or American universities in the decades before. For a long time the word had had a somewhat obscure dictionary existence, primarily carrying legalistic connotations, as in respect to bodies having Boards of Governors, whose institutional role required a designation rather grander than 'administration', less business-like than 'management', and with their 'political' concerns handled discretely but firmly.

But then, all at once, the notion of 'good governance' was there, now to refer to the way in which whole countries, or cities or provinces for that matter, were being 'governed', or to be governed. Contextually, rather than intrinsically, it soon transpired that any references that were made to it somehow pertained to states and other entities in the South, rather than in Western Europe or North America from where the concept was being (re-)launched. Moreover, with the adjective 'good' added to it, it became unmistakably clear that the concept of 'good governance' could be used to invite judgement about *how* the country, city or agency concerned was being 'governed'. It enabled the raising of evaluative questions about proper procedures, transparency, the quality and process of decision-making, and many other such concerns (Doornbos 1995).

Looking back at the interval since the launch of the 'good governance' discourse, it is striking to see how in virtually no time the terms of 'governance' and 'good governance' became household words figuring on top of the list of concerns of aid agencies, governments, researchers and the media. As is often true with new buzz-words, though, there has hardly been a consensus as to its core meaning, and less and less of a common idea as to how it should be applied more concretely. Still, it was and is there and it soon gained a key function by virtue of its capacity all at once to draw attention to a whole range of – largely unspecified – issues concerning processes of public policy-making and authority structures. In that sense it appealed to the imagination of analysts as well as practitioners, and became a focal point for intellectual as well as for policy discourses.

Today, about a decade and a half after its re-birth, various questions have continuing pertinence with regard to the use of 'good governance' as a policy instrument. What exactly was it supposed to mean and what has it been used to refer to? Does it represent a universally valid concept or does it vary from context to context, and from one perspective to another? What meanings has the donor community, led by the World Bank, been attaching to the term over time and how useful have these conceptualizations been? What critique does it invite? What handle did or does it offer when judging countries in connection with the allocation of aid funds? And how opportune has it been to make aid conditional on 'good governance'? By posing conditionalities in terms of practices and structures of governance, changes in the latter respect have tended to become (at least partly) externally determined. Again, is that 'right', and why (or why not) would that be the case?

A reflection on the origins and evolution of the 'good governance' notion, especially as regards its use as a reference point in donor–recipient relations, must thus ask why it emerged at the time it did and what has, since then, been its track record. In the light of the latter, moreover, we may ask whether it is likely to continue receiving the same level of interest as it drew initially.

The pliability of the 'governance' concept

In terms of its scope and potential coverage, the notion of 'governance' semantically had an a priori attractiveness from a global policy-making perspective. Among other things, it could refer to a good deal more than just (sound) administration or management, namely to the dimension of political structuring and the latter's handling, while at the same time including the administrative-managerial element. Though evidently not to be equated with 'politics', let alone 'political leadership', it nonetheless opened a window for focusing on how 'politics' or the political process was embedded and conducted within larger structures. Significantly, in the dichotomous manner in which for years many practitioners and analysts had been used to think about 'politics' and 'administration', there had been hardly a single word connecting these two spheres – distinct yet closely related and overlapping as they are. Part of the term's appeal was that it seemed to be able to fill that gap. Curiously, though, while in principle comprising a political dimension, in actuality the use of 'governance' and 'good governance' on the donor front soon seemed to favour a certain de-politicization of political processes.

Yet it should be borne in mind that the term itself, while pointing to a general area of common concern, hardly carries a specific meaning. Rather, its intrinsic open-ended quality, and inherent lack of specificity have tended to generate a good deal of searching and debate as to what is or should be its 'proper' meaning, prompting multiple efforts to appropriate it and define it in particular ways and directions (Ahrens 1999). But this can never bring all contrasted expectations and interpretations under one common denominator. For bankers, for example, (financial) accountability will represent the crux of 'good governance', while ordinary villagers and citizens in various countries may stress the provision of security as their prime criterion for 'good governance'. Nor is such a priori lack of consensus particularly surprising: a pliable term like 'governance', rather than constituting a concept in its own right, is more like a flexible carrier which can be used to convey varying combinations of messages or ideas, though largely remaining within the same general trade specialization. Thus, there has been a continuing oscillation in the usages entertained, some also more policy-oriented and others more academic.

Interestingly, notions of 'governance' rapidly found their way into academic usage following its adoption in donor circles and in recent times have stimulated lively discussion on various aspects of the themes they denote, pertaining to both forms and practice of the exercise of power (e.g. Hyden and Bratton 1992, Leftwich 1994). It is beyond the scope of this chapter to deal with the academic stream of writing on 'governance'. Suffice it to say that the academic stream has been largely concerned with developing a better understanding of the ways in which power and authority relations are structured in different contexts – thus focusing on different modes of inter-penetration of state–civil society relations. In this connection, one important incentive towards its adoption has been the pervasive privatization and market liberalization policies adopted in many countries, resulting in many novel public–private or 'indirect governance' arrangements (Kooiman 1993). One advantage it thus offered, as Göran Hyden remarked, is that it does not prejudge the locus of actual decision-making – which could be within the state, within an international organization or within some other structural context (Hyden and Bratton 1992: 6). In that regard a concept of 'governance' facilitates analytical pursuits into the exercise of political power, unhindered by formal boundaries, and may fit discourse analysis, embedded structuralism, Marxism and mainstream thinking alike (cf. Van Kersbergen and Van Waarden 2001). Indeed, many political scientists and sociologists, as increasingly also economists, today can hardly do without the term.

In contrast, a donor-directed and policy-oriented discourse on governance has rather been focused on intra-governmental relations and within this context more specifically on state structures designed to ensure accountability, due processes of law and related safeguards. There has naturally been a certain amount of interaction between the two discourses, which can be fruitful as long as both sides remain open to it. But obviously the basic purposes have been different, the academic discourse being primarily oriented towards better analysis and understanding of the institutional linkages between state and society in different contexts, the donor-driven discourse rather being geared towards enhancing policy effectiveness and conceptually preparing the terrain for policy intervention. The guiding motive in this interventionism, it would appear, has been towards the establishment of new global-institutional patterns of hegemony, through a 'disciplining', in a Foucauldian sense – including the governance of 'self' – of state and policy structures in individual countries to conform to the norms set by global institutions, which have been presented as enhancing 'ownership' by the countries concerned.[1] There are indeed intriguing overlaps, though also differences, between the thrust of the 'good governance' discourse and Foucault's 'governmentability'. Both are oriented towards the institutionalization of control mechanisms: the more internalized and self-regulating these can become within a pre-determined design, the more successful they will be. However, historically derived social, economic and institutional structures, or the specific needs and potential of particular countries, would not figure much as points of departure in global 'good governance' designs. Nor was there recognition that there might be different notions, expectations and priorities associated with 'good governance' – no matter how defined – in other political contexts. Instead, one of the key aims appears to have been the promotion, in developing country contexts, of institutional patterns and mechanisms that have been characteristic for Western neo-liberal systems.

The impetus for a renewed interest in having a concept of 'good governance' thus did not primarily originate in an academic context, but from amongst the circle of international donor agencies, in particular the World Bank. Increasingly one had felt a 'need' for such a concept here, though different from that of the academic interest. To better appreciate this, it will be instructive to reconsider the transitions and expectations occurring at the global level at the time.

---

[1] Examples are the PRSPs discussed in Chapter 3 and the New Partnership for Africa's Development (NEPAD), 'a vision and strategic framework for Africa's renewal'.

'Good governance' and political conditionalities

With the demise of the Cold War, the paramount urge to organize the world in opposite camps had come to a halt. Until that moment, the firmer, that is, the more strong-handed, the client states concerned, the easier it had often appeared for global powers and institutions to conclude alliances and aid relations with them. Authoritarianism and dictatorships had been thriving during those years, although in the late 1980s some donors had already begun to attach certain conditions to the granting of development aid. But following the fall of the Berlin Wall (and at least until the aftermath of 'September 11') there no longer seemed to be the same imperative to get the support from, or give support to, regimes with a dubious track record in the handling of their own internal affairs, including human rights issues. Instead, time had come when it seemed quite justified, and when there appeared no more constraints, for global powers and institutions to set conditions to, and prescriptions for, the manner certain client states should be going about the management of their governmental affairs. Rolling back the state systems of many developing countries and reducing the political weight these represented itself also became a key element in the thinking within the global institutions. A new chapter of political conditionalities, that is, of *internally* directed political conditionalities addressed to the structuring and operation of recipient countries' institutions, was being opened. But this required a suitable conceptual framework to justify such interventions.

Until this time, political conditionalities as such had not been unknown: they had been the essence of many client relationships built up during the Cold War. Political support for the West, or for the then so-called East or Soviet-led bloc, in the United Nations, in the field and in other fora, had been a key condition for material and other upkeep of many of the regimes concerned – as in a new era demanding loyalty to the United States in its war against 'terrorism' it is becoming once again. But these conditionalities were basically *externally* oriented. They did not specify how the governments concerned should structure their administration and policy-making processes, what priority they should assign to certain policy initiatives, or how they should handle a whole range of other matters that might now typically come up for 'policy dialogue'. The new, post-Cold War generation of political conditionalities were aimed to do exactly that. The guiding idea was to get a grip on recipient developing countries' handling of policy processes, and more broadly on the way in which government and its constituent political processes – including multi-partyism – would be structured. National sovereignty and non-interference in internal affairs, for long held in high esteem in international politics, were increasingly met with impatience in the light of these initiatives. In World Bank circles at the time, there certainly was an awareness that one was about to step into 'sensitive' matters, as the then Bank President Barber Conable put it. Outlining the new strategy, he declared 'If we are to achieve development, we must aim for growth that cannot be easily reversed through the *political process of imperfect governance*' (Conable 1992: 6; italics added). In other words, the realm and role of politics had to be 'contained'. In 1991, when the Bank for the first time devoted part of its Annual Development Economics Conference to the 'good governance' theme, the anticipations as to what this might imply in terms of the Bank's future agenda were indeed quite high, and in principle comprised nothing less than a 'reform of politics' in aid-dependent countries (World Bank 1992).

In order to be able to raise conditionalities of political and administrative reform, however, some new standard or set of criteria was called for. It is here where the notion of 'good governance' came in, somehow broad enough to comprise public management as well as political dimensions, while at the same time vague enough to allow a fair measure of discretion and flexibility in interpretation as to what 'good' governance would or would not condone. In the donor world led by the World Bank the re-invention of the notion of '(good) governance' thus was meant to enable and justify the launching of a new generation of political conditionalities.

Significantly, the Bank's own already key role in aid co-ordination soon became further enhanced with the adoption of this line, as individual donor countries were not always certain as to what could be subsumed and demanded, and what not, as 'good governance'. They often felt more secure in going 'multilateral', that is, accepting the World Bank's lead and signals in the matter (Uvin 1993: 67). Especially since then the World Bank has cultivated its image as 'the' lead agency in development assistance and thinking, even though other donors such as the European Union may actually have much larger aid budgets to spend.

For the World Bank itself, venturing into these new areas in a way was nonetheless ironic, as its statutes had prohibited it to enter into 'political' lines of action. When the new policy line under the label of good governance cum political conditionalities suggested itself, and was proposed and elaborated by bank staff, the Bank's governors pondered long as to whether the strictly non-political mandate should be maintained or broadened. The outcome was to maintain it, and in its own successive definitions of the concept the Bank for several years then kept to a strictly non-political view of 'governance'. Already, there were significant differences in this regard between some of the staff papers presented at the Bank's 1991 Annual Development Economics Conference, which had departed from a broader understanding that was explicitly inclusive of the interventionist political dimension, and the published versions of the same papers (e.g. the paper by Pierre Landell-Mills and Ismail Serageldin on 'Governance and the External Factor', in World Bank 1992). Only about six years later, with the publication of its 1997 *World Development Report* which included a certain re-appraisal of the role of the state and attention for matters like citizen participation, the Bank moved to a broader, though still essentially 'a-political', conception of 'governance' (Martinussen 1998a).

Nonetheless, the Bank's earlier repositioning had also entailed adoption of a formula which allowed it to play a pivotal role in donor–recipient country relations. While in its own dealings with loan-recipient countries it had to stick to strictly non-political, financial accountability and transparency notions of 'governance', the Bank had accepted the role of secretariat for the consultative meetings of various donor consortia for several countries, which in the end stipulated what political conditionalities would need to be met by the governments concerned (Gibbon 1993: 55–56). In principle this placed the Bank in the strategic position of being able to convey political conditionalities set by the respective consortia to the recipient countries, and subsequently to monitor their implementation, without compromising its own, non-political mandate (ibid.).

'Universality' and globalization

It is important to place the construction of an intervention-oriented 'good governance' agenda within a broader perspective and consider some of its implications. First of all, there is the question of how universal have been the standards of good governance put up by the Western donor community, irrespective of the question how 'deep' these standards reach in reality. One does not need to be an unreserved cultural relativist to recognize that ideas about 'good governance' in principle are conceivable within quite different socio-cultural and political contexts, and may stress different qualities and criteria. Surveying this would in fact constitute a rich field for comparative political anthropology or political science. Historically and across countries at the present time there are numerous different ways in which state–society relations and processes for public policy-making – that is, governance structures – have been given shape. Some of these may be considered 'good', others 'bad'; judgements about this will naturally vary. Most or all governments are likely to score 'good' and 'bad' judgements for different aspects of their policy performance and are likely to meet contrasted expectations in this regard from different sections within their populations. Again, what one opinion, from one background or experience, may consider positive, may be looked upon critically elsewhere. But in actual fact it is unlikely that the world's donor community would want to borrow its standards from comparative political anthropology or different socio-cultural contexts. Rather, donor standards are likely to be derived from the way donors are used to perceive and handle the world around them, that is, from their own particular – and cultural – perspective, even though in the end they may present these as having 'universal' value.

If donor-conceptualized standards of 'good governance' are to be more fully elaborated and operationalized, it thus implies an insistence on Western-derived standards of conduct to be adopted in various non-Western politico-cultural contexts. This is neither new nor particularly surprising, yet it remains important to recognize it for what it is, namely a confrontation of different practices and cultural premises (Martin 1992:15). It is also in this regard that one may note one basic distinction between academic and donor discourses on 'governance'. An academic discourse, at least if it is informed by some cultural sensitivity (Ter Haar 2000:13), presumably would take cultural variation as one of its points of departure, and would try to better understand the merits and demerits of various configurations of 'governance' in different contexts. Donor discourses by contrast are likely to depart from just one general notion of 'governance', and to demand abiding by it.

Related to this is the role which emphasis on 'good governance' principles may take on in globalization processes. Globalization of course has numerous facets, but one particular one is the way in which state functions are getting progressively subsumed under broader trans-national institutional constructs. This plays in all parts of the world, though rather differently so in the developed West as contrasted to the 'developing' South. To the extent that a 'good governance' agenda is actively pursued, it constitutes one more, potentially key, route through which Western-originated policy concepts and processes of institutional globalization are being furthered.

Principle and practice

In retrospect, the early 1990s may come to be viewed as constituting one of the high points in 'good governance' thinking. A broad set of interrelated concepts were formulated delineating areas of concern with policy structures and processes, while more specific issues were put forward for reform in the context of aid packages with conditionalities attached. The dismantling of 'over-developed' state structures in Third World countries thus seemed in easy reach, while multi-party 'democratization' just appeared to be waiting for an external nod and encouragement (cf. Sørensen 1995). Carrot-quality conditionalities, it was anticipated, would help induce these various transformations, bringing about a wholesale overhaul of the developmental state that had been typical for the Cold War era. International expectations were quite high as to what the 'good governance' idea could highlight in terms of needed reforms and what the formulation and application of the new generation of political conditionalities might accomplish. In short, the climate of the time, particularly as perceived from the heights of global institutions, was one full of promise regarding the potential for creating and directing a better, and more 'governable', world.

When putting principle into practice, however, significant complexities became apparent. Basically, the idea of imposing political conditionalities had sounded easier in theory than it would turn out in reality. Not surprisingly, in many countries there turned out to be a lukewarm reception of and compliance with various donor-instigated projects for political reform (Bayart 1993). These projects and proposals were bound to affect stakes in local political processes and balances of power, which the actors concerned would not readily give up. 'Transparency' of political processes and the idea of level playing fields did not easily match with prevailing political cultures and configurations of power, nor lend themselves to smooth translation into operational terms. Step by step the anticipated applicability of conditionalities for 'good governance' began to shrink. Two aspects in particular are worth noting in this respect.

First, one broad area for international 'good governance' attention in the post-Cold War situation was that of democratization and multi-partyism (Abrahamsen 2000). In the early 1990s the launch of the good governance theme, then still conceptualized in a broadly encompassing fashion, became partly focused on the call for multi-partyism. There was then much discussion about this, and there still is some, but it did not change much. Some authoritarian regimes skilfully transformed themselves into dominant parties within facade-type multi-party systems, as in Ethiopia, Zimbabwe and Zambia, demonstrating their resilience as political machines. Others continued, possibly with as little, or as much, by way of development collaboration contacts as they had before. Yet other countries, like Uganda, struggled to get recognition for an alternative to multi-partyism, namely a no-party system, arguing that multi-partyism as it had evolved in the Western experience did not necessarily constitute the sole route to democratic political processes, or to 'good governance' for that matter (Mugaju and Oloka-Onyango 2000, Doornbos 2000). Uganda's own subsequent practices with the 'Movement' system, however, did not do much to sustain faith in the 'no-party' alternative. Uganda's National Resistance Movement has largely transformed itself into a single party and appears to have every intention of staying in power. In contrast, the 2002 Kenyan Presidential elections, prompting the transfer of power from Daniel arap Moi to Mwai Kibaki, like similar transitions in Ghana and Benin earlier, appeared to provide an instance of multi-party democratization and change of government, for which credit should go to the Kenyan voters at least as much as to donors for putting up pressures and 'conditionalities'. Sadly, however, in the Kenyan case, within years of Kibaki's accession to power the laments about the massive extent of corruption within Kenya's government rose to new heights. Basically, as was also observed in Chapter 2, for democratization to be viable and sustainable it needs to receive its impetus from within. Donors may be supportive of democratization processes, but they should not expect to be able to initiate them.

All in all, this particular dimension of the good governance theme does not appear to have lived up to the expectations that had been raised about it. Besides, as already noted, the World Bank had taken a lead in de-emphasizing the 'political' dimensions of 'governance' in its own dealings with aid-recipient countries. To the extent that multi-partyism and democratization (whether or not these two categories should be seen as equivalents) constituted key aspects of the political dimension of the international 'good governance' agenda, they rather appeared to be slipping into the background.

Second, one of the other key intentions with the 'good governance' agenda had been to enable donors to question aid-recipient countries' policy structures and processes, and to get them to alter these – according to 'universal' criteria and conditionalities as set by the donors. How feasible or generally valid this approach would be to begin with could be questioned given the enduring definitional obscurities we have noted. One thing the proponents failed to do was to ask and specify under what conditions – social, economic, political – introducing new governance notions would stand a chance of success (Törnquist 1999: 97–101). Nonetheless, the idea was to ultimately try and transform what donors perceived as 'bad' governance into 'good' governance. More than ten years after, however, the experience with setting conditionalities by and large had become a sobering learning exercise: donors and observers recount many examples of lipservice and less than spontaneous implementation of conditionalities – which should not be too surprising (Bayart 1993). Also, introducing policy conditionalities often meant inserting new elements into highly complex policy processes and situations, leading to fresh complexities for which donors and recipients would henceforth bear joint responsibility. In the process, donors ran the risk of getting more deeply enmeshed in the internal policy processes of recipient countries than they thought they had bargained for (cf. Harrison 1999 for an analysis of the Mozambican example). After several years of interplay between externally initiated conditionalities and government restructuring strategies it became increasingly difficult to disentangle the respective inputs of one and the other. In this light, also, attempts to measure the effectiveness of conditionalities began to turn out rather problematic propositions to begin with and did not produce very illuminating results. Moreover, a strain on resources usually limits the scope for follow-up monitoring. Second thoughts about the practicability of the conditionality instrument as a leverage thus began to preoccupy donors, along with recipients who naturally had had their own reservations about it to begin with. It is now mainly in the context of new sectoral policy involvements which several donors in recent years have opted to concentrate their aid on, that organizational and policy guidelines are being stipulated in relatively greater detail.

Discrepancy between word and reality is also evidenced in other respects, as can be illustrated by the case of Uganda. Uganda is one country chosen by various donors – World Bank/IMF as well as German, Danish, Dutch, British and American aid, among others – for special support in the light of its high growth rate in recent years. This high growth rate has been attributed to 'good governance', which is one way of resolving the definitional question. In actual fact, however, Uganda since the early 1990s had had a notable recovery rate following the devastating years of the Idi Amin and Obote II regimes. But Uganda in recent years has also been competing with countries such as Bangladesh and Nigeria for the top rankings on *Transparency International's* annual list of countries with the highest incidence of corruption. Donors prefer to ignore this and hold on to official growth indicators enabling them to keep betting on a winning horse (Reno 2000b, Hofer 2002). Evidently, therefore, employing the notion of 'good governance' in more than one sense appears to invite double standards. It suggests that for the World Bank, IMF and various other donors, attaining high growth rates irrespective of how these have come about, in the end constitutes a more important indicator of 'good governance' than having a low corruption profile.

What impacts?

If donor policies emphasizing criteria of 'good governance' have been less successful than was anticipated, this is not to say they have had no impact. Interestingly, the phraseology of 'good governance' in some ways has become as common in various remote districts of Africa as it has become in Washington DC or some Western European capitals. This is partly due to a kind of echo effect brought about by many donor agencies – multilateral, bilateral and NGOs – repeating the 'good governance' mantra over and over again, pledging their adherence to it, and projecting it on to their target groups. In an Oxfam-assisted project document on participation and poverty alleviation in Uganda, for example, it was put forward that people at village level demanded 'good governance' in terms of 'transparency and accountability' from their rulers and administrators (Uganda Government 2000). 'Good governance' recurs in a good bit of speechmaking, like in the context of the kind of public admonitions which in earlier periods would have called for proper administration, loyal service, or perhaps pride in the nationalist party. 'Good governance' also figures as a standard item for discussion at numerous seminars for civil servants and NGO staff, organized at a good many hotels in African countries by various ministries with the support of different aid agencies. But it does not necessarily mean that basic *structures* and *processes* of government have been subject to major change. They have not, or have a way of changing only very slowly, if at all. Some local observers may remark that it is a good thing that donors demand 'good governance' and impose their conditionalities, as this may curb gross financial and administrative malpractices to some extent. Perhaps such observations could themselves be seen as signalling that acquaintance with a range of good governance criteria – transparency and accountability, rule of law, respect for human rights, efficiency and effectiveness in service delivery – is slowly percolating in the public awareness, which in turn may result in more critical dispositions towards policy makers' actions. In view of these realities, Graham Harrison suggests that 'we should not only stress the limits of reform or the problematic relations with broader social change, but should also recognize that *any* improvements in the efficiency of state action are significant in a generally difficult environment' (Harrison 2001: 676).

Decentralization

In one respect there has been some notable re-structuring of governmental decision-making in various countries of Africa and Asia and, though perhaps not directly following from the 'good governance' discourse, it is often presented as being closely related to it. With varying degrees of determination, *decentralization* is currently being pursued in a good number of contexts, commonly in response to donor pressures and encouragement, though at times also in conjunction with local interests in achieving greater autonomy for particular regions or groups. Decentralization has developed into a vast terrain of discussion and experimentation (Ribot 2002) and high hopes have been set by various quarters on its success in making 'grassroots participation' a reality. Again, however, it is necessary to recognize that this strategy also has its limitations. Decentralization may provide some scope for enhancing local participation in some situations, but the participation at stake quite often will remain limited to the level of elites and can hardly be a recipe for equity (Meynen and Doornbos 2004). Also, some regions or localities have much better natural resource endowments and/or planning capacities than others to begin with, which in turn may give rise to unequal benefits to be obtained from any enhanced local autonomy. As time passes, these differences may increase due to multiplier effects of unequal baseline capacities and assets. Besides, due to the fragmentation that may follow in the wake of decentralization, wider 'common' interests between different decentralized entities may get neglected or impaired. These realities again underscore the difficulty of devising generally valid formulae for 'good governance'.

From 'conditionality' to 'selectivity' and beyond

Mixed experiences with using 'good governance' as a guiding principle for donor policies and in trying to use aid as an incentive to induce improvements in governance practices, at one point led to a tendency on the donor front to move from 'conditionality' to 'selectivity' (Hout 2004). This was partly to try and avoid the burden of having to monitor attempts at amelioration of policy processes, which require more attention and detailed knowledge than most donors, even the World Bank, can muster. In this connection, the so-called 'Dollar Report' (after its main author, David Dollar), *Assessing Aid* (World Bank 1998), in putting forward the research finding that 'good' performers (in terms of growth rates) are 'best' able to absorb and utilize aid funds effectively, had come to provide a policy rationale for a change of approach. On the basis of the 'scientific' evidence presented in this report, 'selectivity' was being advocated and rationalized as a more cost effective and results-oriented donor strategy. Hence the keen interest with which the recommendations from this report were taken up for discussion and adoption in various donor circuits (e.g. Netherlands Ministry of Foreign Affairs 2000). There were serious criticisms regarding the reliability and relevance of the way these particular findings have been construed (e.g. Lensink and White 1999, Van der Hoeven 1999, WRR 2001). Yet to some donor agencies these shortcomings appeared a lesser concern as compared to the perceived operational advantages on which the report seemed to open a window. These lay in the experience that attempts to steer governance restructuring programmes through conditionalities from the outside had turned out to be far more complicated and laborious engagements than optimistic aid agencies had first assumed they would be. Against these realities, a priori interests to embrace an approach that could help lessen such self-imposed burdens would welcome any 'authoritative' report that appeared to provide a theoretical justification for such a move, as was the case with the 'Dollar report'. But the promises that this policy change seemed to hold out turned out to be short-lived.

'Conditionality' redefined

It is useful to look at what began to happen to the notions of 'good governance' and 'conditionalities' in the light of these shifting insights and priorities. The Dutch policy reversal in favour of concentrating Dutch structural aid to a limited list of aid-receiving countries with strong 'good governance' records signified an interesting example of the new trend. Paradoxically, the encouragement of 'good governance' through political conditionalities itself no longer figured as an area of prime policy attention in the new scenario. 'Good governance' henceforth was assumed present to begin with, in principle elevated now as the key criteria for selection to the status of 'most-favoured' aid-recipient countries as far as Dutch aid was concerned (Netherlands Ministry of Foreign Affairs 2000). Some other donors, notably the United States, similarly indicated intentions to redirect their aid policies in the light of the World Bank's lead to shift from 'conditionality' to 'selectivity', though overall the picture did not result in drastic reversals. Danish and other Scandinavian aid, for example, did not move towards a single criterion of good performance/good governance (Martinussen 1998b), while other donors remained undecided as to whether or to what extent they would incorporate selectivity criteria. The new Dutch policy was to last for only a couple of years, however, and then actually in name only. Ministry officials reportedly had difficulty determining what criteria and indicators to utilize when trying to assess 'good governance' in countries with which Dutch aid had or might have connections (WRR 2001). Aid-recipient countries continued to be selected on a range of other grounds than their 'good governance' records, and the discrepancy between principle and practice of Dutch aid policy was finally resolved by declaring '*a perspective on good governance*', rather than 'good governance' per se, to constitute a sufficient criteria for country selections (Minister voor Ontwikkelingssamenwerking 2003). Henceforth 'track record' country monitoring, based on a (potentially arbitrary) mix of criteria, would determine whether countries would (continue to) qualify for sectoral and macro budget support.

Evidently, as was pointed out in a number of contributions to the report of the Dutch Advisory Council on Government Policy (WRR 2001), to take observance of 'good governance' as an entry criterion for deciding which countries are qualifying for assistance and which are not, was something quite different from trying to demand *improvements* in terms of 'good governance' as a conditionality to aid. But surely even the 'conditionality' towards improvements approach was a fundamentally different proposition from viewing reform of governance, or governance structures, as a meaningful area for development assistance in its own right, like water development or agricultural rehabilitation, without conditions attached. In the then favoured 'selectivity' thinking, at any rate, 'bad' governance in principle would remain bad governance unless the government concerned would be so keen to qualify for Dutch development aid under these conditions that it would feel motivated to readjust its governance structures in order to meet the required criteria – which would be unlikely. Besides, the question would then still arise as to which or whose criteria that would involve: on the side of donors as well as recipients, clarity as to what 'good governance' would imply would be presupposed. But in reality that clarity is difficult to obtain, as the word itself, magic as it may sound, in and of itself does not contain it. Far from constituting a step forward in the operationalization of standards of 'good governance', the policy reversal which embraced 'good governance' as an entry criteria signified a step back in the attempts to come to grips with the complexities of 'good governance' as a policy objective, conceptually and operationally. As Jan Pronk argued in this connection, 'what really matters is not "good policies", but "better policies", better than before, to achieve a greater impact. Policy improvement and better governance should not be seen as pre-conditions for development and for development aid, but also as development objectives themselves' (Pronk 2001: 626).

In the light of the difficulties that donors have been facing in defining and demanding adherence to 'good governance', one may well ask whether 'good governance' still has a future as a guiding concept in the context of aid policies. As it remains difficult to specify or reach consensus about its contents, it seems likely that 'good governance' will continue to figure as a general, fairly open but nonetheless vague phrase with which to register one's approval or disapproval of particular administrative/political practices, or of actual governments, somehow suggesting that there is a reference to particular 'higher standards' in one's judgement. But in that case, the label 'good governance' becomes a tool to justify and rationalize choices that are made on other grounds, such as of *political expediency*. Arbitrary as this may be, it does not lessen the heavy donor involvement in recipient countries' policy processes.

One specific area that has usually come up for special attention in donor–recipient relationships under the heading of 'governance', meanwhile, is that of financial accountability. Indeed, one string of motivations for the raising of 'good governance' on the global policy agenda undoubtedly arose out of this context – for understandable reasons. Quite possibly, when other, less tangible policy concerns have lost their immediate pertinence or self-evidence, or when donors sense they are unable to get a grip on them, the hard core of financial accountability questions will keep standing out as the core of 'good governance' concerns at least as far as donors are concerned. Often, one may see 'good governance', 'transparency' and 'accountability' posing as a trinity of almost synonymous bullet points with particular reference to financial management. It seems quite possible therefore that, if in due course broader notions of 'good governance' were to evaporate, their exit may coincide with increased emphasis on the more tangible issues of financial accountability – which as a matter of fact is any bank's, or donor's, good right if not obligation to raise.

Contemplating alternative priorities

The notion of 'good governance' initially had seemed full of promise to donors as a policy concept and instrument. Donors expected to be able to redirect and improve public policy processes by reference to it, thereby enhancing the effectiveness of their aid policies and programmes. These expectations have turned out a disappointment. The question should be raised, however, whether it was strictly necessary – and prudent – to put forward 'good governance' and 'political conditionalities' in such a closely inter-linked fashion as has been done. If 'good governance', broadly defined and allowing different interpretations, is considered a worthwhile objective, why attach conditionalities? It is this link in particular which has prompted innumerable questions and uncertainties as to what specific meanings of 'good governance' donors would want to have adhered to in the context of aid relationships. Could one not have given greater priority to development assistance programmes in support of governance reforms, such as streamlining bureaucratic procedures or strengthening accountability, though without attaching conditionalities? One relatively simple solution would be to have a section of the relevant donor ministries open to receive proposals for strengthening governance development programmes as a goal by itself, rather than as an instrument towards other objectives. A trend in this direction is actually noticeable, including in the Dutch case, though it remains uncertain what latitude this will offer to unorthodox proposals for governance reform, like propositions that do not strictly adhere to multi-party democratization or other mainstream 'good governance' criteria. Another is the idea advanced by Kanbur and Sandler for a *common pool* approach, in which donors would transfer (part of their) development assistance funds to a central budget without setting specific conditionalities, while recipient countries would be able to draw from it for specific projects and programmes based on their own development strategies, in principle accepted by donors (Kanbur and Sandler 1999).

What would seem called for is a reversal of the relevant relationships concerned. This might be illustrated by the case of (ex-) Somalia, at the present time still without an effective overarching state framework but with initial efforts in different regions to establish basic government services, though other examples could serve the same purpose. The authorities and civic groups in several of these regions are most likely to welcome help in their efforts to reconstitute a (different) kind of state structure, a very complex challenge indeed. But only few donors are (and even then most cautiously) prepared to give this any attention, while most prefer a wait and see attitude. If the position of 'good governance' first, then aid, were to be followed here, then such efforts might not qualify for over a hundred years for anything like structural development assistance towards improved governance. Yet here are instances where 'needs' seem beyond dispute, and where assistance in creating some meaningful form of 'good governance' is likely to be readily received. But then one should say that this constitutes a goal in its own right rather than being the fulfillment of a 'conditionality' in order to qualify for other aid. For cases like these, the question therefore is whether we should not reverse the standard approach in our thinking about international development assistance, trying to see it in terms of recipient–donor rather than donor–recipient relations?

Illusory as this may still seem at present, such a reversal would in principle call for a situation in which donors would be available 'on demand', rather than being 'in command'. Not unlike the idea underlying the common pool proposal of Kanbur and Sadler mentioned above, in such a situation 'demanding' or 'requesting' countries (now usually identified as 'recipients') would be taking the initiative, basically coming forward saying e.g. 'this is our programme for reconstruction, would you be willing to help?' 'Supporting' countries, which through some forum might pledge to be ready in principle to receive such requests, could respond by donating what they can afford, and what they believe constitutes a reasonable contribution. This would reverse the prevailing situation in which typically 'donor' governments develop their programmes, preferences and priorities (and revise them at an ever increasing pace), and in which 'recipient' countries can at best try and sort out how they might fit in, or determine whether they can meet the criteria underlying the latest donors' pre-occupation. The idea would require a good deal more flexibility and adjustment on the 'supplying' side than is generally available right now – which is admittedly difficult from a point of view of budget control. However, it would begin to enable 'demanding' or 'requesting' countries to regain some sense of overall command and genuine ownership over their policy formulation and policy integration. It is this most vital aspect of any governance structure and process which has become seriously eroded due to the massive donor involvement in policy determination in many countries.

Concluding remarks

Notions of 'good governance', in association with 'political conditionalities' as a handle for donor intervention, formed the corner stones for a series of interlocking policy criteria and initiatives that have been prominent on the international aid front for well over a decade. Bestowed in the post-Cold War era with high expectations as to the broadened 'political' policy objectives with respect to aid recipient countries they might help accomplish, it increasingly became apparent that these expectations were over-stretched. Posing political conditionalities as a leverage to induce 'good governance' clearly did not – and could not – work out as envisaged, and as a policy metaphor carrying these instrumental connotations the phrase lost much of its appeal. Conceivably, the 'good governance' metaphor might have had a different career path if donors had not launched it with an eye on being able to attach political conditionalities to it but had treated it as an area for development assistance in its own right.

Today, new kinds of donor–recipient relations are increasingly being favoured, with detailed agreements featuring in-built contractual conditionalities with selected countries about the set-up and implementation of comprehensive donor-supported sector programmes. PRSPs represent the latest incarnation of the attempts to restructure these relationships. Notions of 'good governance' are likely to remain part of donor parlance, though with lessened ambitions about the scope for intervention and political restructuring than had earlier been attached to them. Within the donor discourse, the policy metaphor of 'good governance' thus has undergone a remarkable succession of metamorphoses. While first figuring as a key instrument in donor development and foreign policy to induce reforms in governance through aid as an incentive, some donors subsequently began to consider it as a selection criterion for aid recipient countries. Actual selections could hardly measure up to the standards implied, however, and in the end this particular criterion was ranked down in favour of historical ties or regional concentration of aid involvements, among other things. Meanwhile, the 'good governance' notion more broadly appears to evolve into a general figure of speech which donors use to re-emphasize their calls for policy improvement and reforms in aid relationships, justify their role and interventions in a wide range of engagements, and with reference to which from time to time they threaten 'sanctions'.

5

Of State Collapse and Fresh Starts: Some Critical Reflections

Introduction

Until little more than a decade ago, it would have seemed almost inconceivable even to professional political analysts that incidences of state collapse should be on the increase, that the prospect of short-lived or more enduring statelessness should become more common, and that discussion about these phenomena should be rapidly spreading. For a long time, states were accepted as 'normal' in a very basic sense and scholarly perspectives commonly took such 'normalcy' as their point of departure (Doornbos 1994). As already noted in Chapter 1, an extensive literature (in history, archaeology, anthropology and political science) developed on the dynamics of state *formation* – discussing and weighing variables that may have given rise to it, such as conquest, trade routes, population pressure and a range of other factors (see, e.g., Claessen and Skalnik 1978, Doornbos and Kaviraj 1997, Tilly 1990) – but generally there was little writing on state *collapse*. Normatively, once states had come into existence they were expected to last – and, in recent decades, to help sustain the international system that had in turn come to be based on them. A notable exception to this continuity-based perspective was the historical, and the historians', interest in the collapse of *empires* (e.g., Eisenstadt 1988, Gibbon 1952, Lieven 2000). But there are important qualitative differences between empires and state systems, and by implication in the nature of their possible collapse. Empires may fall apart into distinct entities, in principle re-combinable in different arrangements. States in contrast supposedly represent core and indivisible units, even though there have been a good number of examples to the contrary. The Ottoman, Austrian-Hungarian and Soviet empires illustrate the point, while the erstwhile Ethiopian empire continues to struggle to try and transform itself into a state. Nonetheless, the collapse of an empire may also trigger the breakdown of one or more of its vassal states, as was happening in Tadzjikistan in 1992 (Lieven 2000: 393).

Yet understanding the dynamics of state *collapse* may be no less important than appreciating those at work in state *formation*. A better grasp of processes leading to collapse should give us additional insights into what makes states work, and what fails to do so. Moreover, although they seem to be situated at opposite ends of a continuum, there are several key connections between the dynamics of state 'formation' and state 'collapse', which, on closer inspection, may not be as far apart as they first appear. Again, Eisenstadt as already noted in Chapter 1, aptly called for attention to what lies 'beyond collapse', as state (and empire) collapse is likely to inaugurate fresh or renewed processes of state formation, thus signifying 'not the end of social institutions, but almost always the beginning of new ones' (Eisenstadt 1988: 293). Similarly, Ali Mazrui, referring to the contemporary drama in Africa, asked the cardinal question, 'Have Somalia, Rwanda, Liberia, Angola, Burundi been experiencing the death pangs of an old order dying and groaning for refuge? Or are we witnessing the birth pangs of a real but devastating birth of a genuinely post-colonial order?' (Mazrui 1995: 22). Depending on one's understanding of 'collapse' and the political dynamics that give rise to it, it is indeed conceivable to regard collapse as *part of* processes of state reconfiguration and formation. Certainly, a better understanding of processes of collapse is crucial to determine how political reconstruction might best be approached.

If incidences of state collapse appear to be on the increase, then obviously answers are needed to a number of 'why and how' questions. However, it is equally important to ask *what* is being referred to as state collapse and whether different understandings and definitions of the phenomenon may influence our assumptions about its incidence. What are the significant features of state collapse? How do we (and should we) define it? What triggers it? Are some state systems, or contexts, more prone to it than others, and if so, under what kind of conditions? What are the implications of collapse – both internally within the state system concerned, and externally with respect to the relations with the world outside? At another level, questions raised include what does state collapse and the disappearance of the state mean for the idea of 'normalcy' and sovereignty of states, as now enshrined in the UN system? What is the international system's response to state collapse? What lies beyond collapse and how should we visualize and propose to handle the connections between state collapse and state formation, or political reconstruction, in the contemporary era? Clearly, the phenomenon prompts a virtual avalanche of questions.

Two main themes are central to these various queries, one concerned with the search for causalities and a second one concerned with appropriate responses. Discussion of these themes requires examination of the connections that may be postulated between the two. There is often a tendency to look for single causes and explanations of state collapse, and to propose single, preferably 'quick-fix' or 'one size fits all' solutions. In fact, what may be called for is a more differentiating scrutiny of the factors leading to collapse in specific instances, and, in this light, a (re-)consideration of responses and possible external actor involvement.

This chapter therefore first tries to disentangle 'collapse', a term that, unwittingly perhaps, has come to be used to describe quite a range of different things, which is not helpful for clarity of analysis. Following this, the chapter addresses two related concerns. First, even if we adhere to a strict definition, which would talk of collapse only when 'the basic functions of the state are no longer performed', to use Zartman's terms (1995: 5), we are likely to find some quite distinct patterns of and *different and contrasted trajectories to* collapse. It is thus important to look into the complex web of conditioning and facilitating factors that may (or may not) set in motion a chain reaction eventually leading to state collapse. This may contribute to a better understanding not only of why certain dynamics tend to end in state collapse, but also of the extent to which we can identify any different patterns emerging, which could have significant implications for further analysis and policy.

The second concern to be addressed is the response side, specifically external responses. External actors, notably the 'donor community', are trying to better prepare themselves for the eventualities of crises of governance and state collapse in various countries and to design more effective strategies and instruments of response. Their actions seem to be generally guided by assumptions as to how state systems in the contemporary world should be structured and how they ought to function, and by what appears to be called for – in that light – in order to restore or establish effective government. The big question here is whether there will be a 'fit' between the determinants and dynamics of state collapse in various situations and the responses and solutions for restoration which are offered. When contemplating appropriate responses to instances of state collapse, one would imagine, for example, that a key pre-condition for meaningful action must be a careful scrutiny of the background and dynamics leading to the collapse. The achievement of such an optimal 'fit' may, however, be seriously hampered by a variety of factors, including fundamentally different premises from which the crises may be viewed.

Understanding state collapse

To get a better grip on some of these questions, it will be useful to further unpack the notion of collapse as such and see what different kinds of understanding about the failure of state functions it tends to convey. There is a good chance of a need for some sifting here, however, as within the social sciences there is often an inclination to subsume additional meanings and dimensions under 'new' concepts. Rapidly advancing claims of extended relevance and prevalence for the notion concerned in the end may lead to 'collapse' symptoms being spotted almost everywhere, thus making the term rather meaningless.

Some definitional problems influencing our understanding of state collapse can be illustrated at the hand of the work of William Zartman, who brought out the first symposium on the subject. In the Introduction to his edited volume, *Collapsed States*, he submits that 'collapse means that the basic functions of the state are no longer performed, as analysed in various theories of the state' (Zartman 1995: 5). By itself, that understanding would appear beyond question and to provide a ready-made shorthand for what seems at stake. When further specifying his concept, however, Zartman writes that '[s]tate collapse ... is the breakdown of good governance, law and order' (ibid., p. 6). This is more problematic, first of all as it tends to relate the signalling of instances of state collapse to our understanding of 'good governance', which is an essentially judgemental and normative matter (and as noted in Chapter 4 above quite controversial at that). What is more, one imagines that 'collapse' should not be used to refer only to the breakdown of 'good governance', but to that of any pattern of governance, good or bad. If one fails to do that, one might first of all get far too many instances of 'collapse' covered – as indeed seems to be the case with Zartman, who refers to 'many' current instances of collapse. Moreover, employing such a normative notion could lead to endless quibbles and disputes as to whether particular instances of deterioration in 'good governance' illustrate 'state collapse'. Historically, there have been not a few sobering examples of 'bad' governance in which the functioning of the state system as such was in no way impaired, but where in true Machiavellian (or neutral Weberian) spirit it remained geared towards the implementation of the rulers' chosen objectives. In contrast, instances of complete collapse, in the sense of the grinding to a halt and virtual disappearance of a once functioning state system, still seem rather exceptional. Somalia and Sierra Leone in recent years have provided the most clear-cut examples, closely followed by others like Bosnia, Liberia, Congo, Cambodia and Afghanistan. Still, even if these remain exceptional cases, what is not necessarily disputed is that the incidence seems to be on the increase.

However, there are additional reasons for a closer look at notions of breakdown of '(good) governance, law and order', in Zartman's term, as defining the essence of state collapse, as it directly relates to our understanding of the phenomena at stake. Leaving the question of 'good' or 'bad' governance aside, can we assume that when a state no longer functions this necessarily implies a breakdown of 'order', or even of 'law and order'? Easily as these terms may come to mind to describe imagined situations of state collapse, postulating direct connections here tends to imply viewing 'order' as 'state-given', essentially a Hobbesian view: take away the state, and 'order' too will disappear. True as this may well be for various situations, for example, Liberia, Sierra Leone and DR Congo at different recent intervals, it might yet be wrong too readily to assume such one to one relationships. Even the United States once essentially emerged out of a setting in which 'free and equal' individuals – future citizens – in what by and large appears to have been an orderly fashion, were searching for meaningful ways of governing themselves before it, or they, became a state. Historically, various other examples could be cited. Also, early anthropologists contributed greatly to our understanding of these questions by pointing to the existence of meaningful forms of government without state structures, the 'stateless societies' first described by Evans-Pritchard and Fortes in their classic *African Political Systems* (1940). The distinction then developed between 'states' and 'stateless societies' now seems to deserve renewed theoretical interest in the light of the increasing incidence of uncertain political futures following cases of state collapse. Within this perspective, as was noted in Chapter 1, one would expect attention to be devoted to the kind of factors that may either facilitate or block new departures in state formation in contemporary situations, while similarly one should anticipate fresh interest in the study of political processes within the 'new' stateless societies of our time.

Constituting one prime example of the dilemmas this throws up, for more than ten years since 1991 Somalia has done without the benefit of a state system, a situation which, one may say, still largely obtains notwithstanding the fact that as of 2000 several attempts have been made to reintroduce a central government. This followed on prolonged negotiations among a number of, though by no means all, contending parties, mediated in 2000 by the government of neighbouring Djibouti, and as of 2003 again in Nairobi, Kenya. The attempts to arrive at renewed state formation in the Somali context are complicated due to a clash between two different conceptions underlying such efforts – a centralist line in favour of restoration of the erstwhile state structures, and a 'decentralized' line favouring initiatives to create autonomous regional states, which in due course might become constituent units within a relatively loose federal framework (Doornbos 2001). That dilemma has continued to haunt Somali state reconstruction efforts. Whatever it might finally lead to, we can note that in several Somali regions people for well over a decade had managed to cope, and to cope relatively well and in relatively orderly ways, without a functioning state system – some might even say 'better' than when the previous state system was still intact (WSP 1998).

To illustrate this, statelessness as long as it has obtained in the Somali situation could be taken to mean, quite literally, that one could/can walk into the territory from Ethiopia or Kenya without being met by any immigration or customs officials; that no taxes are being collected; that there have been no government schools or hospitals running; that indeed there has been no functioning government police or army, nor any other functioning government office. Still, in several regions trade and commerce have been going on in various sectors: there is import of oil, bottled water, the favourite addictive *quat* and numerous utensils, and export of livestock, frankincense, shellfish and some other products. People harvest, have their domestic activities, marry, give birth, and so on; they send their children to private schools, and take language or other courses. They have efficient and economic satellite telecommunication facilities with the rest of the world; they can have money transactions executed in any currency, and receive or send money from/to abroad as easily as from anywhere in Europe. In short, in various regions there has been a fairly normal set of activities, except that there was no state.

Whatever useful functions states may have to offer, the presence of a 'state' and of 'order' thus cannot always be equated. Besides, one should take note of the opposite possibility, that of 'state terror' coinciding with severe 'disorder', which Somalia experienced at an earlier stage and which similarly has been the fate of Uganda under Idi Amin (1971–79), Ethiopia under Mengistu (1974–91), Cambodia under Pol Pot (1975–79) and has occurred in numerous other situations historically. For definitional clarity, therefore, there would seem to be a point in limiting the notion of 'state collapse' to the kind of situation in which a functioning state system ceases to exist – whatever that situation may or may not imply in terms of 'order'. For less than complete collapse it might be better to refer to 'state failure', another recent addition to our vocabulary, though this may require further specification as to which particular state functions have been 'failing' – the failure to deliver essential public welfare services, the failure to provide basic security (vis-à-vis internal as well as external threats), the failure to act as a moderator of opposed interests, among others. Finally, though, while taking note of seemingly non-problematic 'deviant' patterns, this is not to deny the possibility of state collapse turning into a situation of frightening anarchy.

Closely connected to this we may also note some other distinctions. Aside from instances of 'total' collapse of state frameworks, there have been some recent cases of 'partial' collapse, that is, of some state functions but not all, like in DRC, and of territorially restricted collapse due to ethnic or other conflict, like in Sudan (1973–present) and Sri Lanka (1983–2001). Furthermore, we might distinguish between temporary versus enduring state collapse, as illustrated by the cases of Albania and Somalia, and to the occurrence of situations featuring a presence of state authority during the day, and rebel authority during the night.

Theoretically a more significant difference is that implied in the notions of 'twilight institutions' and 'twilight states' (Lund 2006), which points to the occurrence and at times co-existence of different kinds of institutions with a claim to public authority within the same general territory, like traditional chiefs, state representatives, rebel leaders, and others. Recognizing the plurality of public authorities in any given situation is important, among other things, to get a better idea of the stretch and limits of 'normal' state power, which usually is indeed limited.

Dynamics of civil conflict and state collapse

The collapse of a state can hardly occur spontaneously, or all at once. If and where it happens, it is likely to have been preceded and initiated by complex and conflict-ridden processes of deterioration, decline and erosion of state functions. Actual collapse is likely to constitute the final moment of such processes, and to occur when a certain point of no return has been passed. These processes have their own dynamics, which is not to say that they are strictly internal processes. Indeed, the precise ways in which external and internal determinants interact and coalesce in prompting processes leading to state collapse are extremely important for a better understanding of the phenomenon. (The fact that they are often insufficiently understood, incidentally, makes it easier for each side, internal or external, to blame the other.)

As processes, dynamics of decline are theoretically reversible, and one can only speculate about the number of instances where timely intervention – from below or from above, from inside or outside – may have stopped a chain of events that could have culminated in state collapse. A trite yet relevant truism would be to say that proper performance and maintenance of state functions and institutions provides the best protection against state collapse. But the dynamic quality of the processes concerned also makes it difficult to identify with any certainty at what point in a spiral of potential collapse a state system may find itself. As with historical state formation processes, where one may recognize in retrospect that a state has emerged out of various formative processes (Claessen 1993), the 'root causes' of state collapse will similarly have been at work well before any actual collapse manifests itself.

If a cursory look at definitional elements suggests that generalizing about 'state collapse' is rather hazardous, this seems equally true when trying to identify its causes and consequences. Although in a sense the end result may appear to be the same in all cases – the absence of a once functioning state system – the dynamics leading to that condition may be vastly different from one situation to the next. Nor should this be surprising. The fragile Sierra Leonean situation, for example, with its massive insecurity and violence at the hands of armed rebel groups enjoying significant external support (Reno 2000a), appeared qualitatively different from the fragmentation of the erstwhile Somali state system into different regional entities vying with each other for power (Doornbos 2002). Superficially, the common element in both cases seemed to be the presence of 'warlords' capturing control and continuing to play a dominant role; but a closer look would show that there has been a good deal more to it, and many differences between these two situations.

In the Somali case, it was the inability to accommodate conflicting interests, often articulated on a clan basis, and the instrumental use to which the state apparatus was put in the pursuit of this inter-clan violence, that caused the disintegration of the fragile system. For all its repressive qualities, the Somali state had a relatively 'thin' presence within the society, which meant that it could all the more easily collapse and be thrown off when inter-clan conflict and repression came to a head (Doornbos and Markakis 1994). In Sierra Leone, it was the greed for profit from control over the lucrative illegal diamond trade that became a key factor fuelling the rebellion and by implication the progressive undermining of the state system (Ellis 2001, Reno 2000a). However, this still leaves open the question of why the rebellion started, for which very different explanations have been offered, notably ethnic grievances spurred by unequal access to power and resources (Richards 1996). The Somali context in recent times has comprised several regions with ambitions for either far-reaching political autonomy (like Puntland) or full-fledged independence (i.e. Somaliland) – thus for statehood in one form or another. This again differs sharply from the Sierra Leonean situation, which is argued to have comprised various powerful groups known to be negatively disposed to any resurrection of the state framework (Reno 2000a).

Both the Sierra Leonean and Somali examples, meanwhile, stand in contrast to the pattern of the relatively short-lived, but no less dramatic, collapse of the Albanian state in 1996–97. In this case, collapse followed in the wake of the crisis triggered by the infamous pyramid schemes which had invalidated the savings and securities of so many people, in the end causing a massive popular uprising against the 'failing' state (De Gaay Fortman 2000, Vaughan-Whitehead 1999). Thus, taking only these three instances of state collapse, the differences involved seem to represent a good deal more than 'incidental' factors. Rather, they underscore the need to explore more fully the emergence of different patterns in, or tracks to, state collapse.

Other examples also illustrate this differentiation of patterns. For instance, the complex dynamics that led to the crisis and collapse of the Cambodian state framework followed on years of protracted and destructive struggle between the Pol Pot government and liberation forces, and eventually required a complex UN-led effort to restructure a state system expected to be reasonably open to and representative of the various political strands in the country (Utting 1994). Other recent configurations of collapsing states have included the compound crises which occurred – and in several instances still continue – in Haiti, Bosnia, Liberia, Congo, and indeed Afghanistan. Each of these evidently requires its own explanation of what went wrong in terms of failing state systems no longer able to provide basic security, ending up in final collapse. In several of these cases, like Haiti or Congo, state power had for so long been personalized, based on non-formal militias loyal only to the president, that the degeneration of the system caused the fragile state structure to become largely irrelevant and eventually to collapse. In Afghanistan, prolonged violent conflict had started as a late 'Cold War' proxy war in 1979, resulting in ongoing stalemate among the conflicting groups and pervasive social disorientation within the population. In the wake of this, and in the face of non-state forces with an entirely different cultural and ideological agenda – the Taliban – the state largely lost its function, and in the end lost out. Since then, the world has witnessed how that trajectory was brought to completion with the externally induced collapse of the Taliban regime, which exposed the state system it had controlled to be in ruins (Rubin 2002). The Iraq case, finally, represents yet another step, reversing the sequence we would normally expect to run from state collapse to the establishment of a new order into one in which a basic (external) drive to want a new order instils a determination and move to effectuate a wholesale state collapse.

Trying to better understand state collapse, therefore, must mean getting a better grip on the conditioning factors. What makes some political and economic contexts more vulnerable than others to dynamics leading to state collapse, and what variables in this regard may lead to different tracks? Internally, as noted, there are various distinct factors to explore, such as a lack of meaningful linkages between state and society, greed for resources, excessive concentration of power and gross institutional mismanagement. More generally still there are the nature and dynamics of social cleavages and civil conflict along class, ethnic, religious or regional lines, or some combination of these.

Externally, again, several recurrent patterns present themselves, working alone or in concert with others. One is the strategy of deliberate destabilization on the part of neighbouring powers, either for geopolitical reasons as in Lebanon or Cambodia, or for economic gain as in Congo and Sierra Leone (Reno 1998). Another is the general vulnerability of poor countries, especially African countries, vis-à-vis forces emanating from the world economy. With regard to Rwanda, for example, though strictly speaking not a case of complete 'collapse', there has been some debate about the role played by the slump in international coffee prices, together with IMF/World Bank imposed austerity measures, shortly before the 1994 genocide. According to Chossudovsky (1999) this had set the pre-conditions for a sharpening of ethnic tensions and eventual crisis. This argument is qualified by Storey, who, while conceding that there is 'some substance' to it, submits that the World Bank's policy had been to increase state resources to the Rwandan government during the relevant period (Storey 2001: 375–376). Yet, consumer prices and fees for health and education had indeed been rising in the context of austerity policies, adding to economic hardships. A 'social insecurity' aspect which may have played a role in the background to the Rwandese genocide is also suggested by the research of Philip Verwimp, who found that Hutu households with less security in terms of land holdings and other assets have been more actively taking part in the massacres, though usually encouraged by more powerful landlords (Verwimp 2003). The Albanian case was more unique in terms of its precipitants, though here, too, severe austerity measures demanded as conditionalities for foreign aid had preceded the crisis that erupted in 1996 (Tarifa and Spoor 2000). The Afghan case was special in its own way, with a state system that had by and large ceased functioning as a 'normal' state, though in the end receiving its *coup de grace* with the American intervention.

State–society linkages under threat

Clearly, the discussion about state collapse in most cases is closely related to that of the causes and consequences of civil conflict. However, the latter evidently represents a much broader field than that concerned with state collapse as such. If we strictly keep to a bottom line definition of state collapse as referring to situations where all normal state functions have ceased to exist, then most or all recent patterns of state collapse will have been preceded by sub-state conflict and violence of one kind or another. An all-out civil war for example, may seriously weaken the central state and eventually cause its collapse. Ethnic or religious strife and other forms of sub-national conflict may severely affect the chances of survival of the state system as a whole. Again, widening socio-economic gaps within the population, induced or aggravated by factors emanating from the global economy, may likewise fuel conflicts and eventually incapacitate the state system to handle them.

State collapse may itself constitute a moment in ongoing civil conflict, inaugurating new episodes in the strife, such as in Liberia. Again, as suggested earlier, state collapse in due course may conceivably open up processes of renewed state formation. But the relation between state collapse and civil conflict is not a chicken and egg one. If we reverse the equation, it is by no means the case that all instances of civil conflict, no matter how severe, will lead to state collapse. Historically, there have been numerous cases of prolonged or profound civil conflict which have *not* led to ultimate state collapse. If it appears to have done so more frequently in recent times, this may be due to particular conditions resulting from the fragility of state systems within the current global context having come to play a larger role, a point to which we shall return.

In discussing dynamics that may lead to state collapse, Zartman (1995) points to a 'necessary' factor which is contained in the paradox of 'the effectiveness of the state before collapse, through repression and neglect, in destroying the regulative and regenerative capacities of society: [T]he collapsing state contracts, isolates itself, retreats. As it implodes, it saps the vital functions of society' (Zartman 1995: 7). Zartman thus views state collapse here as one side of a coin of which societal collapse is the other: the fabric of linkages and feedback mechanisms between state and society, vital for any meaningful 'governance', gets irreparably ruptured. There is much to be said for this conceptualization, which links the (mal-)functioning of the state to that of societal processes and capacities. Nonetheless, that kind of crisis can arguably occur more easily in some situations than in others, notably in those where the fabric of linkages and two way mechanisms between state and society has not grown into a dense or thick cluster of connections but has remained fairly thin and superficial. Indeed (enduring) collapse may be more readily anticipated in contexts where there is a limited and still somewhat artificial state presence within the society, in Somalia or Chad, for example, than in others where the idea and reality of statehood has a long-standing background and integration, like in Ethiopia, India, or various other contexts. This would remain true even if ex-imperial Ethiopia, for example, might fall apart at some point as a territorial entity: the ideas of 'state' and 'stateness' are likely to reassert themselves among several of the parts into which it might then fragment. Generally speaking, as the incidence of state collapse in recent years has been stronger in Africa than in Asia and other world regions, it seems reasonable to assume that this may be related to the existence of weaker state–society linkages in Africa than elsewhere.

In this connection, Zartman suggests that there is insufficient evidence to say that collapse results from inadequate or inadequately functioning institutions, that is, maladapted and mal-functioning 'Western-style' colonially derived state institutions. It is certainly true that some inconsistency between implanted institutions and their new contexts has been present in numerous situations, sometimes even with major implications such as in India and South Asia generally. And indeed, maladapted as they have been, they have often nonetheless continued to 'function' and create new streams of interaction, resource management and power structures. Zartman concludes from this that this 'mal-functioning' by itself constitutes no cause of collapse, since so many other 'mal-functioning' institutions do not lead to collapse (ibid., p. 6). Again, however, it may not so much be the 'mal-functioning' of implanted institutions that may have fuelled collapse, but rather the extent of mismatch of novel institutions with their environment. This may have allowed only few meaningful linkages between state and society to develop and thus have left the state structure as a fairly artificial body hanging over society. Within the society concerned distinctive socio-political processes would continuously evolve and may naturally re-assert themselves once the 'alien body' of the state system is thrown off. If in addition 'mal-functioning' in such instances also means arbitrary rule, enhancing people's insecurity, and engendering gross inequities in the access to resources, then a process leading towards ultimate collapse may only get accelerated, as in the Somali case.

Different trajectories

The examples reviewed thus far suggest that short of, or beyond, one or another mega explanation pointing to changed global (pre-)conditions that have prompted an increased incidence of state collapse, it is important to identify to what extent different political and economic constellations may have given rise to different trajectories to collapse. Such an approach is akin to the way in which complex political emergencies have been distinguished from one another (Cliffe and Luckham 2000), and avoids starting out from a priori assumptions about the causes of state collapse. Put differently, it is difficult to postulate that there is a single 'recipe' for collapse, and hardly realistic to assume a single path or set of determinants. At the same time, what evolves does not seem to be *random*: recent examples suggest there are some recognizable and potentially recurrent patterns. Therefore, there appears to be justification for the premise that instances of state collapse, even if superficially similar, represent the provisional end-result of different sets of dynamic processes, subject to different clusters of contextual variables and forces. Trying to chart out and categorize such different paths, provisional and incomplete as it may be, should therefore be a crucial step in any attempt to theorize about state collapse.

Yet it is important to note that the present global context – in which the major powers no longer have the same interest in maintaining inter-state balances of power, and by implication in maintaining states that they did during the Cold War – appears much more prone to the incidence of state collapse than was previously the case, especially in Africa. As Dennis Dijkzeul observes, '[the] central strategic shift in international relations during the 1990s went from a bipolar system based on strong sovereign states with strong strategic and economic interests to a system with one superpower, the United States, and an increasing number of weak or failed states, which lacked clear strategic and economic relevance' (Dijkzeul 2004: 75). In the years following 'September 11' the picture has not essentially changed in this regard, except that the chances of external intervention in existing state systems, followed by their collapse, have evidently increased – witness the case of Iraq in 2003 and Afghanistan before it.

Generally, the rapidly changing global context, characterized by the drive towards economic liberalization and privatization, the pursuit of global market relations, the propagation of the rolling back of the state, the demanding role of the international financial institutions, and related features such as the global communications transformation, can certainly be viewed as offering a mega explanation of sorts, setting global pre-conditions, for various recent instances of state collapse. In general, of course, whenever there happens to be an increased incidence of whatever phenomenon, it is quite natural to look for common or over-arching causes. The end of the Cold War, together with the changed rationales of big power politics in the international arena and the new global conditions by which these have been accompanied, indeed appears to figure as one such 'general' explanatory cluster of variables.

However, causalities are complex and may involve different levels of determinants and conditioning factors. Thus, the lifting of Cold War hegemonic 'support' structures might need to be primarily understood as implying that different social and political state systems – some of them more robust, others more fragile and vulnerable, yet each embedded within its own historically endowed socio-political and cultural context – were laid open to a whole range of political and economic forces and interests, internal as well as external. However, such a major change of (pre-)conditions should not be expected to promote or induce broadly parallel tracks. A common cause does not necessarily trigger common results. The kind of pattern that might ensue, if any, would depend on factors such as the structuring of political forces, societal divisions, resource endowments and so on. In facing the forces of post-Cold War globalization, state systems with different fault lines in their social or economic structures may exhibit contrasted patterns of fragmentation (if it comes to that). Exploring such different contexts and possible trajectories is important, also with an eye on assessing the appropriateness of external responses, or for understanding new conflicts that might arise out of conflicting scenarios for political rebuilding (Doornbos 2002).

When trying to reconnoitre different chain reactions to collapse, partly on the basis of the discussion above, a number of distinct patterns begin to suggest themselves. In the following, the first four are more 'basic' in character, the last two conceivably more 'supplementary':

1. states in which the privatization of state assets and prerogatives of state rulers has become extreme, and in which there are deepening challenges to that rule from former associates as well as from various liberation fronts (Zaire/Congo under Mobutu, Haiti under Duvalier, Uganda under Amin, Somalia under Barre)
2. states with a marked historical mismatch between the nature and orientation of state institutions and the socio-political processes and divisions within the society concerned (e.g., Somalia, Chad, Georgia, Rwanda)
3. states in which there are deepening fights over the control of strategic resources – diamonds, oil, timber, and others – involving rebel groups and privatized armies, making state institutions irrelevant (Congo, Sierra Leone, Liberia, potentially Nigeria)
4. states undergoing a major struggle over power and over the political and cultural orientation and organization of society (Cambodia, Afghanistan, Tadzjikistan, potentially Sudan)
5. states in which secession attempts run out of hand, potentially affecting the continuity of the state system as a whole (e.g., Congo, potentially Indonesia)
6. fragile states suddenly facing deteriorating economic conditions which seriously affect the livelihood of a large majority of the population, leading to a breakdown of state institutions (Albania at the time of the pyramid games, Rwanda allegedly prior to the genocide).

In addition to these specific variants, we could think of states in which institutional failures to provide basic security in one or more respects (physical security, health, nutrition) have gone beyond a point of repair – due to whatever specific reasons – thus invoking a state bankruptcy of sorts. This more general variant may figure as both a manifestation and determinant of collapse, the latter as deteriorating conditions become a factor in their own right.

Of course such a tentative listing does not make any claims to completeness. It is easy to imagine that other tracks will be 'discovered' in due course. It should also be understood that any such preliminary categorization does not imply strictly separate tracks. Rather, several of these dynamics could be operative at the same time, reinforcing one another. In this connection, one of the most important, and most difficult, distinctions to be made arises from mutations that may occur over time. Rebel activity in Congo or Sierra Leone may have been born out of grievances based on ethnic inequalities, for example, but might in due course have become transformed into coercive systems of primitive accumulation. The resulting trajectory is therefore not necessarily strictly linear or singular. Furthermore, some determining patterns are conceivably more profound than others, and may require other facilitating or conditioning factors for their mobilization – a topic that would take us back to the analysis of social movements (Dwivedi 2001, Landsberger 1968, Salih 1999). Finally, we can never be certain until it has happened that any of these 'tracks' will result in collapse. A whole range of chance factors may in the end make all the difference between collapse and a state which lingers, or limps, on.

Trying to map out different trajectories to collapse is important also for the choice of possible remedial or preventive action, and should take note of the mix of internal and external factors and actors involved. For instance, if the key problem in a given situation were identified as one of grossly malfunctioning institutions (as is often assumed), then presumably there would be a case for major internal institutional repair or overhaul – even though this might leave unattended the root causes of arbitrary rule, ethnic grievances or other conflicts that may have been responsible for the failing institutions in the first place. But if collapse has occurred or is threatening due to a state system's extreme vulnerability to changing externally driven economic conditions, then obviously the focus for remedial action should be shifted into different directions. Again, if a basic mismatch between a country's state framework and societal structure lies at the root of collapse, then it may well be more prudent to allow fresh departures to emerge out of that situation than insisting on re-instatement of the previous failing state structures. In other words, the routes for possible remedial or preventive action may need to be just as different as the tracks leading to collapse. Mistakes in identifying the pattern of causality, and thus the solution, can be grave and may worsen already precarious situations.

Unsurprisingly, several instances of collapse in recent years have been followed by international calls for restoration of 'order', sanctions, or even advocacy of some form of international trusteeship for certain situations. The latter had been advocated for Sierra Leone, for example, and in a de facto way began to be implemented with the British intervention there (Ellis 2001). It is certainly conceivable that some contexts may require a basic restoration of order to start with and that external actors may have a key role to play in that. In some situations of state collapse, combined with profound stalemate between rival parties, there may simply be no alternative to some form of third party engagement, at the negotiating table or otherwise.

However, the option of intervention and international trusteeship has been advanced as a possible form of international action for wider clusters of countries more generally (Helman and Rattner 1993, Pfaff 1995, among others) and apparently has been tentatively contemplated in general terms within several multilateral circles, including the World Bank (cf. Moore 2000). In somewhat similar vein, there have been proposals for a 'de-certification' of certain categories of countries, a measure meant to exclude them from normal privileges and reciprocities among UN-members (Herbst 1996). Such generalized calls or proposals become problematic, because they do not regard the merits or demerits of specific situations or how they have come about. Rather, they seem to be based on an assumption that the order which had previously existed – such as that under the erstwhile Sierra Leone government – was in itself legitimate but was derailed and destroyed at the hands of unlawful elements. As a hypothesis, such a reading of the route to collapse emphasizes institutional failures as a root cause, while as a remedy it recommends redressing proper institutional mechanisms and procedures, thus putting the state back into place. This is not necessarily wrong, but that still does not make it right, or sufficient. Pointing to institutional failures may not add much to the analysis, as the question still remains as to how those institutional mechanisms (that is, state structures) came to be undermined, and at the hands of what forces. Although 'collapse' at one level may seem synonymous with 'disorder', it may not always require a reflex reaction intent on putting that same order back in place.

The strand of writing which places particular emphasis on institutional failures and mismanagement as an explanation of state collapse is related to a good deal of donor critique which in recent years has been levelled at the performance of, in particular, African governments in terms of 'governance' failures. The ease and pace with which the 'good governance' discourse was embraced in donor circles has indeed been remarkable (Abrahamsen 2000, Doornbos 1995 and Chapter 4), yet it hardly offers a tool for better understanding of different socio-political contexts to which state systems must try to relate, or why they may be failing at this.

Again, it is important not to fall into the trap that social researchers are capable of laying for themselves: keen to generalize and categorize on the basis of limited case-study material, claims are often made for a much wider validity of a particular type of phenomenon than the data concerned might strictly justify. Not unrelated to the discussion about breakdown and state collapse, for example, this kind of methodological shortcut – and shortcoming – would seem to be at play with respect to the 'criminalization of African politics' thesis advanced by Bayart *et al.* (1999). Even a demonstrable or increased incidence of criminalization in specific contexts cannot provide a valid basis for generalizations or for broadly depicting African politics in those terms. Nor can the occurrence of greed-driven, hence basically criminal rebel activity such as that which has been haunting Sierra Leone and Liberia, provide sufficient ground to equate *all* rebel action in Africa with criminal activity, as Paul Collier (1999, 2001) would like us to accept. Moreover, in the context of the greed versus grievance debate which has recently been initiated (Berdal and Malone 2000), it could be quite wrong to assume that rebel activity in various situations was *started* on the basis of the greed motive, like a business enterprise. Again, there may be different layers of causality within one and the same context, requiring careful analysis that can reach below the surface.

Some other 'early warning' signals may not be out of place here, and may be flagged even after 'September 11'. External actors should beware of rapid and overwhelming interventions which could in turn create new internal–external dichotomies. Instead, internal actors as a matter of course must be allowed – and should themselves claim – a central role in any efforts at political reconstruction. Also, following collapse, agonizing re-appraisal of the nature of the (collapsed) state system by those most concerned may need to run its course, and should be allowed the time it needs. As suggested earlier, any straight-jacketing back into the previous state forms that failed should be avoided if the key problem has been a lack of fit between political forces and societal structures. In such cases, a situation of statelessness lasting for some time should not by definition be viewed as problematic, but might in fact allow much-needed re-appraisal of alternative structures, and futures. Significantly in this vein, a tentative conclusion drawn in a recent report by the German *Gesellschaft für Technische Zusammenarbeit* (GTZ) was that '[the] collapse of states in crisis need not be prevented, since a "better state" cannot emerge until that collapse has taken place' (Mehler and Ribaux 2000: 107).

Statelessness and the international context

'Statelessness', the situation that may follow for longer or shorter periods after collapse, represents a conceptual category that may deserve a good deal more attention than it is normally being accorded.

Implications that external actors should draw from situations of statelessness are, first, to resist the urge to rush in because there happens to be no government in place, and second, if novel forms of government are emerging, to give them a fair chance. Of course, conditions may vary dramatically from one context to another and there are some, like East Timor at the height of crisis (2000), in which a timely international presence is essential. It is also hard to imagine Afghanistan today – and in the foreseeable future – without a strong international presence. Yet in the longer run it is important that Afghans themselves regain control over their own affairs, in ways which will be most consistent with their societal and political divisions. Again, the Iraq situation is different from virtually everything that has gone before, but now appears to be turning into a nightmare for those who seemed so keen to come and set things 'straight'.

The implications of collapse and statelessness vis-à-vis the external environment seem full of contradictions, as can be illustrated with the example of Somalia. Over more than a ten year period during which major parts of Somali society seemed to have concluded that no useful purpose would be served by a return to the former unified Somali state, the United Nations and other international agencies, as well as foreign governments, have kept holding on to the myth of the sovereignty of the former Somali state. They maintained working relations on the ground in various regions, but the image of undivided Somali sovereignty was strenuously upheld by the international community. Meanwhile, Somaliland, the former British protectorate that had merged with Italian-controlled Somalia at independence in 1961, took the position that it wanted to revert to its own, separate status at the collapse of the Somali state in 1991, thus (re-)declaring its independence. It has done so in view of the traumatic experiences to which it had been subjected following the merger, but all its calls for international recognition tabled with the United Nations have fallen on deaf ears (Yannis 1997). By contrast, the United Nations and other international actors were quick to give their support to the short-lived government restored in Mogadishu in 2000, which claimed control over all of Somalia even though these claims remained highly controversial in various regions, and again to the Transitional Federal Government (TFG) set up in Nairobi in 2004 and led by controversial Col. Abdullahi Yusuf, which has been lacking any effective base within Somalia until (at least) well into 2005. Somaliland's legitimate claims to international recognition are thus being sidestepped in favour of the larger goal of trying to restore the collapsed Somali republic. What explains these different responses?

Although this must be a matter of conjecture, several pre-occupations would seem to be playing a role. First, at an intuitive level, which surely counts among key players in the international arena, there appears to be a sense of unease at the sight of blank spaces emerging on the world's maps. With the end of colonialism, all global territory was supposedly divided into formally recognized states. This has become a bottom-line to the new world order, representing a new, prescriptive normalcy. There is now even an emerging, yet largely unsubstantiated assumption that where there are no states, there might be 'terrorists', as has been suggested with respect to Somalia following '9/11' (Hagmann 2004).[1] By contrast, the idea that the ubiquity of states might no longer be so normal, must be frightening from the perspective of a world system that for its own existence has come to depend on the premise of normalcy of states.

More practically, there are other concerns – the international system needs mailboxes and addressees for each entity within its orbit. In that light, no constituent unit should be allowed to disappear or to go underground. But also, there must be a natural fear for precedents: if one weak state collapses and is allowed to get away with it, others might follow, a prospect that some would say must be prevented from a perspective of system maintenance. More serious, and more difficult to resolve, is the fact that all countries, even the poorest and most vulnerable, have become tied to a whole web of treaties and international obligations through the sheer fact of their independent status and membership in the international order. Last but not least, if a collapsing state has incurred huge debts, such as presumably had been the case with Somalia which during the Cold War received vast deliveries of arms from the big powers, who is to be held responsible for those debts? The idea of debtor countries one by one disappearing, dissolving, leaving no address whatsoever, must be an international banker's nightmare. Presumably, therefore, the myth of uninterrupted sovereignty is also necessary to ensure that some body or entity, with some kind of address, remains accountable for the debts and obligations of previous governments of the former state.

Looking at these questions in terms of sovereignty, two points seem to call for attention. Sovereignty supposedly embodies a nation's ultimate

---

[1] Accordingly, at an American think-tank discussion in 2004, it was suggested that 'Engagement in Somalia is risky, but must be weighed against the potential for terrorist activity there. The establishment of the TPG should provide an opportunity for increased American involvement' (West 2005: 21).

self-determining powers about its own future, which is entrusted in conditional custody by its people to the state (Brons 2001, Buzan 1991). In the case of collapsed states like Somalia, however, it now appears that the international system, specifically the United Nations Security Council, is putting itself up as an alternative custodian, empowered to withhold sovereignty and to grant it to successor rulers when it considers that the appropriate moment has come. The case of Iraq is even further removed from any conceivable norms or substitute norms like a role for the United Nations, with the US government taking the position that *it* will decide on the steps required for re-instatement of an Iraqi government.

Second and not unrelated to the first point, as already noted in Chapter 3 with reference to many of Africa's post-colonial states, one notion which held ground for some time is that their survival as independent states would have come to a halt had it not been for the international recognition of their sovereignty (and the big powers' interests in propping it up) (Jackson and Rosberg 1982, Jackson 1990). While this thesis tended to disregard the role of international actors themselves in narrowing the room for manoeuvre and the sovereign scope for policy initiatives and policy co-ordination by post-independence African governments, sovereignty in this perspective could be viewed as a saving grace for otherwise failing or collapsing states. It is ironic therefore that, having arrived at a point where collapse has run its full course and former constituent units of a collapsed state may see no more future for it, it is the international recognition of sovereignty which tends to hamper the exploration of alternative futures.

With collapse, therefore, new kinds of situations arise: international recognition may no longer serve as a protective umbrella for weak regimes, but may become a potential stumbling bloc to fresh starts and rejuvenation by insisting on holding on to old territorial boundaries and political entities. By implication, renewed efforts at state formation would need to be cast in the mould of the previous state system, even if it has proved unworkable, in order to comply with the demands of international recognition. This departs sharply from the usual pattern of international recognition following the logic of internal evolution and paths of reconfiguration and state formation, which one imagines has been a basic historical pattern. Inevitably, therefore, this raises new questions about the scope for political re-starts in situations where external recognition plays an increasingly decisive role.

If the incidence of state collapse and non-recognition of newly emerging entities were to increase, it is conceivable that earlier (pre-UN) patterns in international relations might be repeated once again: recognition of 'states' by some other (neighbouring or like-minded) partners, but not necessarily by the system as a whole. This would add to a recent trend towards unilateral action on the international front in other respects, threatening the aspirations to universality for the United Nations and its institutions (Yannis 1999). The US invasion of Iraq has brought this out dramatically. If the United Nations in the long run is to retain a central role in these matters, it may be important for it to try to develop some measure of positive flexibility in this regard.

International actors

Recognizing different trajectories and their respective (potential) outcomes thus appears to be of the utmost importance when considering what responses, international or otherwise, are most appropriate in a given situation.[2] That message, however, does not always seem to be heeded. A recipe-thirsty international community rather appears inclined to search for readily available programmes of intervention, at times apparently irrespective of the factors that have led to actual crisis situations.

It is not difficult to understand how such inclinations may have come about. While the international community often feels it has a role to play in the redress of severe crisis with respect to particular countries, the time, interest and capacity to investigate how particular routes have led to collapse is often lacking. In lieu of this, and analogous to the idea that a broken leg needs a standard cure no matter how it came to be broken, external actors quickly resort to the view that collapse is collapse and in need of repair and reconstruction. In addition, a kind of reverse reasoning may come into play: if there is a preferred 'solution' to state collapse, there may also be a preferred 'cause' – or at least, insufficient interest in understanding how state collapse came about in a particular situation and in trying to develop responses in that light.

As a result of the perceived challenges of failing states and instances of state collapse, many multilateral and bilateral aid agencies have in recent years set up their own programmes meant to respond to the complex political emergencies to which these give rise. A common strategy is to try to be prepared for rapid and effective action. Significantly, these tendencies have acquired a dynamic of their own, and in their pursuit of

---

[2] Junne and Verkoren rightly warn against 'one-size-fits-all' approaches to post-conflict development generally (Junne and Verkoren 2005).

effectiveness and co-ordinated action may paradoxically lead away from, rather than towards, developing capacities to design context- and trajectory-specific approaches. Moreover, external agendas and an interest in capturing the moment and bringing about fundamental change may enter the equation, irrespective of the dynamics that led to a given situation. As GTZ authors Mehler and Ribaux recently noted, and recommended:

> [post]-conflict situations often provide special opportunities for political, legal, economic and administrative reforms to change past systems and structures which may have contributed to economic and social inequities and conflict ... In the wake of conflict, donors should seize opportunities to help promote and maintain the momentum for reconciliation and needed reforms. (Mehler and Ribaux 2000: 37)

Evidently, active interests keen to make 'fresh starts' in war-torn societies, from fresh designs, exist not only on the 'receiving' end, but also on the donor front.

On the donor front, several features deserve attention. One is the tendency to search for common strategies, in part as a corrective to situations in which different external agencies were all doing their own thing, resulting in proverbial inter-agency confusion (Moore 1996). Through co-ordinated interventions, as advocated by Foreman *et al.* (2000), among others, it is anticipated that effectiveness, strength, and impact can be optimized. Second and closely related is a tendency to work towards set recipes, which can be deployed at once and in all situations, again in response to perceived urgencies and demands of effectiveness (ibid.). Third, some authors and agencies are becoming less inhibited about suggesting the need to sideline the 'sovereignty' of some of the affected countries, proposing to have it temporarily replaced through a United Nations or some other 'mandate' (for instance, Helman and Ratner 1992, Pfaff 1995). Fourth, there is a trend among leading multilateral agencies to see post-conflict contexts as a suitable ground, and moment, to install market-friendly frameworks, thus seeing fresh starts as the moment for fresh designs of a particular kind. The GTZ document cited earlier goes in this direction. Similarly, a Carnegie/UNHCR document authored by John Stremlau, after noting that it 'foresees the need for fundamental changes in the definition and defense of [the] principles of sovereign equality', goes on to suggest that 'sustainable development based on legitimate combinations of market economics, democratic values and a healthy civil society can eventually provide the means for any nation to resolve internal conflicts peacefully and fairly' (Stremlau 1998: 2). A guiding hand is also offered by the newly opened State Department Office of the Co-ordinator for Reconstruction and Stabilization (S/CRS), tasked 'to lead and coordinate U.S. Government planning, and institutionalize U.S. capacity, to help stabilize and reconstruct societies in transition from conflict or civil strife so they can reach a sustainable path towards peace, democracy and a market economy' (West 2005: 30 and http://www.state.gov/s/crs/). Related policy projections are increasingly articulated in other official and semi-official statements.

The combined effect of these dynamic features presents us with a paradox: as international agencies become more and more prepared to intervene, ready to move in with co-ordinated programmes and interested in re-creating political space in ways that promise accelerated political and economic liberalization, there will be less chance of responses being tailored to take account of specific situations, or of leaving the initiative to internal actors with their own visions of a different future. It may at best allow lip service to the idea that reconstruction at a national or regional scale might require an involvement of 'local' leadership, joint action, or whatever. There is little a priori preparedness to consider that different contexts might need different approaches and priorities, to be worked out in mutual consultation, let alone that national leadership should be given the necessary scope for its own strategies. Likewise, there is little sense, it seems, in which donors might be prepared to see themselves not so much 'in command' but available 'on demand', either for emergency situations or otherwise.

A new field of discourse and engagement thus appears to be shaping up around the 'politics of reconstruction', with multilateral agencies and other donors partly in competition amongst each other – though basically moving towards co-ordinated action – and with the leadership(s) of affected countries often having very limited chances to manifest themselves or to be heard. Afghanistan today has all the ingredients to become an illustration of this point. External–internal dividing lines may become deepened and sharpened in the process, and novel forms of domination may emerge around the introduction of new frameworks of political and economic accountability and control. Iraq, too, though presenting a situation not quite like those of other 'normally' collapsed states, illustrates this kind of divide in no uncertain terms.

Conclusion: imagining fresh starts

What, then, could lie beyond collapse, and what lessons can be drawn from past experiences? Historically speaking, one would expect a new political order to come to surface from amidst the ruins of the old, possibly building on elements that had been suppressed or ignored. As noted earlier, the connections between the old and the new can be extremely important in understanding the emergence and evolution of new political forms. In European history, state formation processes often re-started in new directions and in new constellations following the demise of a previous order. Today in various settings in the South it is important that political re-starts should be given a realistic chance of succeeding, as well as the space they may require for working out new and viable arrangements. This implies, among other things, that whatever well-intentioned plans are being made for international assistance to rehabilitation, a key point of departure must be that internal social and political actors and dynamics play a central, not a spectator's role. Another implication is a need on all sides to recognize that fundamental political change, including that involved in processes of state formation, may in the long run need to be reflected in revised political maps and atlases. Stifling such processes for the sake of global 'stability' could in the end prove counter-productive.

So what could be done to reverse tendencies that block fresh openings and political re-starts, allowing constructive interactions on policy priorities in rehabilitation? First and foremost, there is a need to *de-generalize*, that is, for external actors and analysts to resist the temptation to overly generalize about causes of state collapse and their solutions. Instead, due attention should be given in analyses as well as in policy outlines to the implications of contrasted contexts, different dynamics and different trajectories that may continue to play crucial roles when trying to move from collapse to recovery. Responses should be context- and trajectory-sensitive, and must not start out from a priori positions. Donor agencies should, in this light, refrain from investing much time and energy in the generation of generalized policy responses and blueprints, which to some extent might alleviate their primary pre-occupation with the merits and adequacy of their policy instruments. Instead, they should consider collapse and re-start situations in more specific terms, beginning with an understanding of the trajectories that gave rise to them, and with an adaptive position as to what they might require in terms of redress or rehabilitation. Such a more receptive posture might in turn invoke more modest ambitions among external actors with respect to their scope and capacity to influence processes of political reconstruction. With a less programmatic orientation determining an agency's responses and actions, there would be more chance of external actors concentrating on how they could best respond to demands arising from specific situations, developing a reactive rather than a pro-active stance.

Fresh start moments, almost by definition, are delicate. They may be full of promise and expectations of brighter futures, distanced from the past. At the same time, they are extremely fragile, as the conflicts and violence that were inherent in the processes of breakdown and collapse will still be alive in the memory, and could conceivably be re-ignited. Fresh starts therefore need careful handling by all, and sound understandings of the circumstances that gave rise to them. External actors have important roles to play in these episodes, especially in advisory and moderating capacities geared towards consensus and confidence building among previously hostile parties. But they should be aware of the risks of complicating the process if they expect *their* designs for new political futures and structures to play a primary role.

6
Linking the Future to the Past: Ethnicity, Reforms and Pluralism

Introduction

Strategies of state restructuring promoted by global powers and institutions in recent times have focused on two broad avenues of 'good governance' reform – multi-partyism and decentralization. Among various implications of these reforms, their potential effects in terms of shifting political identities and bringing ethnic demands and conflicts to the fore are significant. In Africa in particular, though not only there, this translates itself into the need to examine the politics of ethnicity in the context of state restructuring. The present chapter seeks to address this task.

Among the various themes that have constituted the discourse on African states and societies, that of ethnicity has been noted for its remarkable record. The 'resilient paradigm', as Timothy Shaw (1986) once called it, was part of the stock in trade at the very genesis of modern African studies. Presently, it is still, or again, very much up front. It has, however, been a very controversial theme with its existence and legitimacy over the years in frequent dispute. Held up in some quarters as the final explanatory variable of just about everything happening on the African political scene, ethnicity has often with equal vehemence been discarded by radical researchers as an irrelevant conceptual obstruction to proper analysis of the politics of transformation, or as simply an American invention. Through the years the theme has thus definitely drawn its share of debate, resulting from changing waves of academic interest, from new political circumstances and pre-occupations and from the interplay between them. Significantly, though, at the end of each cycle of debate, ethnicity, the elusive factor, has often seemed to simply re-emerge, chameleon-fashion: featuring new colours and in a

119

different guise, it has continued to provoke new questions and debate as to its true nature and proper conceptualization.

Following the drastically changing political conditions within and around African states in the wake of liberalization, structural adjustment and its repercussions, a new wave of questions about ethnicity has been emerging. Specifically, with the declining hegemony of the centralized state, the pressures to go multi-party and the moves to adopt new forms of decentralization in various countries, questions have been raised with increasing frequency as to how ethnicity would be evolving and manifesting itself within these changing parameters. The questions have been echoed from Kenya to Cameroon, from Angola to Ethiopia and from Sudan to Zimbabwe. And evidently the echoes – or possibly some of the original queries – have been actively transmitted among Africa-watchers in Europe, North America and elsewhere. The questions concerned have come in different versions and just as in previous rounds of debate, answers to them would tend to vary significantly, reflecting respondents' perceptions as to what seemed at issue and/or their inclination to highlight particular concerns while, intentionally or unintentionally, de-emphasizing others. This chapter attempts to explore the terrain, considering recent questions and tendencies against the background of changing state–society relationships in Africa.

Recurrent questions

Following the demise of the Cold War, manifold uncertainties about the implications of the new global conjuncture for the trajectories of African political systems became reflected in the nature of questions that mushroomed concerning the role and significance of ethnicity. Many of these queries were not exactly novel, but reflected ongoing presuppositions that became re-articulated with reference to changing contexts, such as: would party formation and political mobilization be more likely to take shape along ethnic lines under conditions of political pluralism? Would Africa be going to see a kind of ethnic resurgence and militancy, a spurt of ethnically based mini-nationalisms, and/or a pervasive rethinking of ethnic consciousness and identity? Will there be increasing demands for the right of self-determination by African nationalities, to begin with by those which got squeezed in colonial or post-colonial territorial arrangements, but possibly also by others? Can ethnic expression take any 'fundamentalist' turn, however this should be understood exactly? Or would it be conceivable that radically different ways of structuring ethnicity might be emerging in various African political contexts? What would be the implications for the post-colonial state and for the nature of politics? Is one witnessing the preliminary steps in processes of basic restructuring of African state systems, beginning with the most ancient of all, Ethiopia? Or are most of these queries addressed to simply transient phenomena, likely to disappear soon enough as they get 'satisfied', partly perhaps through their very articulation? What *is* one observing in the first place and how should we interpret it? Many such questions have been surfacing in recent years concerning the role of ethnicity and how one should understand it.

A sharpening of the questions posed is essential if we want to gain greater clarity of the processes concerned. Cautious questioners, therefore, would first want to ask whether there would in fact be any likelihood of ethnicity becoming articulated and politicized more vigorously under multi-partyism and decentralization than under previous or alternative conditions. What if political reform were not on the agenda? Would this leave, or have left, articulations of ethnicity comfortably dormant, 'neutral', or alternatively more easily contained and controlled? Or would they follow their own logic and evolution in any event, shaped as has often been the case by forces of domination and control and marred already in many instances by a prolonged history of ethnic conflict? Raising these questions is to begin to answer them and to suggest that too narrow a focus on ethnicity per se, without due attention for its political and historical context, may not be very helpful. But if there is no a priori reason why ethnic mobilization must necessarily be more on the increase in pluralist and decentralized frameworks, one cannot assume either that there will be no relationship and effect whatsoever. To the extent that they represent substantive rather than formal changes, moves towards reform and decentralization may themselves perhaps be seen as a response to, and an attempt to accommodate, growing ethnic pressures resulting from various kinds of motivations. More generally, restructuring of existing institutional arrangements, as must be the case with any shift towards political pluralism and decentralization, may contribute to changes in state–civil society relationships and thus to changes in the political context of ethnicity. What different forms of ethnic articulation could this then induce and what significance should be attached to it?

Some questions about the relative significance of ethnicity vis-à-vis the retreat of the central state and any prospects of multi-partyism, however, appear to deserve as much attention as the phenomena they enquire about. This would be true for example, for questions which bluntly ask 'will tribalism be unleashed again?', or for the assertion of the inevitability of ethnic conflict under more pluralistic systems (which for some time had constituted the defence-line of various regimes – Kenya, Zimbabwe, Zambia – worried to lose their carefully nurtured power base). It might be recalled in passing, however, that the latter kind of argument is not exactly new. Independence itself was delayed in a number of instances on the strength of similar forebodings of 'tribal' conflict and the argument has since been advanced in more than one place at more than one time.

But questions in this vein about ethnicity are themselves problematic. Their phrasing seems to anticipate certain kinds of truths, such as the expectation that open political processes will necessarily degenerate at the hands of erratic, 'tribal' sentiments. This appears indicative of a pre-occupation with certain aspects or phenomena only, that is, mainly the 'visible', emotive and violent ones, while tending or wanting to ignore concrete social issues and grievances which may underlie ethnically expressed political action. Again, for those in power advancing this kind of argument, playing the 'tribalist' card usually amounts to emphasizing a single and 'threatening' emotive dimension, as if this had an autonomous role, while at the same time trying to avoid confronting any inequities in the exercise of power or resource distribution that might have given rise to expressions of frustration and consciousness to begin with.

Problems with conceptualization

When trying to come to grips with the problematic of ethnicity, a few preliminary points, not unlike those that were pertinent during earlier phases when ethnicity was drawing attention, will be useful. One is that ethnicity as such does not explain anything: it needs to be explained. If this requires re-emphasizing, it should be clear that such reiteration is addressed to two otherwise quite opposite modes of thinking. One is that of any latter-day adherents to the primordial loyalties school that entertain an a priori expectation that the dissolution of one-party states will 'naturally' lead to multi-ethnic multi-partyism and, through this, to a blossoming of ethnicity generally. The other is that of various Marxist researchers who, from an overriding preoccupation with the harder facts of political economy, have tended to dismiss ethnicity as just an instance of false consciousness, positing that manifestations of ethnic identity, ethnic ideology and ethnic conflict are mere epiphenomena not really worthy of serious attention. Significantly, modernization theorists and orthodox Marxists at one time also shared another per-spective. Both conceived of ethnicity as an anachronistic mode of thinking soon to become surpassed and engulfed by either – and here they differed again – the spirit of rationality and modernity or by mature class consciousness, itself also a token of rationality. The primordialists, however, should understand that, of course, various groups will try to strengthen their social and political position and claims by invoking tradition, mythical charters of origin, or what not – and that not a few examples of these have actually been especially invented for the purpose (Ranger 1983). Marxist researchers, on the other hand, would have rendered greater service through exercising more conceptual flexibility, which might have allowed the recognition of particular expressions of ethnicity as protest against subordination, and others as attempts to underpin positions of power and hegemony (Stavenhagen 1991).

Closely related is a similarly elementary point. Ethnicity as such, or the so-called ethnic factor, does not exist independently: it essentially represents a single element, aspect or dimension lifted out of a more complex reality. It derives its meaning and significance from the interplay between other variables such as class, state and power, while in turn it can (but does not necessarily do so) infuse such dimensions with meaning and political clout. Discussion of ethnicity per se actually does not make too much sense, therefore, as there is no way of establishing what orientation or underlying motive any ethnic consciousness raising may have without first understanding the context and interplay of the social forces and the issues concerned. Any 'blind' discussion of ethnicity may in fact entail some very risky and problematic forms of reification. Thus, ethnicity should always be considered in its dynamic relation to and interaction with other social dynamics.

Finally, if expressions of ethnicity, whether as identity, ideology or competitiveness need to be contextualized, it is also necessary to recognize its essentially fluid and manipulable properties. Ethnicity as constructed identity is one of a multiple set of potential identities and usually also itself has multiple facets and faces. Whether any one or more of these will actually be called upon to give expression to specific social demands or to a political front, is again a matter of contextual variables – which may explain quite unexpected changes in asserted identities, allegiances or coalitions by particular groups. Thus, novel identities may be asserted, or new coalitions entered into under a common label, in response to the changing needs and opportunities in the political arena. At times, it can indeed be striking to note how 'rediscoveries' of common interests and common bonds may be clothed and rationalized from a well-stocked supply of, often quite original, 'cultural' attributes. Ethnic consciousness, in short, is in no way 'fixed'.

Generally, ethnic configurations, the generation of ethnic consciousness and the impetus to ethnic protest, must all be understood in the context of the changing relationships between state and society from which they derive their significance and orientation. One key problem in understanding ethnicity, however, lies in the wide mix of tendencies, strategies and reactions comprised under the 'ethnic' phenomenon and therefore, again, in the virtual impossibility to associate ethnicity, unlike class for example, with any singular kind of social or political thrust. Inkatha represented one expression of ethnicity, but so did/does the Amhara and now the Tigrayan resistance to the demand for political equality by Ethiopia's other nationalities – and the latters' struggles for precisely these goals. Again, Tuareg demands for independence, shelved in lieu of enhanced autonomy; the complex manoeuvering that culminated in the reinstatement of Buganda kingship in Uganda, followed by that in Bunyoro and Toro as well as by continuing and deepening dispute about it in Ankole; the articulation of protest in the dispute around the Dagomba paramount chieftaincy in northern Ghana; the ethnic defence line of vulnerable communities in the Cameroonian and Congolese rainforests and similarly, the political networking of various pastoralist groups in the Horn – all represent different instances of ethnicity at play. Numerous other examples abound, of course. Other than signifying an ethnic articulation of 'something' political, however, they do not necessarily have too much in common.

What must be appreciated is that the social basis and structuring of ethnicity in Africa comprises widely different forms, including potentially self-standing nationalities, ethnic strata, small vulnerable communities and various clan and kinship networks. Besides, and above all, ethnicity and class articulate in giving shape to new ruling strata and subordinate categories in various countries. All this tends to stretch the category to a rather amorphous and seemingly meaningless catch-all. Still, to restrict the analysis to the category of 'nationalities' (Mamdani 1983) is to preclude consideration of the critical problems that have been arising in connection with ethnic stratification or re-stratification in different parts of the continent, or with the struggle for survival of distinct but vulnerable groups. Using a broader concept, then, one must anticipate entirely different issues imposing themselves in each case.

It should also be noted, though, that while in many different cases (such as struggles over access to resources or over political representation) a political strategy – offensive or defensive, as the case may be – may be pursued with an explicit reference to ethnic identity, even such a choice is contextual. Some groups, collectivities or social movements at particular junctures will have good grounds to emphasize ethnicity, or to 'ethnicize' issues, while others instead may seek to de-emphasize it. Moreover, the motivations for choosing different forms of identity articulation are likely to vary in crucial respects and often may be diametrically opposed.

The specificity of the African case

An understanding of ethnicity in context first requires a proper grasp of the specificity of its configuration in the African case, as compared, for example, to its occurrence in the Andean region and in Central America, or in various countries of South and South East Asia. In several Andean countries, for instance, indigenous ethnic peasant communities find themselves largely differentiated from the dominant urban-based national middle classes and other social forces associated with the state, while remaining largely unrelated also to the massive numbers of urban poor. Ethnicity here has a more overt class dimension, though it does not link up to a single, comprehensive class structure (Stavenhagen 1991). In India and other South Asian countries, by contrast, ethnicity is essentially taken to refer to the articulation of cultural identity and diversity of a whole range of minority communities, such as language, religious and tribal groupings and distinct nationalities. Many of these, it is felt, stand to lose their cultural distinctiveness in the face of homogenizing technological forces, while, moreover, their pluriformity and coexistence is endangered by what Kothari and others have described as the politics of majoritarianism (Kothari 1988a). Articulations of ethnicity thus also tend to be related to the processes by which cultural distinctiveness and diversity are under threat. At the same time, however, there are also opposite and assertive forms of ethnicity, seeking political dominance and exclusive rights for particular communities. Promoted by the forces of majority politics, these include chauvinist movements such as Hindutva in India today (Sharma 2003) and the movement towards constructing an exclusive Sinhalese-Buddhist identity in Sri Lanka which ran until some years ago.

In Africa, in contrast, ethnicity by and large rarely figures as an attribute confined to minorities vis-à-vis nationally dominant social strata identifying and asserting themselves in similar fashion as elsewhere. Nor is ethnicity in Africa predominantly an expression of any traditional distinctiveness vis-à-vis technologically and culturally homogenizing forces. Rather, it figures, and is perceived to figure, as one basic constitutive element prevalent in and throughout virtually all societies.

Essentially, it underscores how, in one respect, the social fabric of most African countries comprises a fairly complex and fluid ensemble of different peoples, nations and nationalities, ethnic strata and in some cases caste-like divisions. At the same time, there has been a rapidly accelerating pace of urban and rural class differentiation in most parts of Africa, at times articulated with ethnic differentiation though generally cutting across the ethnic matrix. Thus, while social differentiation in some instances is coterminous with ethnic differentiation, there is no necessary one-to-one correspondence between them.

Nonetheless, perhaps one of the most significant long-term social transformations affecting the nature and focus of ethnic articulations in Africa is the emergence and manifestation of a kind of proto national bourgeoisie in various parts of the continent. Members of these strata may themselves (selectively) de-emphasize ethnic backgrounds, identifying instead more strongly with national characteristics and points of orientation – from which they will often indeed have had a good deal to gain. Alternatively, if they are themselves drawn largely from one dominant ethnic category, as is often the case, they may be inclined to project the cultural identity of that group on to the multi-ethnic state as a whole. In either case, one important consequence of the crystallization of a dominant national bourgeoisie is the possible gradual peripheralization of various weaker ethnic communities. Ultimately these communities may come to resemble the indigenous peasant communities in, say, Guatemala, Mexico or Bolivia, or several minority groups in India, thus adding new political significance and meaning to the reality and articulation of their ethnicity.

Ethnicity and the politics of pluralism

At stake today is the wider search for a redefinition and restructuring of the relationships between state and society, which at times have been dubbed problematic, dichotomous and precarious (Rothchild and Chazan 1988). There has been frequent expression of the need to find a different balance within this duality, favouring societal rather than state forms of organization, and giving more concrete content to the concept and reality of civil society in the African context. However, the range of possible state–civil society relationships in Africa represents a highly variable complex, which, moreover, has by no means been fully crystallized conceptually (Doornbos, 1990 and Chapter 3). To complicate matters further, the politics of ethnicity in many places has been blurring rather than accentuating the civil society–state equation, precisely through the pervasive infusion of ethnic calculus into the control over and the operations of the state. A key question is to what extent ethnicity may provide a basis for future, relatively autonomous socio-political organization and alternative development strategies (Hettne 1991). All blanket predictions are hazardous. Still, it seems inconceivable that ethnically defined social entities will not somehow come to figure, perhaps even quite prominently in some places, as a possible basis for politico-organizational forms. After all, ethnic mobilization and patronage provide one of a relatively limited number of possible bases for decentralized political organization and also for party formation. Also, in decentralized operations and actions through NGOs, ethnic communities may serve as a basis for organization and self-help action, as they will often do through the simple fact of being locally and therefore community based. In so far as 'civil society' can denote 'grassroots' organizational forms, clan, kinship and other local community association forms may at times seem to present themselves as ready-made points of departure in this regard. However, there is a need to take care in making too ready equations between decentralization and 'community' participation, as often there are sharp social divisions running right through the communities concerned (Meynen and Doornbos 2004).

Generally, with so many self-help organizations springing up based on ethnic constituencies, it seems possible that the concept of civil society will increasingly gain specificity. But those for whom 'grassroots' organizations and 'civil society' imply participatory processes and voluntary action will do well to remember, and to anticipate, that a move to local and supposedly traditional forms of social organization may also signify the (re-)emergence and proliferation of (male) chauvinistic roles, outlooks and manners of exercising power, with little scope for open exchange and popular involvement or liberal/progressive, relativizing and gender-neutral perspectives. Moves that are meant to be forward-looking and opening social space may thus in fact turn out to be quite regressive.

With respect to the possible effects on the articulation of ethnicity of changing African political structures (notably the eclipse of one-party systems, the shrinking of central state involvement and – in varying degrees – their replacement by substantially decentralized structures), at least two broad areas of attention stand out. One is that of the search for new organizational forms which might bridge the state–society division, and for institutional alternatives to the structures and linkages once provided through the single party and centralizing state. It is difficult to anticipate whether any particular pattern will finally emerge as dominant in this respect. Quite conceivably a variety of patterns may in fact develop. Two broad possibilities, however, suggest themselves as likely. One is that dominant ruling groups that were represented in single party structures may split up into two or more fractions, though to some extent still representing 'more of the same' and in coalition continuing their control over the state. The other is that, given generally weakening central state structures and the need to accommodate and recognize vocal constituent units, stronger ethnic groupings, language communities and nationalities may emerge as possible constituencies within the changing political frameworks. In this connection there has been a good deal of attention for the Ethiopian constitution promulgated in 1994, which supposedly is based on representation by nationality and spoke even of self-determination for nationalities. Ethiopian realities since then have turned out vastly differently however. Another was the emergence of embryonic regional states such as Puntland (in addition to Somaliland which has reclaimed its independence) on the ruins of the Somali state with its highly centralized concentration of power, which had collapsed in 1991. At one point, there was also a rapid but ephemeral proliferation of new, mostly ethnically circumscribed candidate parties in the post-Mobutu context in DRC Congo, totalling in the hundreds before polling. In Uganda in 2005 there have been increasing calls for separate districts by ethnically defined communities, stimulated by an interplay of decentralization policies and pre-election calls for concessions from the centre. Additional examples would illustrate how expression is often sought for political representation of popular interests under ethnic or other banners, but also how dominant power-holders often seek to counter, divert or make use of these pressures.

Whether the new state forms that are emerging, such as de-centralized structures or new electoral and party systems, will actually represent more democratic forms and practices, is a question of evident interest, but one likely to remain topical for a long time to come in a good many cases. Presently the various attempts at reform under way in several countries signify notably weakened central structures, inviting, as it were, alternative ways of filling in the political space. The manifest external interest in the measurable aspects of democracy, as in the insistence on counting more than one party as a yardstick for progress, stands in contrast to the relative silence displayed as regards the more qualitative aspects of democracy. These latter would include more attention for ways in which popular involvement and feedback might have been, or might be, enhanced in existing political structures and policy practices at local and national levels.

Another problem area which has inevitably come into play in the wake of the dismantling of single party and state structures in various countries, derives from the accommodations and political settlements made in the past among different ethnic groups, or more usually imposed upon them. In many instances, conflicting interests and demands regarding issues like access to land and other resources, the structuring of representation, the location of roads and services, or the distribution of other benefits, have resulted in political settlements which have strongly favoured some ethnic groups or strata, or at least some of their members, while proving detrimental to others. Often, the development and growth of central state and party structures was based on a kind of pecking order among competing ethnic groups and a freezing of these differential privileges and entitlements among them – or again, among their notables. Many enduring ethnic grievances and expressions of protest are essentially about such inequities in the distribution of public goods. Clearly, therefore, one should expect any loosening or alteration of state structures to be accompanied by a resurfacing of old sores and the emergence of fresh ones, and by numerous demands and pressures to redress perceived ethnic inequalities and disadvantages. In various instances, no doubt, the relative positions of power and privilege may themselves be up for revision. The outcomes of such challenges and struggles are likely to be determined by the relative strength of social forces at the local or regional level, often with, though at times without the potential intervention of the central state.

The facade of one-party unity was hardly possible without the cement of patronage. By offering rewards to and through influential elites, patronage served to make up for not a few inequities between ethnic winners and losers and thus was instrumental in institutionalizing multi-ethnic representation into single-party structures. With a move to other, theoretically more pluralist state and institutional forms, patronage is likely to be equally, if not more, salient in the mobilization of followings and coalitions (Eriksen 2001). One should thus not be too surprised if, in a number of instances, political entrepreneurship will lead some former regional party notables to change flags and form new 'ethnic' constituencies.

The future of ethnicity

When trying to anticipate future modes of ethnicity articulation, it is also important to note that not only the political structures through which interests may be expressed have been subject to transformation, but to some extent the stakes themselves are changing. Several decades ago one of the key routes to individual wealth and aggrandisement was through political or bureaucratic office, in turn based largely on ethnic patronage. Political and bureaucratic positions could then be translated into business and wealth. Today this route, though evidently still there, does not always hold out similar promises. Business wealth in a number of countries has begun to reproduce itself without an immediate political base to start from. Though 'connections' remain invariably helpful, if not essential, overt emphasis on ethnic identity and patronage is not necessarily called for and may actually constrain the scope for business transactions and expansion. Second and third generations, meanwhile, have grown up in urban milieus or abroad, often entertaining very different images of the ethnic linkage altogether (including, at times, some surprisingly militant 'ethnic' positions). While in some regards, therefore, there would seem to be lessened chances of ethnicity being politicized, unexpected ethnic responses may well be triggered in other areas.

At another end, various categories of activists and urban workers may seek to avoid and de-emphasize ethnicity as a basis for social action, as indeed they have done in many cases. During the anti-apartheid struggle, for example, the ANC in South Africa was a major example of a deliberately non-racial and non-ethnic organization. Also, in various areas of industrial activity elsewhere, the scope for collective bargaining may be impaired by fragmentation of union strength along ethnic lines and is therefore avoided. Similarly, human rights actions and the safeguarding of essential freedoms generally demand the transcending of ethnic frames of operation and the mobilization of broader social solidarity. Here too, there is no logic to ethnic mobilization and action, neither before nor after any institutional changes towards political pluralism. Nor were, for all the inevitable emotive reactions they provoked, the bread riots following structural adjustment programmes in Khartoum, Lusaka or Tunis at one time particularly noted for articulating their protests in terms of ethnicity (Seddon 1989).

Still, a resurgence of ethnicity may come in basically two, again opposite, ways. One is emanating from ethnic communities under threat and from groups that have lost out in their dealings with the state or with more powerful neighbours and rivals. Here one should remember that it is by no means certain that political reforms will entail the replacement of politically dominant groups, locally or nationally. Most ruling groups will actively try to prevent such from happening. If somehow a momentum of this kind were nonetheless to develop, however, then many disadvantaged ethnic groups and strata will no doubt want to give voice to demands for redress of their grievances. Under such circumstances, ethnicity cannot but flourish: few things are as favourable for ethnic or national self-identity as freshly remembered sufferance linked to the prospect or expectation of redress and justice. In such cases ethnicity may come to be perceived as a framework and source of solidarity and liberation. There might be a sense, then, of how relations with rival groups and/or the centre might be open for renegotiation, on the basis of parity and mutual recognition. Visions of alternative arrangements and relationships between constituent groups, ethnic or otherwise, based on equity, reciprocity and mutual respect for cultural distinctiveness (Hettne 1991) could then come on the horizon. If fulfilled, these might give rise to dramatically different political forms and formations in Africa. Admittedly, however, this has not occurred too often in practice as yet.

Some groups, even under such circumstances, however, would face difficulties in articulating their most basic concerns and indeed their very identity. This is the problem of weak cultures being interrogated by dominant cultures, which is made additionally problematic as the interrogation is conducted – and inevitably distorted – in the language and conceptual categories of dominant social forces, colonial or post-colonial. In this connection Ashis Nandy (1987) asked the crucial question: 'what are the obstacles a culture faces which seek to redefine its identity?'. With reference to Africa the answer was given, in part, by Mudimbe when he pointed out how 'the forms and formulations of the colonial culture and its aims were somehow the means of trivialising the whole traditional mode of life and its spiritual framework' (Mudimbe 1988: 4).

It is possible, if not probable, that the problems and contradictions implied in this respect will become more rather than less manifest as time passes by. As noted already, the emergence of a proto-national bourgeoisie may well entail a further peripheralization of various ethnic communities from the mainstream of 'development'. But it is not just that cleavages between dominant and subordinate groups may widen and be increasingly reflected in novel forms of cultural differentiation – often, incidentally, based on narrowing and formalistic extrapolations of Western-derived dominant culture on the one hand as against increasingly eroded forms and expressions of marginalized traditions on the other. It is also that many of Africa's new elites have not been especially noted for their empathy for the cultural distinctiveness of weaker ethnic groups. Pastoralist groups in the Horn of Africa and elsewhere are a case in point. Perceived as an embarrassment to the national identity of new, 'modern' ruling elites, the latter more often than not have been quick to devise policies of sedentarization in order to remove the pastoralists' 'backwardness' from sight (Doornbos and Markakis 1991). Generally, *ethnic* pluralism and coexistence – as Africa has in fact known for most of remembered time in most of its regions – would require and presuppose a give-and-take attitude on the part of all social groupings and strata concerned. In its absence, insistence on conformity to the emerging cultural standards of new national elites is likely to engender increasingly embittered articulations of ethnic consciousness and the expressed need for cultural survival on the part of peripheralized groups.

Conclusion

If ethnicity can indicate a route to the rediscovery of meaning, a recapturing of cultural identity and the recreation of solidarity, there can be no dispute about its enigmatic force and its liberating potential. Such in any case seems to be its promise and revitalizing power to various social movements seeking escape from oppression and arbitrary rule in different parts of Africa. These movements might further gain in significance and depth if they were to link up to other 'new social movements', such as ecological, human rights, or spiritual movements. But the other, uglier face of ethnicity is one that, while purporting to deliver such ultimate ends, actually presents itself in narrowly parochial terms for which powerful political patrons may arrogate themselves the right to be the sole legitimate interpreters.

Not unlike 'liberation ethnicity', its more parochially oriented 'chauvinist' alter ego tends to share several universal features, which are also pursued by similar groups in Asian and European contexts: the search for and re-emphasis on 'roots', the true tradition and the reconstitution and salvation of the community, and so on. The dividing line between 'liberating' and 'chauvinistic' versions of ethnic perspectives on a just future can actually be extremely thin and at times only a careful analysis of the language and symbols chosen may give a clue as to the social basis from which a particular perspective is being advanced. Basically this is the consequence of the different and shifting social realities concerned: opposition groups as well as dominant forces, even within a single political context, may both draw from one and the same body of spiritual traditions to generate support for the particular position they advocate, which in the final analysis amounts to either a challenge to or an effort to uphold the status quo. What makes analysis even more precarious is that the positions themselves may be shifting almost imperceptibly from the one into the other. As with nationalism, articulations of ethnicity and ethnic identity may go through cyclical processes: emerging as populist, tentatively progressive forces, they may increasingly come to represent narrow conservative tendencies and interests in maintaining the social order by dominant strata. The politics of pluralism thus is likely to engender not a few misreadings of coded ethnic messages in the years ahead.

Perhaps one of the major causes of the failure of the post-colonial state in Africa has been its gross neglect of its cultural basis. In the urge to create political unity, the tendency has been to negate ethnic, regional and cultural diversities rather than recognize them as ingredients in the construction of a new society. The result has often been a facade of seeming unity at the cost of many unsettled wounds and denied identities. Fatally in the long run, the state project had no meaningful or alternative sources of cultural inspiration to draw on, leaving it in the end without a vision and empty-handed in the face of impending crisis and disintegration. 'Official nationalism', to use Benedict Anderson's (1983) term – which had been extremely narrowly conceived from the start – simply ran out of steam.

In reaction, one current trend is to opt for political pluralism, decentralization and possibly for according ethnicity a prime place as a basis for political organization. The trend coincides with and is encouraged by current state restructuring agendas in the wake of globalization, emphasizing multipartyism and decentralization. This pendulum swing in the opposite direction might stimulate expectations that such an alternative starting point could provide a superior basis for long-term political projects. This could turn out to be a grave misconception, however. If ethnicity were to be assigned any paramount, 'constitutional' role in this scheme of things, renewed disillusionment will be difficult to avoid: ethnicity can only provide an alternative basis for political organization at the cost of a whole new wave of misrepresentations, distortions and inequities. Drawing that conclusion is not to imply an argument against pluralism per se, and certainly not against seeking democratic alternatives or the basic need to overcome past and emerging ethnic inequities and to respect ethnic identities. But that reification of ethnic structures inevitably implies new forms of symbolic and other inequities and potential discrimination. Writing with the hindsight of lessons drawn from experiences with state partitions across the globe, Robert Schaeffer concludes in similar vein:

> Unless social movements and governments find a way to promote democracy in heterogeneous states, to deconstruct social identities

defined by historical animosities and shaped by contemporary problems, and to find peaceful alternatives to conflict within and between states, the divisions created by partition will deepen and the wall dividing people will continue to rise. (Schaeffer 1999: 258)

Similarly, reification of ethnicity is only likely to add up to further fragmentation of state frameworks into micro-universes, far away from any broad new visions that could assemble narrowly defined entities behind a common set of goals and cause the assertion of local identities and demands to recede into the background.

7
State and Identity in Europe and India: Comparative Dynamics

Introduction

Though the dynamics of globalization have been with us for centuries (Wallerstein 1974, Robertson 2003), in recent times social consciousness of the centrality of global forces – through exposure to communication technologies, global marketing channels, macro-institutional linkages and changing lifestyles – has been on the rise in most parts of the world. In Europe and India such global consciousness has risen as much as anywhere else. Within the overall welter of forces involved, the interplay of different dynamic aspects of globalization, institutional and cognitive, is here of particular importance and interest. Taking globalization as a set of pervasive forces – economic, cultural and political – transforming patterns of interaction between different collectivities, including 'nation-states', one point of special relevance concerns the institutional dynamics and their impacts on collective identities. These institutional dynamics include processes of state formation as well as of state restructuring, which in both cases entail recurrent formative processes, including the emergence of state-like institutions as in Europe or major restructuring of centre–periphery relations as in India. In turn the impacts of these processes in terms of socio-cultural identities may manifest themselves through shifting conceptions and expressions of self at individual as well as at collective levels, including that of the state, or through a hardening of communal identifications felt to have come under threat.

This chapter explores this interest by pursuing two sets of comparative questions. One is to try and better understand how global forces impinge upon processes of state formation and state restructuring specifically in Europe and India. The focus here is on the changing role and position of the two geo-political entities within the global context and on the patterns of institutional extension and adjustment they display in the face of global challenges. The other and main question is to try and assess how transitions in the role of the state at the global level and modifications in the respective state frameworks impact upon the nature and expression of political orientations and identities. In both the European and Indian cases, therefore, the focus is on the interactions between institutional changes, actual or projected, and the social responses they engender in terms of popular identities or social movements.

In Europe and India today, longer-term political transitions and projections of alternative future political frameworks, at the (sub-)continental as well as at state and regional levels, have been raising expectations, anxieties and queries in terms of collective identities – identities that may be defended, desired or denied. In both cases, questions are also raised as to what is and what should be the identity of the broader entities that are emerging as global players. These processes as well as the contexts within which they occur are distinct and different in a number of important respects in the two cases, even though at times some of the issues put forward may be formulated in surprisingly analogous terms. For various reasons, including precisely the differences involved, it seems useful therefore to venture a parallel discussion of these transitional experiences.

Taking this as a point of departure, any more specific discussion of changing cultural and political identities in Europe or India must confront a multitude of currents and undercurrents in either context. In Europe, both Central and Eastern as well as Western, new assertions of collective identity – nationalist, regional and 'continental' – and new questions about the long-term significance and implications of these assertions have been advanced with increasing vigour in recent years. Central in this complex of different dynamics has been the emergence and expansion of the European Union as a new type of supra-state, partly in operation, partly projected to undertake additional roles and to embrace more member-states. The growth of this body raises vexed questions about what will finally constitute its identity and what will distinguish it from the world around it. In India, key transitions and issues in recent years have included the rise to prominence of the politico-religious movement of Hindutva, seeking to redefine the foundations of 'India', in addition to the continued action and relevance of sub-national 'proto-nationalist' movements in different parts of the country and far-reaching moves towards decentralization. Again, these transitions raise complex questions about India's identity and its key defining characteristics within a broader context. In the two different settings, all of these currents, sometimes mixing, sometimes separately, thus have been provoking profound queries about cultural identities and orientations in the face of uncertain future circumstances.

Beyond this, questions regarding the redefinition of social identities in both contexts have come to be linked conceptually to transitions in the role of the state framework under the impact of neo-liberal policies, and more broadly to the role of India and Europe in a globalizing world. Both Europe and India have been emerging as key players in the global market arena, having China, the United States and Japan (and to an extent each other) as their main competitors. Both face major challenges to maintain and strengthen themselves vis-à-vis these rival blocs, economically and increasingly politically, and with considerable implications in terms of the dynamics providing for internal social and political cohesion. Paradoxically, the heightening prominence of 'Europe' and 'India' as global players may be said to have arisen in reaction to the challenges of globalization, while at the same time constituting one of its manifestations and contributing to its dynamics. In various ways, changes and clashes of identities appear reflective of such broader transitions in Indian and European society, and of changing conceptions of the state in India and Europe. It should not be too surprising, therefore, that in both contexts one also finds increasing questioning and debate at this juncture around the 'idea of Europe' and the 'idea of India' (Castells 2001: ch. 5, Khilnani 1999, Villain Gandossi 1990).

At a general level, concern has often been expressed in both contexts that distinctive cultural identities face obliteration as a result of homogenizing forces: market, institutional and technological. But one question this raises is whether a dichotomy between perceived homogenization and cultural distinctiveness is the best way of understanding some of the contradictions in contemporary identity processes. The relation between identity formation and social contexts is undoubtedly complex and subject to continuous change, due to a whole array of factors including homogenizing institutional and technological forces. Nonetheless, in lieu of the homogenization thesis, an alternative analysis could focus more directly on the dynamic relationships between identity and power. This would allow and, indeed, require a perspective on how identities are articulated in confrontation to others in changing contexts, and must address the question of power processes and the competition for hegemony in defining collective identities.

Now, the current abundance of manifestations on the supply side of identity, political and cultural, is both perplexing and deceptive, taxing many an analyst and observer alike. But processes of identity formation largely derive their significance and orientation from the way they are being prodded and mobilized as part of processes of social and political differentiation, conflict and transformation. Notwithstanding frequent appearances to the contrary, therefore, the articulation of cultural and political identity cannot be understood on its own terms or as an autonomous outflow from basic cultural roots either in Europe or in India, but essentially comprises contextually determined processes ultimately related to questions of power and domination. It goes without saying that if we accept this as a point of departure, it should be valid in its application in both the European and the Indian contexts. Still, any such enquiry first raises preliminary questions about comparative analysis as such. What do we actually mean by 'comparability' and is comparison realistic to begin with? To what extent is it justified to try and draw parallels between processes occurring in vastly different contexts or, if this would still appear to be the case, in what ways can the two experiences be made more instructive to one another?

Taking up this area of interest, this chapter will first address the question of comparability and then move on with a general background of contemporary issues of state and identity formation in Europe and India, trying to relate questions about identity formation to the discussion of changing centre–state and central–regional relationships in Europe and India. Given the vast subject-matter, however, it will be evident that the aim can only be to highlight some key points of comparative interest concerning the two contexts and their dynamics.

On comparability

If we were to heed John Stuart Mill's words of caution, we should not even contemplate any comparative analysis of state formation/ restructuring and identity processes in contexts as complex and different as Europe and India. In his essay on 'Two Methods of Comparison', Mill wrote:

> [In] the case of political phenomena, the supposition of unity of cause is not only wide of the truth, but at an immeasurable distance from it. The causes of every social phenomenon which we are particularly interested about, security, wealth, freedom, good government, public virtue, general intelligence, or their opposites, are infinitely numerous, especially the external or remote causes, which alone are, for the most part, accessible to direct observation. (Mill 1888/1970: 213)

Strictly speaking Mill had a point of course, and if we wanted to establish any final 'truth' about the connections or causalities we are interested in, we had better abstain from too ambitious comparative exercises. Besides, if any such exercise were to invoke historical analogy, Ravinder Kumar warns us that '[n]obody knows better than the historian, that if history repeats itself, then it does so as a monumental farce!' (Kumar 1997: 407).

Still, the purpose here may be less demanding than the ones Mill may have been presupposing at the time. A more limited, and limiting, purpose would be to try and spot instructive parallels, highlighting that particular response patterns are not unique but explicable in terms of wider and more universally valid understandings. This is in no way to expect the same kinds of manifestations to occur, or to occur simultaneously. Conceivably, similar kinds of transitional processes and the impacts or repercussions they may engender could occur in quite different historical contexts in different settings. Besides, comparative research is not just intended to look for similarities, as significant contrasts can be equally (or more) enlightening, as has been the case with frequent comparative studies of India and China. Comparative research with China has not only highlighted various aspects of the two countries' contrasted development trajectories (e.g. Swamy 2003), but has provided space for such esoteric interests as Xinru Liu's *Ancient India and Ancient China: Trade and Religious Exchanges AD 1–600* (1988).[1]

More specifically regarding the plausibility of Indian–European comparative perspectives, Ravinder Kumar cautiously observed that India's post-independence record with state formation 'may not altogether be an experience devoid of interest to the scholar, or the political actor, within the wider European community in our times' (Kumar 1997: 408). And on the same question, Sudipta Kaviraj, in reflecting on the complex interrelations between religion, politics and modernity in India, writes that 'the specific trajectory that modernity is taking in Indian history

---

[1] Today, on the question as to 'how India compares with China', it is observed that 'China's social sector policy since its early years has led to dramatic improvements in literacy, health, longevity, and infant mortality rates while its switch to an outward-oriented strategy that encouraged exports, foreign investment and the private sector led to a sustained growth of 9 per cent over two decades. In contrast, the growth rate in India averaged 5 per cent during the last two decades and its social indicators remain far below China's .... Despite such figures, there are economists and analysts who see India holding a greater potential in the longer term. ... India's strength is seen as lying in its large pool of university educated workers and strong institutions' (*The Hindu/The Guardian*, 12 July 2005).

[...] cannot be understood as a mere complicated re-enactment of modernity in the West. At the same time, it cannot be understood without reference to it' (Kaviraj 1995: 316). To which Sunil Khilnani, reversing the equation, adds, in his *The Idea of India*, that not only did

> the West's present delineate ... the image of India's future, [but that] the odd twist is that India's present may actually contain more than a premonitory hint of the West's own political future. The themes and conflicts that animate India's politics today have a surprisingly wide resonance – the assertion of community and group rights and the use of democracy to affirm collective identities; the difficulties of maintaining large-scale, multi-cultural political unions; the compulsion to make democracy work despite economic adversity, to sustain democracy without prosperity. The older democracies might recognize that each of these stands uncomfortably close to their own doorsteps. (Khilnani 1999: 8–9)

Khilnani may yet come to be proven right, who knows. Though the last 50 years or so have by and large given the appearance of an upbeat 'integration' dynamic as far as the European Union's formation has been concerned, there is no certainty that this imagery is to last. And notwithstanding India's demonstrated staying power to date, there is no guarantee that this will remain unchallenged in the times ahead either.

One potentially suitable entry point for the kind of comparative analysis we might envisage in this connection seems the focus once proposed by Hopkins and Wallerstein, who referred to 'the national or society-wide level of social organization as continually subject to two fundamental kinds of disturbing influences, one of which emanates from sub-national levels of organization and one from supra-national levels of organization' (Hopkins and Wallerstein, 1970: 202). Though their notion of 'disturbing influences' may suggest more of a situation, and norm, of stability than will often seem justified, the two contrasted types of pressures and potential frictions between different levels of state action and political engagement they identify do represent recognizable tendencies that can be seen to recur within different epochs and contexts, including those of Europe and India. More specifically, they put forward:

> Among the various local-level or more generally sub-national processes are some which continually exert centrifugal pressures on the society and which would eventually divide it into two or more

smaller-scale entities if they were not countered. And among the various supra-national processes are some which constantly exert incorporative pressures and which tend in the short-run to diminish a national society's autonomy or independence in some respect or another and in the long-run to absorb it completely into a larger whole. (Ibid.)

Contrasted processes as outlined above may be found at work within a single political entity, pulling in opposite directions while keeping each other in balance, in the end having a relative political 'stability' as its result. But one or the other of such tendencies may also be stronger within a particular setting, evoking pictures of either integration or disintegration, or of state formation or breakdown, as a general characterization of the processes concerned. While the net effect may then be to push the process into one direction or another, one should not forget that opposite forces have been lying at its basis.

With respect to Europe and India such opposite tendencies are indeed of interest in terms of comparative analysis. In the European case, the project to expand and deepen the European Union, currently in crisis following the French and Dutch referenda held in 2005 over the proposed European Constitution as well as growing disagreements among member-states as to how to proceed further, so far has been very much a case involving '*supra-national processes ... which constantly exert incorporative pressures and ... diminish a national society's autonomy or independence in some respect or another and in the long-run [may] absorb it completely into a larger whole*' (ibid). And on the Indian side, still in the vein of Hopkins' and Wallerstein's equation, there appears no lack of '*sub-national processes ... which continually exert centrifugal pressures on the society and which would eventually divide it into two or more smaller-scale entities if they were not countered*' (ibid). In both cases one can also identify a whole set of forces pulling in opposite directions, at times suggesting an 'impasse' or 'reversal' of the dynamics concerned, with only vague prospects of the outcomes in the longer-run. But, in a nutshell, this twin set of dynamic cycles appears an a priori useful lens through which to probe Europe and India's experiences with centripetal and centrifugal forces, even though it cannot answer with any certainty whether the two will continue the trajectories they started out from or might yet turn into a different direction.

In the light of the above, there are several pitfalls to note when considering comparative ventures. First, if we are interested in comparing processes of state and identity formation in Europe and India, we should guard against any compulsion to spot and establish *concurrent parallels* as, for example, with respect to the manifestation of regional identities in opposition to centralizing states. Though there are numerous historical examples of regional cultural identities that have been mobilized and sensitized in opposition to powerful and demanding centres, a blurred analysis might result from any a priori assumption of simultaneous occurrences in this regard. Cyclical movements of autonomy versus domination may not be synchronic but may run in opposite directions in different situations which are occurring at one and the same time. In brief, comparison of events should not be mistaken for comparison of processes. More concretely, though still hypothetically, it is conceivable that exponents of European nationality based movements, like the Basks, the Scottish, or the Ukranians for that matter, might – as long as promises of returns seem to be forthcoming – turn out supportive of processes of unification and incorporation into an enlarging European Union, while at the same time their Indian counterparts are increasingly resisting the centre's demands for incorporation or demanding the opposite, namely increased autonomy. But at any subsequent stages in a European integration process, increasing competitiveness for political space and benefits plus fear of losing out and becoming marginalized might well give rise to similar kinds of withdrawal, opposition and articulation of national, regional or ethnic protests as have frequently been manifested in India. An integration–disintegration cycle would then complete its turn, perhaps leading to renewed but different questioning of the concept of European identity, among other things. At that point a key question may concern the internal redistribution of benefits from unification policies, as has already come up in preliminary debates. To better understand similarities and comparabilities of *processes*, therefore, we need to allow ourselves a fair measure of latitude in choosing and comparing different historical periods and contexts. Seen in that light, the euphoric phase of the European unification project might come to look remotely reminiscent of the optimistic, self-confident days of early Indian central planning, or the early 'integrative' yet centre-oriented years of African independent statehood, both of which happened to be exemplary for the prevalence of the idea of the 'relative autonomy of the state'. For the EU project such parallels could therefore provide a relevant point of reference. As Ravinder Kumar suggested (as cited above), it is from that perspective that it could be of interest for EU observers and actors to look at what strategies for integration were adopted in India following 1947, and with what consequences.

A second route with pitfalls would be to start instead from an assumption of *qualitative differences* in the processes concerned. This is not to deny important actual differences that have existed between processes of state and identity formation, derived as they have been from entirely different historical scenarios. Any comparative analysis between Europe and India at this point must start from the simple fact that India is an existing political unit and Europe, also the European Union, is not, or at least not fully. India came about by an act of legislation in 1947. With its unity assumed from the start, different state, linguistic and regional interests have since been pressuring the centre for recognition and accommodation of their demands, nibbling away from the overall united framework. Europe instead started out from an amalgam of different entities, trying to come to a broader unity, and for the time being must be expected to run a different, in principle opposite, scenario. But that distinction precisely contains the interesting and potentially revealing difference between the two processes.

There are also other differences of basic significance. One is of course that India as presently constituted is a product of European domination and amalgamation, whereas most of Europe has not had any such comparable experience (unless we were to go back to Roman times). There would be closer parallels if Europe had been similarly invaded and controlled by external forces, with an administrative grid, schools, railways and communications left behind and continuing to shape intra-European interactions and European identities. Any such historically derived differences are real and important and it would be short-sighted not to address them. Yet taking these into account is not the same as hypothesizing basic a priori differences in which the 'other side' is brought in not so much in order to enhance our understanding of it or to explore commonalities, but to formulate and re-emphasize difference, 'otherness'. In essence, that would be the Orientalist discourse, which has been narrowed down to a denial of the possibility of general patterns of social intercourse and, by implication, of the necessity to try and understand them as such (Said 1978, Kaviraj 1989). Instead, when embracing Europe and India within a single perspective, the questions raised should, in the first place, try to recognize the universality (in the sense of general comprehensibility and logic) of the processes concerned. Only then can an exploration of comparable variables and their effects in terms of patterns of social interaction and symbolic behaviour be meaningfully undertaken.

Finally, in trying to explore any broadly comparable configurations and complexities of identity articulation, it is important to enquire to what extent there seems to be comparability in terms of patterns and dynamics of centre–periphery relations, of political domination and of centrifugal and centripetal forces at play over time. To this end, we need to have a proper understanding of actual and potential variations in terms of the impact of socio-economic transformations in different situations, as the projections of collective positions within a given socio-economic framework are likely to remain key determinants of identity formation, whether defined as class or in terms of ethnicity or other descriptive categories. It is in such terms that we may better appreciate the nature of any parallels and contrasts in searches for collective self-identification in response to changing social norms and contextual givens.

Europe

Europe's relation to globalization, specifically the European Union's, is highly paradoxical: 'European integration is, at the same time, a reaction to the process of globalization and its most advanced expression' (Castells 2001: 348). At the present time it is as yet difficult to see how exactly the European Union will overcome the impasse that emerged in 2005 around its further expansion and long-term direction, including questions about re-distributing its burdens and benefits. Nonetheless, there is by and large still a widely held assumption, as in the words of one leading analyst of the European project, that 'Europe is in the process of inventing a new political form, something more than a confederation but less than a federation – an association of sovereign states which pool their sovereignty only in very restricted areas to varying degrees, an association which does not seek to have the coercive power to act directly on individuals in the fashion of nation states' (Siedentop 2001: 1).

The relative uniqueness of the adopted form – which in fact amounts to a continuous and fairly open-ended process of state and institution building rather than a concretely envisaged edifice as end goal – has been attracting the attention of many analysts and observers. Manuel Castells calls it 'the network state', 'characterized by the sharing of authority (that is, in the last resort, the capacity to impose legitimized violence) along a network' (Castells 2001: 363). Networks, he adds, do not have a centre, but 'nodes'. This seems a basically valid characterization to distinguish the process from more conventional state-building experiences, yet one should not overlook that 'Brussels' in the EU context unmistakably appears to be developing itself as a kind of prime 'node among nodes'. And as to the presumed novelty of the European form and process, one preliminary comparative note from India may not be altogether out of place. Historically, 'Indian society', writes Sudipta Kaviraj, 'was characterized by a type of social organization ... which accorded to the state less centrality than the standard European practice ... The state that existed in this kind of marginality to the social organization [was] without a clear locus of sovereign power' (Kaviraj 1995: 301). Leaving aside the vast differences of social organization in the two cases, the parallel in this respect can already help guard against too Eurocentric a view of what is presently evolving.

Regarding the parameters within which the process is being engineered, Siedentop reiterated – consistent with experience elsewhere – that one of the key conditions for the emergence of a successful federalism is consensus over the question as to which areas of policy-making should be given to the centre and which should be left to the constituent parts. In the case of the European Union, though, that question is more complicated than usual as it is by no means clear yet whether the framework is moving towards a form of federalism or some other form of collective policy-making. The European Union has formulated its 'subsidiarity' principle (broadly saying that the centre should refrain from entering into policy areas that are best left to the competence of the constituent units) to govern the handling of some of the choices concerned, but again it is left open whether this will apply to member-states or to regions – within or across states – for various purposes. In this connection it might be observed that one of the aims of the Treaty of Maastricht (1992) in preparing the ground for the EU was to provide Europe with a set of common structures and institutional arrangements essentially devoted to market regulation, not unlike those of India. The importance of the large Indian home market had often been stressed by Indian economists from the days of Nehruvian central planning onwards (Chakravarty 1987), and in a sense a similarly enlarged market is what was initially being sought in Europe as well, while today we can see both the European Union and India increasingly preparing for outward-oriented global competitiveness.

The first impetus towards European integration had been political, however, striving for political unity through economic collaboration in selected areas like coal and steel, followed by agriculture, to avoid the possibility of resumption of preparations for warfare. Analysing the process at the time, Ernst Haas concluded that European integration in the early years was facilitated by the existence of considerable agreement on objectives among the elites of various social and economic groups within each of the participating states as well as among the elites at the interstate level. Moreover, roughly identical social and economic structures allowed a linking up of these national systems at various levels (Haas 1967: 320). At later stages this consensus would be more difficult to achieve among an enlarged and more varied membership. The process was expanded into various other fields and at a subsequent stage European policies were actually given priority over policies of member-states, covering areas ranging from infrastructure, technology and research to education, environment, regional development, immigration, justice and police (Castells 2001: 345). In the light of the European Union's ascending role, national member-states have gradually been shedding some of their key functions, and a European state of sorts has been slowly emerging and beginning to occupy some of this space. It is an unusual kind of state, theoretically leaving the sovereignty and jurisdiction of its member-states (first 15, presently 25) untouched, but claiming final control especially over the 'economic space' and increasingly over other areas. Experience to date, however, has been that 'economic space' is a rather elastic notion and entry point for intervention, and that policies governing it may easily infringe upon other spheres. Critical commentaries over the past several years, however, have cited many examples of misgivings evolving from the implementation of the European Union's detailed policy guidelines in historically derived local and regional production processes, as in the areas of food processing.

Significant consequences, even if mainly indirectly, have been anticipated in the cultural sphere as well. The European Union, though not exactly designed to fulfill any long-cherished dreams of cultural unification, has led many people on the continent to ponder the implications for individual and collective identities – culturally and politically. Questions of changing identities in the European context, not unlike in India, have often been posed in terms of a contradiction between processes of homogenization versus national cultural diversity. Would a technocratic, market-homogenizing Europe obliterate national cultures and identities? Or is the fear of homogenization unwarranted and are primary identifications unlikely to shift towards 'Europe' to begin with? Among the various queries raised a central one concerns the very idea and proposition of European identity itself. What constitutes the core of 'European-ness' and how meaningful is any such root denominator, are questions that have been asked for decades (Berting and Van de Braak 1988). Essentially, one concern in this discussion has been whether national and sub-national cultural identities and distinctiveness will be able to withstand the anticipated integrative thrust of an emerging

European state framework, or whether instead they are likely to be levelled out as a corollary of the latter's emergence, or alternatively whether the two kinds of orientations can coexist without harming one another.

While the level of generality of these queries hardly allows unequivocal answers, we should appreciate the fact of substantially contrasting perceptions of 'Europe', 'European-ness' and 'European identity' prevailing across Europe (Berting 1997). Within most of Europe the presence of notable variations in national and regional cultures, languages and religious patterns, often accentuated by prolonged historical divisions, in a sense makes the idea of any amalgamating 'Europeanization' appear an abstract, almost far-fetched prospect. This is not to underrate numerous shared aspects, including shared histories either at the same or at opposite sides in the battlefield among different nations, like around Waterloo. Significantly, however, this has not alleviated some of the prevailing apprehensions about a 'homogenization' of sorts. Though the European Union so far has not been particularly trying to boost a political identity of its own at the expense of its member-states, part of an underlying uneasiness appears to arise from the fact that for various fields constituent members' policy frameworks are becoming increasingly irrelevant, in the end losing their significance as protective social umbrellas and symbols of identification. Besides, the use of the English language has been rapidly spreading on the continent in conjunction with market integration, internet and education, strengthening a sense of loss of cultural distinctiveness among majority speakers of several other language groups. Though the European Union can hardly be held directly responsible for all such transformations, for various groups it has nonetheless come to serve as a bogeyman in this respect.

Except for the abortive proposal for a European Constitution in 2005, the European Union did not yet seek too much of a role in terms of trying to build a strengthened institutional identity, an attitude which some observers believe has been a key source of its success, while others see it as its Achilles heel. Nonetheless, its steadily increasing presence indirectly did probably instil a sense that national identities, and the institutions and symbols underlying them, matter less than they did before. As border controls within Europe have largely vanished and the common currency on the continent is increasingly the Euro, some of the more visible co-ordinates of nationality are disappearing, triggering 'liberating' as well as 'alienating' sentiments among different population groups. Not surprisingly, in reaction to the increasing EU presence one can note a re-emergence and re-assertion of 'national' identifications in a number of respects, such as the searches for a national history 'canon' in the Netherlands, the steeply increased popularity and sales of 'national' history books in several countries, and the re-assertion of numerous local and regional cultural forms of expression, whether inherited or invented. In the light of these tendencies, Castells suggests that 'nationalism, not federalism, is the concomitant development of European integration'. And he adds that 'only if the EU is able to handle, and accommodate, nationalism will it survive as a political construction' (Castells 2001: 359).

In part the 'No' vote to the proposed European Constitution in the French and Dutch referenda of 2005 could indeed be explainable by apprehensions among part of the populace for potential loss of their 'national' identity and sense of security, underlining a discrepancy between Europe's 'nations' and 'states' in their respective appreciations of the EU project. The 'states', that is the member governments and bureaucracies, for years were busily participating in new joint endeavours and mutual adjustments of their legislations, while the 'nations' or respective popular constituencies had no part in this except at the receiving end. When it came to voting, evidently a whole range of motivations determined the negative outcome of these votes, put in from the far left as well as the far right, yet three in particular played a role, namely: (i) feelings of threat of globalization (not realizing that EU policies try to work against that threat); (ii) the European Union's enlargement policy, thought to be too rapid and too ambitious, especially with respect to Turkey; and (iii) EU's image as that of an excessively interfering bureaucracy, known in short as 'Brussels'. Each of these stands could be said to have reflected as well as reinforced lingering 'national' misgivings about the EU project. Besides, one specific factor contributing to a critical disposition among voters appears to have been the novelty and idea of a European 'constitution'. Several commentators thought this had been much too grand a concept for what was actually required (a summation of existing treaties mainly). As a result, various voters may unnecessarily have been led to puzzle how this was to affect the status and significance of existing national constitutions, while others took the opportunity to express their frustration about a whole range of misgivings, including about their national government's performance. Nonetheless, many 'No'-voters emphasized they were not against Europe or the European Union per se but objected to the codification of a neo-liberal market outlook within the proposed Constitution.

In time to come some of these manifestations may yet change. If the European Union is to move further from a market framework towards some kind of political unity, which is what many would argue will be needed to put in some weight in global discussions, then it would have to assert itself more forcefully as the *European Union*. But precisely then the question of its social constituency and the parameters of its 'European' identity become important, and will need to be based on a more directly democratic mandate, among other things. In this respect, despite some of the setbacks to unification incurred, Europe is likely to remain in transition in several respects, politically and institutionally, and it is not unreasonable to expect that processes of state and identity formation which have been characteristic for the continent may yet enter, and need to enter, a new and enlarging phase. Reflecting on this, Jürgen Habermas commented some years ago, with historical hindsight:

> There are two lessons to be learnt from the history of the European nation-states. If the emergence of national consciousness involved a painful process of abstraction, leading from local and dynastic identities to national and democratic ones, why, firstly, should this generation of a highly artificial kind of civic solidarity – 'a solidarity among strangers' – be doomed to come to a final halt just at the borders of our classical nation-states? And secondly: the artificial conditions in which national consciousness came into existence recall the empirical circumstances necessary for an extension of that process of identity-formation beyond national boundaries. These are: the emergence of a European civil society; the construction of a European-wide public sphere; and the shaping of a political culture that can be shared by all European citizens. (Habermas 2001: 8)

Habermas may have seemed somewhat over-optimistic about the ease with which 'artificial' constructions like national identity might recede and make room for identity-formation at the European level, at least more optimistic than subsequent manifestations have appeared to warrant. Still, given time, identity formation at a European level, complementing national, regional and other popular identities, in the end might well be on the increase. In this respect the EU founders may have pragmatically expected that citizens of European countries in due course would get accustomed to the new, overarching framework and assimilate a sense or layer of European identification. Perhaps, too, they started from the premise that harmonization of economic policies would not necessarily create friction with national identifications and cultures. Nevertheless, one of the principal architects of the European Union, Jean Monnet, once remarked that 'if we had to do it again, I would begin with "culture" ' (Villain Gandossi 1990: 9, cited in Berting 1997: 413). In the aftermath of the negative 2005 referenda results on the proposed European Constitution, however, many commentaries concluded that the proponents of the EU project had insufficiently recognized how critical the gap was that had been growing between their own conceptions for an enlarging and more integrated Europe on the one hand and popular experiences and perceptions of the same on the other. Euphemistically identified as the result of a 'pedagogical deficit', more squarely criticized as a 'democratic deficit', the gap's reality was nonetheless revealing.

These circumstances, although tempered by the fact that the European unification processes are contracted by as yet sovereign states, cannot but underscore the essential link between political democracy and identity. It is unrealistic to expect genuine popular identification with policies and institutions which offer little scope for popular involvement. Elections for the European Parliament, for example, have largely reflected its relatively marginal role so far: it has been mostly *national* issues which have been brought forward for contestation during election campaigns. Whether Europe's technocratic institutions will be able to find their way to a democratization of policy processes, or alternatively, whether democratic popular movements succeed in effectively gaining control over European policy processes, will prove decisive not only for the future of European democracy, but also for its political identity. In its absence it has been observed that today's 'Eurocrats' enjoy a latitude of governance matched only by European princes of earlier epochs. The questions this raises are particularly compelling given that there are no other conceivable bases on which to form a genuine European solidarity and identity. In this connection Castells observes 'by and large, there is no European identity. But it could be built, not in contradiction, but complementary to national, regional and local identities', with the EU process of social construction figuring as 'project identity' (Castells 2001: 365). Yet it is ironic of course that the first effort to come to a democratic consultation, on the draft European Constitution, misfired partly out of a voters' revenge for the European Union's institutional aloofness.

Regionalization

It is important to look also at the emergence of the European Union in regional terms, and see how 'sub-national' regions have begun to relate to the European Union, and vice versa. The European Union, at one level posing as a purely neutral and technocratic body which tries to avoid offending member states by refraining from entering into discussions on sensitive cultural issues, at another level appears to be quietly building up a political support base of its own through its policies for regional development, bypassing and limiting the role of national-level policy-making. Through special grants from the European Regional Development Fund and other funds under Community Initiatives, already totalling some 36 per cent of its overall budget in the late 1990s (John 2000: 880), the EU Commission has gained increasing leverage to engage in special relations with supposedly 'backward' regions in various European countries. The EU Commission has also been strongly encouraging initiatives towards inter-regional collaboration, including cross-border projects involving regions of different national member-states, and at one time it gave its explicit support to the idea of a 'Europe of regions' advocated by some regions. The term implied that national institutions would give way to the merging European state, and that regions in due course would get direct access to European policy-making processes (John 2000: 882). Several of the most active regions concerned, such as Scotland, Wales and Brittany, from their part have used the opportunity to expand their own room for manoeuvre, thus enhancing their own regional and nationalist ambitions vis-à-vis their respective national governments. Some observers have thus seen regionalization in its various forms contributing significantly to the 'Europeanization' of governance and the 'denationalization' of space (Brenner 1999: 435). Others, however, would caution that 'finding the right scale at which to manage a competitive European economy, solve environmental problems and ensure social cohesion is no nearer now than at the beginning of the 1990s when the prospect of a Europe of regions seemed to provide the answer' (Newman 2000: 895). Whatever the record so far, the European Union as an emerging state is clearly trying to develop supportive relations with different regions across Europe, trying to engage in a long-term constituency building distinct from its connections with the official member-states (John 2000).

Regions which are not necessarily 'backward' (such as Flanders, Bavaria, Catalonia), have also been identifying opportunities for an enlarged role and identity in the new European constellation. They see it as a chance to reduce the reach of national re-distributive state structures, and to develop trade and cultural links with other regions 'abroad'. There has been some euphoria about strengthening linkages between Brittany and Flanders (stimulated also by high-speed rail links), and the Basques have been demonstrating a keen interest in what the European Union may have in stock for them in terms of autonomy or more. Similarly, the Scottish Constitutional Convention and the Standing Commission on the Scottish Economy have been developing alternative paths for Scottish autonomy within *Europe*, for rethinking their economic and political scenarios in the context of European integration, and for examining ways of modifying their ties within the United Kingdom (Mitchell and Leicester 1999). These initiatives in Scotland were facilitated by openings at the EU level, which provided a welcome focus and channel for dealing with points on which the Scottish felt their position had been compromised over the years within the United Kingdom and were calling for amelioration. Thus, a certain dual development of supra-state and regional structures, to some extent reflected in the articulation of corresponding identities, is being pursued in Europe, comprising an interesting footnote to historical patterns of centralization.

However, the European Union's patronage of regional development and identities, channelled in part through its Committee of the Regions, a body with representatives of European regional and local authorities, does not necessarily represent, or result in, unqualified liberalism and enhancement of cultural pluralism. As experience in India and elsewhere has shown, regional autonomy has the potential of sheltering narrow interests, championed by regionally dominant and often conservatively oriented classes. A relative dominance of such groups may get enhanced as they face fewer restrictions and occasions demanding engagement in political compromise with other political groups – industrial labour, urban classes, the tertiary sector – under the aegis of national metropolitan politics. Any prospects of a more regionalized European political framework, though quite theoretical at the present stage, would therefore need to be critically assessed in terms of their implications for a political and cultural climate favouring civil liberties, cultural pluralism and social compromise. Again, any chances of success in this regard may largely depend on whether or not the emergent European political institutions will be subjected to substantive democratization.

Western, Eastern and Central Europe

In Western Europe generally, specifically as regards the forces and identifications supporting or opposing the emergence of European level political institutions, one can note some deviations from 'normal' dialectical patterns. Impressionistically, the European Union as the most established institution of an emerging European state, by and large enjoys neither broad popular support nor widespread opposition. A European movement, which explicitly presented itself as the torch-bearer of European integration and identity in the early years of unification, has largely dissipated more or less in unison with the emergence of European institutions. Western European nationalisms by and large have lost much of their strengths, and opposition in national or nationalist terms to European integration remains relatively limited.

In Central and Eastern Europe (CEE), the transformations that have been occurring since 1989 in more than one way have been of major importance to the ongoing EU project and the questions of identity it throws up. Somehow in contrast to the older EU member states it appears there is both a fresh and stronger support for EU integration and at the same time a stronger sense of national distinctiveness in the CEE states. The countries concerned (Estonia, Lithuania, Latvia, Poland, Hungary, Czech Republic, Slovakia, Slovenia) have in fact gone through a double transition, one of un-doing their political, economic and administrative ties with the former Soviet Union and the Comecon-bloc, and second that of entering the EU (and NATO) and adopting numerous EU regulations which have had to be integrated into their own legal-administrative frameworks. The latter operation has been quite massive as an exercise in state (re)formation and it has been noted that 'the increase of "administrative capacity", that is public adminis-tration reforms geared towards high quality, is primarily EU-driven in CEE' (Drechsler 2005: 100). This observation in turn may testify to the extent to which CEE countries have already reoriented themselves towards public policy-making in accordance with EU standards, a trans-formation that seems underscored by the fact that the tasks involved are largely carried by a new and surprisingly young cohort of senior administrators in several countries.

In terms of changing state-identity reciprocities, a casual impression is that these have not been particularly dramatic in CEE, which may be for several reasons. In the first place, the countries concerned only recently regained their independence and national identity and clearly are not too keen to abandon them. More than in most Western European coun-tries, national identity and a sense of nationalism have remained impor-tant in CEE countries, though in several cases this has been heightened in the opposition to former Russian dominance. With some stretching of concepts, the transformations that have taken place thus could be perceived as arising out of the intersection of a politically homogenizing grid, that of the former communist bloc of states, on the one hand and various pressures emanating from a revival of national and cultural identities on the other. The dramatic developments in Eastern Europe and the former Soviet Union that led to the collapse and dismantling of this grid have called for multiple interpretations (Motyl 1992, Prazauskas 1991). Several of these would refer to dynamics and confrontations that took place in terms of political identity, such as civil society versus the state (Poland), or nationality as a rationale for state reunification (the Germanies) as well as for state dismantling (Yugoslavia), all paralleled by the loss of appeal, and actual removal, of numerous symbols of identity from the era of state socialism (such as statues, party symbols and other icons).

The 1989 German reunification was of special significance with respect to both the Eastern and Western European contexts. The reunification urge was based on flexible and shifting nationalist identity constructs, especially the notion of 'Heimat' (Applegate 1990). German longings for the 'Heimat' appeared to share a nostalgic element with the search for 'Bharat' in India. In the newly added states as part of the German Federal Republic, the latter constituted one factor undermining the projected hegemony defined in terms of state socialism. At the same time, German reunification momentarily put the EU integration project under some pressure, as it was by no means immediately clear whether the two projects would be compatible. The choice boiled down to either a reunited Germany opting out of the European Union (which would have been the end of it) or of the other EU members reconciling themselves to the inclusion of one particularly strong, central and dominant member, which is what happened. At the same time, the German reunification urge itself provided a significant corrective to assumptions that (Western) Europe had become post-nationalist, highlighting a dimension of potential fragility in EU arrangements and projections which perhaps had been underestimated.

More broadly, the Central and Eastern European examples (though also the Russian case) appear to offer some significant lessons concerning the longer term impacts of homogenizing grids elsewhere. Vis-à-vis Western European concerns about the threat of homogenization, they seem to issue a note of reassurance that a decline in cultural identity and resilience due to politico-technocratic homogenization need not be too readily anticipated. This may still leave unanswered the chicken and egg question as to what came first. Did the Central and Eastern European (and also Russian) examples indicate undiminished cultural resilience and identity of sorts, in the end breaking through the grid, or did they exemplify a weakened 'grid' which had been losing its homogenizing strength and could thus give way to a reassertion of 'natural' categories such as nationality, ethnicity and civil society with which to organize political alternatives to the state? The answer is probably both and is likely to remain somewhat ambiguous inasmuch as it may be cast in terms that rest on a projection of preferred readings of history. Of key importance, however, is the fact that Central and Eastern European countries had not voluntarily joined a political union of sorts but had been incorporated into it against their will, which naturally stimulated their interest to opt out once given a chance.

European identities and Europe's identity

The question of European identities is not just a matter of the extent of people's identifications with 'Europe' and the stimuli they receive in favour or against adopting any such added identities. Identity processes – the amalgam of stimuli that influence and shape collective consciousness – proceed along internal as well as external dimensions: 'internal' with respect to the way people relate to regional, national or continental levels of identity – or to religious, cultural or other foci of solidarity – 'external' with respect to other entities in the world outside. The question therefore is also about Europe's – and the EU's – own identity and its social, cultural or political basis and what distinguishes it from what lies 'beyond'. With its amorphous and porous boundaries, Europe and the EU cannot refer to a clearly defined geographical entity. Linguistically the continent is a mosaic, defying any proposals for a singular identity. Due to all the linguistic divisions English increasingly becomes the European *lingua franca* and even within bilingual countries like Belgium, English has become the second language for both French and Dutch speakers.

Culturally, the question as to what Europe or EU members have in common is inordinately complex. It was raised at the time of drafting the proposed European Constitution, in the course of which there was some debate as to whether the preamble should make some reference to fundamental values shared throughout Europe, and how. At that point the Vatican reiterated its position that there can only be a Christian Europe or no Europe at all. In this position it could count on the support from predominantly Roman-Catholic countries like Poland, Hungary, Ireland, Spain and Portugal in particular, followed by a good number of others, though countries like France and Belgium (also with large majorities of Roman-Catholics) indicated they would strongly oppose this on account of the principle of separation of church and state that has been entrenched within their secular constitutional frameworks. As a compromise the draft preamble only contained a watered-down reference to the 'cultural, religious and humanist inheritance of Europe'. The question is likely to reassert itself in one form or another, however, especially in the light of recent swings to the political right in several member countries.

Of far-reaching consequence therefore remains the question of what kind of identity profiles are likely to be encouraged in Europe in the years ahead or which may emerge in response to enlarging state designs in accordance with its status as an emerging regional superpower. Will dominant forces opt for strictly neutral or secular definitions of self-identity, or is Europe likely to be increasingly presented as rooted in Judeo-Christian culture (Gordon 1989)? Such portrayals would imply further internal as well as external boundary definitions vis-à-vis Muslim communities in particular. In Europe this would entail defining, once again, what or who is 'non-European', a task which would not be without problems nor without historical precedent. As from the days of the Crusades, some sense of European identity has partly been formed in offensive as well as defensive postures vis-à-vis Islam (Bruyning 1991). From outside Europe, exclusionary efforts towards unification may conceivably be perceived in the light of a tradition going back to 1492, when the Spanish monarchy evicted the Moors from the Iberian Peninsula and 'Christian' Europe henceforth began to mould itself apart from its North African and Asian neighbours – in doing so putting a halt in the process to the highly innovative and cosmopolitan Christian–Jewish–Muslim era which had made Andalusia blossom intellectually and physically from the tenth century onwards.

Europe's diffuse geographical borders with Muslim regions have been repeatedly pushed backward and forward on the Balkans as well. As a reminder, Vienna still has a street called *Turkenschanz*, referring to the defence barrier put up against besieging Turks in 1683. Reservations to the Turks entering Europe are topical again today, as witnessed by widespread European reluctance to accept predominantly Muslim Turkey as a prospective member of the European Union. The EU Commission in its efforts to promote market expansion initiated the groundwork for Turkey's membership application long ago, and formal negotiations, expected to take as long as a ten-year period, have been scheduled to begin in 2005. However, due to its large population Turkey's application for EU membership would at once make it the biggest member country with proportionally the strongest voting power, and given its predominantly Muslim population would not fail to affect the nature of the community's collective identity if it were to be implemented. Hence the initiative was not received with great enthusiasm in present member countries and has instead added to the puzzles and reservations that people in these countries have about the longer-term political identity of the European Union. If in the end the application is turned down it is likely to entail serious internal social and identity conflicts within Turkey itself, as many members of its educated elite presumably would feel more at home within Europe than having to reorient themselves to former Ottoman linkages. Whether Turkey's less vocal Muslim majority would be equally keen to become part of the European Union and Europe is less certain.

In coping with its future, therefore, the European Union in the years ahead is bound to continue grappling with two major questions concerning its existence and evolution. One concerns, again, the kind of relations it should try to develop with its constituent members, in particular to what extent it should initiate pan-European legislation regarding issues that could equally well or better be taken up by individual member-states. Indications are that the European Union is trying to be more prudent and avoiding intrusions into areas of potential national competence where choices are at stake. Second remains the question of European identity. The final paradox here is that the European Union will somehow need to develop more of an identity of its own if it is to evolve as one of the key global players, and further proposals to that end may well be expected in the times to come. Yet trying to define a European identity remains problematic given the inadequacies attached to virtually any common denominator that might be proposed. As a result almost any attempts to create a common European imprimatur of one kind or another is bound to turn out a narrowing one, closing rather than widening horizons and potentially alienating some of its current constituencies. An 'open-ended' definition of European identity thus would seem most fitting to what has been an open-ended development trajectory in the case of the European Union so far.

India

In contrast to the European Union's phased and open-ended state building process, a seemingly opposite kind of dynamic has been at work in India. 'India' was established by an act of law at independence, not as the product of a deliberate state-building project requiring negotiation and consensus at numerous stages and intervals as in the case of the EU. As a focus for social and cultural identity, the idea of 'India' for a long time probably carried rather remote and abstract dimensions to many of its inhabitants, though it was plausibly argued that for all its variety of cultures, languages and religions, it nonetheless constituted a kind of 'civilisational state' (Kumar 1997). Nehru's 'idea of India' significantly has more than once since come to serve as a focus for epistemological exploration of India's origins and identity. Thus, in his 1999 study, *The Idea of India*, Sunil Khilnani traces the conceptual roots of a state form that was essentially meant to be pluralist – 'seeking to coordinate within the form of a modern state a variety of values: democracy, religious tolerance, economic development and cultural pluralism'. Khilnani observes that '[the] arrival of the modern state on the Indian landscape ... and its growth and consolidation as a stable entity after 1947 ... mark a shift from a society where authority was secured by diverse local methods to one where it is located in a single sovereign agency' (Khilnani 1999: 3). And in a recent address on the occasion of receiving an honorary doctorate at Oxford, India's Prime Minister Manmohan Singh submitted that '[the] idea of India as enshrined in our Constitution, with its emphasis on the principles of secularism, democracy, the rule of law, and above all, the equality of all human beings irrespective of caste, community, language or ethnicity, has deep roots in India's ancient civilisation' (Singh 2005).

The fact that the country since then has held together suggests a remarkable achievement in the light of major challenges it has been facing to its territorial integrity, and also when taking into account the break-up of Pakistan following its Partition from India in 1947. But not only did the country itself keep together despite threats of fragmentation, the 'idea of India' as such, Khilnani submits, similarly has had a remarkable tenacity. 'Indians of vastly different backgrounds and ambitions today all wish to claim it for themselves. [But even] as they divide, these struggles themselves testify to the presence of a common history, a shared Indian past. The struggle for that past is of course a struggle to determine the future ideas of India' (Khilnani 1999: 13).[2]

In India pervasive processes of transformation as well as continuing tussles for power have been strongly affecting the relationship between the federal centre and the states since the early years of independence. In recent decades these have led to various attempts to re-assert political centralization, most notably during the governments of Indira Gandhi (1966–77 and 1980–84), while at the same time there has been a deepening

---

[2] Not all observers of the Indian political scene might be ready to agree to disagree in this respect. One reviewer of Khilnani's *The Idea of India*, Subhash Kak, noted that one 'can speak of the idea of the Bharatvarsha of the Puranic imagination, the Hindustan of the Mughal empire, and more recent Indias of the Marxists, the Congressmen, the socialists, the Muslim League, the Shiv Sena, the BJP, and so on', critiquing Khilnani for privileging the Nehruvian vision of India instead of speaking of the idea of a nation in the plural (Kak 2005).

political gravity of state level politics and influence. Exemplary for the shifts that have been taking place is the decline in the role and position of the Indian Administrative Service (IAS), the all-India elite administrative corps inherited from British times at independence, which for a number of years continued to provide co-ordination and unity of policy on behalf of the central government in a wide range of policy areas. Gradually, however, various state governments have been usurping many of the IAS's functions and powers, causing the role of the centre to become increasingly transformed from one of initiating and co-ordinating common policies to one of negotiating and mediating between different state and regional interests.

In conjunction with these transitions, various kinds of identity issues have also come to the fore. The sharpening of conflicts in and over Kashmir has been but one indication of the intensification of confrontations around political identities on regional, communal and religious levels. The articulation of distinctive political identities in opposition to the centre underlay the claims to Khalistan in the 1980s, the various nationality movements in the northeast and regional movements elsewhere in India (such as the one demanding at one time 'Maharashtra for the Maharashtrians'). Moreover, deepening Hindu and Muslim fundamentalism has amounted, fundamentally, to increasingly vocal assertions of reconstructed identity, unearthing vexing long-term questions about the content and definition of national unity. In these debates, observers with otherwise different perspectives on the crisis have frequently shared an apprehension of 'things falling apart', to use Achebe's phrase from a different context.

With respect to the institutional and cultural grid that has been underlying India's unity, two broad critiques can be discerned: the first raising basic questions about its distorting homogenizing impacts on various nationality, ethnic and cultural configurations (Kothari 1988a); the second questioning whether the grid itself is sufficiently self-sustaining to accommodate challenges and demands arising from various culturally based centrifugal forces. There has also been concern, from different quarters, about the impact of technological change on socio-cultural structures. Nevertheless, there is some debate as to whether such impacts should be directly associated with the interventionist thrust of India's political–institutional 'grid', or whether the rapid rise of technological empires in some spheres might itself be explicable in terms of a weakened political 'grid'. India's autonomously operating dairy development policy structures provide a case in point for the pivotal role claimed by semi-public organizations in development and policy making (Doornbos and Nair 1990), while other examples could be found in the institutions operating in the energy sector.

Ongoing centre–state rivalries for power have often been focused on other, 'sub-national' entities, defined as cultural, language, religious or caste communities. It is these for which increasing room, representation and recognition has frequently been demanded over the years, some-times with a call for extended autonomy or separate statehood, in a few cases with an outright bid for secession. This has been commonly accompanied by heightened tensions within the affected regions and constituencies of the country, though generally one has sought – and succeeded – to accommodate some space for the language, caste, tribal, or religious community concerned within the overall context of the Indian union. Groups feeling deprived within particular states would characteristically appeal to the central government for a change of status, and might be able to count on a responsive ear from the centre especially if the state government concerned was dominated by another political party than the one in power at the centre.

Partha Chatterjee has related the policy responses that were given to these situations as flowing directly from the rational planning model adopted at Indian independence. Not unlike the technocratic, neutrally bureaucratic approach that has often been noted as the EU's trademark, Indian central planning similarly had a decisively a-political orientation, often seeking to de-politicize intensely political issues. As Chatterjee describes the process, the central state's strategy in these situations characteristically was:

> to insist that all conflicts between particular interests admit of an 'economic' solution – 'economic' in the sense of allocations to each part that are consistent with the overall constraints of the whole. Thus, a particular interest, whether expressed in terms of class, language, region, caste, tribe, or community, is to be recognized and given a place within the framework of the general by being assigned a priority and an allocation relative to all other parts. (Chatterjee 1994: 214–215)

The resulting trend and picture has been one of continuing fragmentation of the Indian body politic, requiring ever more concessions to ever more specifically articulated demands from groups claiming to have been neglected. The way this dynamic works out can be gleaned from one such case reported in *The Hindu* of 6 July 2005:

> The West Bengal Government has attempted to buy peace in the Darjeeling hills by conceding, at various stages over the past

seven months, the demands of Subash Ghisingh for greater powers to the Darjeeling Gorkha Hill Council (DGHC) of which he is caretaker Chairman. The Government is now confronted with a fresh challenge. Having extracted an affirmative response to the additional powers he has been seeking, Mr. Ghisingh is now asking for a re-drawing of the political map. He wants more areas included under the Council in what appears a throwback to the days of the agitation for a separate Gorkhaland State.

As a follow-up to his outright rejection of the State Government's proposal to grant the Council a constitutional guarantee with the incorporation of a fresh clause to Article 371 to upgrade the DGHC, the Centre and the State government have agreed to grant Sixth Schedule status to the Council. Despite this, at the end of the fifth round of tripartite talks convened by the Union Home Minister in New Delhi last week, Mr. Ghisingh asked that the Council's jurisdiction be extended to cover the entire Darjeeling district.

This particular case is one of many that have come up in the course of the years since independence. While registering the strikingly legalistic and seemingly a-political procedures and terminology in which these demands are being handled, it is important to note the longer-term implications which the pattern of these pressures and conflicts has had for the nature of the Indian state and the forms in which some of its political processes have been moulded. As the idiom used in the above excerpt may already indicate, one of those forms has actually been to divert various issues requiring complex decision-making to the courts, often overburdening the latter with tasks they were not exactly set up for. More broadly, the implications of these patterns have been sketched by Khilnani, who commented:

> The steady political mobilization instigated by democratic competition was bringing lower and poorer people into politics, many who were organizing themselves into groups defined by legally ascribed public identities: the Backward and Other Backward Classes, the Scheduled Castes and others. They considered their interests framed by local horizons, and from the 1970s began to find a voice in a multiplicity of regional parties and political formations. (Khilnani 1999: 181)

Actually, the process of clamouring for recognition as deprived groups does not necessarily end with the granting of constitutionally classified status, but may proceed further through the targeting of internal differentiations for government attention and uplifting. Some Dalit groups illustrate this tendency towards a pattern of involution of sorts. During colonial and pre-colonial days, Dalits did not so much speak up for themselves but were 'spoken about' by other social groups, as 'untouchables' mainly. After independence they were, more neutrally, constitutionally designated as 'Scheduled Castes' (Yurlova 1990), while in recent times they have themselves taken up the term 'Dalits' as a more strident self-designation (Oomen 2004: 163). However, as P.L. Dharma observes, divisions and rivalry among different groups of Dalits, though all struggling to escape from their 'identity-less identity', frequently cause the scope for joint action under one common (Dalit) denominator to become overshadowed by identity struggles amongst themselves. This has been the case, for example, with the Balagai and Yedagai Scheduled Castes in Karnataka, each claiming 'superiority' vis-à-vis each other but in the end both losing out due to unwillingness to make joint appeals in terms of a broader Dalit solidarity (Dharma 2003: 48).

Essentially, India's constitutionally enshrined reservation policy, designed to make 'unequals' equal, has thus become profoundly politicized in the course of the years, leading a perplexed ILO mission at one time to make the understatement that India's affirmative action system is 'very complex' (Rajeev Dhavan in *The Hindu*, 13 June 2003). Significantly, most of the groups involved in the demands concerned did not seek to opt out, except for some in Kashmir and in the Northeast, and in Tamil Nadu during earlier periods. In most cases their horizon was rather oriented towards obtaining special concessions from the centre, which per definition reinforced their disposition to stay in. Allowing concessions by way of special grants or increased representation at the central level thus often proved a suitable antidote for the central government to claims for autonomy, not unlike the mechanisms that had been at work in France with regional protest movements at an earlier time. There, various social movements which drew their inspiration from regional cultures, such as in Brittany, Occitan or Savoy, for some time were very vocal in calling for enlarged autonomies, but tended to disappear from the scene upon receiving increased central government support (Touraine 1981). The Indian state framework likewise has proved so far resilient enough to keep together in the face of these challenges, defying threats of easy fragmentation into two or more parts.

Still, an important question remains as to who in the end have been the beneficiaries of these concessions. As Rajni Kothari observed in regard to the 'Directive Principles and Fundamental Rights' (the constitutional provisions governing the grants concerned), 'what has in fact happened is that the rights of the poor are being trampled all over the place, whether they are the landless, or the *dalits*, the *adivasis* and the forest people, or those who are displaced by dams and projects' (Kothari 1988a: 225). As has similarly been an experience in various other contexts, representative leaders and lesser officials may quietly agree to shift their roles from one of giving voice to popular demands to soothing those same demands in a more system-dependent stance in exchange for receiving personal benefits. India's Congress Party, the ruling party for the first several decades after independence, has proved particularly accommodative in these respects.

Significantly, the tendency towards increasing fragmentation has not changed with India's adoption of economic liberalization from the 1990s onwards. The argument has been advanced that the fiscal retreat of the central state which this has entailed has widened interregional inequalities and is hurting poor and weak regions relatively more. Implying a direct link between globalization and the restructuring of Indian States, Guljit Arora observed that

> such a situation is easily exploitable by an elite political class and its allied groups. Since it is easy to identify people in terms of small regional identities, one may find a number of economic and political formations culminating into regional movements raising more demands for smaller administrative and political units to be run by them independently. Pressures already being exerted by geographic units like Bodoland, Gorkhaland, Harit Pradesh, Mithilanchal, Telengana, and Vidarbha cannot be easily dismissed. (Arora 2004: 171)

Evidently, the scramble for political rewards at constituency level continues its course more or less irrespective of some of the broader strategy changes at the centre.

Decentralization

If India's political experience since independence has been one of increasing regionalization and power struggles between the centre and the states, leading to a more fragmented political framework, decentralization policies adopted in more recent years have not reduced the resulting complexity of the overall policy process. To the contrary, for all the laudable objectives of 'bringing government closer to the people' and promoting popular participation, decentralization in India as elsewhere has often actually been accentuating some of the adverse communal rivalries at stake in local politics. These effects have been noted particularly in respect of the policies concerning the management of natural resources (Meynen and Doornbos 2004).

In India, considerable pressure had been put on the central government by various people's movements and NGOs to decentralize the management of natural resources and increase people's participation in this management (Dwivedi 2001). At the same time, the central government initiated decentralization of natural resource management along *sectoral* lines, parallel to the recommendations advocated worldwide by the international financial institutions. As in the context of economic globalization local economies have been increasingly forced to open up; however, local natural resource management practices in various parts of the country have become reoriented to commercial exploitation without due regard to the protection of natural resources or the subsistence needs of the poor. Besides, decentralization of government itself was also undertaken through the *panchayati raj* programme for local government reform. The way these different forms of decentralization should relate to one another in practice has remained unresolved, however – a problem which has been compounded as a result of the political strife between the central and state governments. As a result, there have been numerous instances of administrative confusion about responsibilities and jurisdictions (Baumann 1998). Moreover, with the general idea of devolving issues for decision-making to lower administrative levels, actual decision-making powers about a range of vital resource questions have often come to lie with community representations, within which the interests of traders and wealthier farmers usually prove strongest. As higher-level authorities no longer exercise a final arbiter say in situations of conflict between different kinds of resource use patterns, decentralization often results in augmentation of local strife over resources as well as in further empowering the categories who are already economically strongest (Meynen and Doornbos 2004). Indirectly this has had important implications in terms of aggravating social conflicts at grassroots levels.

Hindutva

The Hindutva challenge of recent years is very different in nature from the risks of fragmentation and the challenges of centre–state rivalries which India has increasingly been facing since independence. Not only does it put forward, and demand recognition for, a very particular and 'fundamentalist' reading of history – which has been severely criticized for its basic flaws and distortions (Sen 2002, Thapar 2003) – but its demands almost per definition cannot be accommodated within the prevailing framework. Instead it calls for no less than drastic revision and overhaul of the entire political framework, seeking to have it recognized as being based on Hindu identity, a claim which rests on what has come to be known as electoral majoritarianism in India. In nurturing its position, Hindutva essentially puts India's secular state framework under attack (Juergensmeyer 1994), demanding recognition of India as a 'Hindu' state with far-reaching implications for the position of other religious communities like Muslims, Sikhs, Christians and Buddhists. Hinduization feeds on and instils fear and enmity towards 'Others', in the process seeking to create a unison of vision and action which India's variegated forms of Hindu worship actually never had before. Hindutva's emergence as a political force, which has been a slow but steady incremental growth, has indeed been accompanied by increased violence against other religious groups and symbols. One of the most notorious actions in this respect was the mob destruction of the sixteenth-century Babri Masjid in Ayodhya in 1992, on the grounds that it had been built on the site of a Hindu temple devoted to the Hindu deity Lord Ram – who, incidentally, is being accorded an increasingly central and martial position within Hindutva's pantheon. There are many aspects to the emergence and manifestation of this pervasive Hindu-inspired political movement which call for attention, in some way constituting a resumption of the political dynamics and Hindu–Muslim frictions that had led to Partition at the time of independence. In recent years, the Bharatiya Janata Party (BJP), whose rise has largely benefited from Hindutva sentiments and which led a national coalition government from 1998–2004, has emerged as a formidable force and will need to be counted as a major opponent to Congress at future electoral tests. Indeed, no discussion of Indian history, politics and society in recent years has been possible without substantial attention for the phenomenon of the rise of Hindutva, which in recent times has been extremely vocal politically (e.g. Khilnani 1999, Malik and Singh 1994, Oomen 2004, Sharma 2003, Thapar 2003).

One possible albeit indirect approach to an understanding of Hindutva is to relate it to India's experience with the West. A central theme in Indian discourses on identity formation concerns the interpretation of India's relations with the West, specifically India's prolonged exposure to the West's culture of technology and rationality but also of course the way in which its institutions, educational and language patterns have been shaped in interaction with the West, specifically Britain.

In the theorizing about the nature and impact of this exposure, two opposite positions can be identified in India. The first recognizes and basically accepts the Western experience as something which has pervasively influenced the shape of and become part of the complex of Indian society, accepting secularism as a basic principle for its state formation. The second position as a matter of principle would want to reject India's experience with the West, defining it as something alien which India should distance itself from. This position comprises a variety of perspectives, some more nuanced than others, but in its most fundamental form it questions the concept of 'India' as such while, spiritually at least, engaging in the search for 'Bharat', the Hindu homeland. This has in essence been the position of the Hindutva movement, which draws its initial spiritual inspiration from the writings of Swami Vivekanda, Vinayak Damodar Savarkar, Dayananda Saraswati, Sri Aurobindo and contemporaries in the early twentieth century (Sharma 2003). Except for Vinayak Savarkar, however, most of these thinkers might have found Hindutva giving a highly distorted representation of their ideas.

In the light of the challenges to which 'the idea of India' has been subjected especially from the side of Hindutva in recent years, one may note frequent references being made to the founding principles of the Indian state, with the idea of secularism being one of its keystones, and to which the British legacy made significant contributions. In his 2005 Oxford address referred to above, Prime Minister Manmohan Singh, upon reflecting on India's civilizational roots of the 'idea of India', went on to say that 'it is undeniable that the founding fathers of our republic were also greatly influenced by the ideas associated with the age of enlightenment in Europe. Our Constitution remains a testimony to the enduring interplay between what is essentially Indian and what is very British in our intellectual heritage' (Singh 2005). Upon delivering his speech Manmohan Singh was at once thoroughly criticized in the Indian press for having been excessively kind about British rule and refraining from being equally candid about its evils (*The Hindu*, 19 July 2005). Yet the perspective he articulated fundamentally had been the Nehruvian point of departure for India's state building, starting out from recognition of India's enormous cultural and historical diversity and representing an attempt to create and maintain an institutional platform which could serve the purposes of tolerance, dialogue and mutual respect among its many population groups. Secularism is a central element in this conception, but has become increasingly controversial in the Indian context. Many Indian intellectuals in recent years have felt forced to define their position on this highly sensitized question, and have spoken out about it in their writings with more or less nuance and accuracy. In the context of a sharp dissection and refutation of Hindutva's majoritarian identity claims, for example, Amartya Sen brings in the vision of Tagore in support of the basic Nehruvian perspective. Tagore, the towering Indian poet and thinker, had argued that the 'idea of India' itself militated against a culturally separatist view – 'against the intense consciousness of the separateness of one's own people from others' (Sen 2002: 48). Yet, the social dynamics on the ground often display a growing discrepancy with those in the world of ideas.

Searching for an explanation for the rise of Hindutva that might be informed by historical sociology, Sudipta Kaviraj traces some determinants of that discrepancy in the Indian context. Linking several critical developments that have successively affected the Indian state and society, he first draws attention to the fact that '[since] the sixties, Indian politics [had] seen a massive alteration in style, language, modes of behavior, reflecting far more the actual cultural understandings of rural Indian society rather than the Westernist cultivation of the elite which inherited power in the Nehru years' (Kaviraj 1995: 313). But he adds that that particular development

> was compounded by the forgetfulness and negligence of the Nehruvian state itself about the process of the cultural reproduction of the nation. It not merely failed to create conditions for a common sense in Indian politics, through which liberal, secular political ideas could be communicated dialogically to them, rather, its neglect of cultural institutions like primary education contributed to a further division between a Westernist English-using social aristocracy and a disadvantaged vernacular culture condemned to backwardness and self-deprecation. (Ibid.: 313–314)

This bifurcation, in Kaviraj's analysis, prepared the ground for two types of political dissent, 'an economic critique of class and an indigenist critique of modernist cultural privilege'. And it is this second kind of resentment which 'predominantly found cultural expression through regionalist and communal politics, through the politics of Hindi and Hinduism' (ibid.: 314). Hindutva, which grew larger subsequent to this analysis, represents an immensely swollen expression of that resentment, and will take some time before it finds an accommodation with other realities on the ground.

India, not unlike Europe, in the years ahead thus will continue to face challenges emanating from its considerable political and regional diversity as well as from popular reactions to its identity constructs. But the political forces involved and the targets at stake are highly contrasted in the two cases. If in Europe regionalization has been one of the (EU) centre's strategies to widen its policy sway over the Union's collective space, in India states and regions have been seeking increased policy involvement at the cost of the centre's powers. And whereas in Europe the idea of developing a common identity is problematic and may not materialize due to popular dissent, thus leaving the question open-ended, in India popular forces intent subjecting to its identity to drastic redefinition will continue to press for change, and are likely to find the central state in favour of retaining openness.

Comparative observations

As the experiences in Europe and India have illustrated, collective identities are being shaped and reshaped in innumerable ways, while their basic determinants must be sought in strategies to reconfirm or gain hegemony on the one hand, and people's search for equity, dignity and recognition on the other. These dialectical processes and the socio-political transformations they give rise to are invariably reflected in changing articulations of political identity, popular and/or official. Ultimately, they determine the definition of the political community itself. At times, though, as the previous sections have illustrated, these dialectical and dialogical interactions may halt and stagnate if the state, or the main forces opposing it, lose touch with broader social dynamics occurring around them. Distorted dialogue then results.

Europe and India clearly have both had prolonged and profound experiences with the interplay between state forms and identity, and with the clashes or juxtapositions of official and popular identities that may result from them. State forms may give rise to – in due course – to collective identities, while conversely collective identities have at times served as a springboard for new ventures in state formation. The two kinds of dynamics may also relate to one another sequentially, for which again both Europe and India historically provide examples. While generalization in this respect is hazardous, the proposition might be ventured that there have been more frequent instances of state forms giving rise to social responses in identity terms than the other way around. On the Indian side, for example, Partition gave rise to state forms shaping India and Pakistan, opening possibilities to discover, or re-discover, their respective identities. Subsequently a whole range of social movements within both countries sought further adjustments within the newly established frameworks. This still leaves aside the question of what basically triggered Partition, and whether this was primarily a question of popular struggles or of lack of consensus among the political elites. The question continues to engage the minds of historians and others on the sub-continent and, while one answer is that Partition itself was a product of claimed political identity (Pakistan), another would emphasize that a different set of interactions between Nehru, Gandhi and the Muslim leader Jinnah might have prevented it. In Europe at roughly the same time the post-Second World War division of the continent unmistakably laid down state forms which subsequently became reflected in new official designations associated with the two respective blocs of countries, while the fall of the Berlin Wall in 1989 constituted a rather more exceptional case of popular sentiments and identities asserting themselves and initiating processes of fundamental state reform.

In the European case, the loss of legitimacy and hegemony of socialist frameworks created room for articulations of identity in terms of nationality, ethnicity and civil organization. In the South Asian context, there would be a hypothetical parallel if one day religion were to lose its commanding appeal to popular consciousnesses and identity, allowing reassertion of commonalities in terms of Punjabi or Bengali identities across borders. As regards the comparative dynamics in the two contexts, one might say that on the European side the initiative over the past 60 years has been with the introduction of new (EU) state forms, leading in turn to a variety of popular reactions in identity terms, affirmative as well as negative, while in the Indian context the initiative has rather been with popular movements of various description, with the state seeking to play a reactive, in principle accommodating, role.

The point of departure in this chapter was the observation that both in Europe and India today, having both been involved in major state formation and state restructuring exercises, there are basic searches for new definitions of collective identity. Though prompted by different stimuli, in both instances the searches involve multi-stranded dialogues in which state policies and hegemonic projections, mobilization of cultural and religious sentiments, articulations of popular identities and autonomy, and academic analysis and debate provide key inputs. In both cases a major question concerns the relations between secularism and cultural identity. India as presently constituted has essentially represented a secular institutional framework overlaying considerable cultural diversity – its core being formed by the colonial legacy and subsequently given a new thrust and rationale through new conceptions of national unity and planning during the Nehru era. At the present juncture India has reached a point where according to some of its observers its national institutional framework no longer appears as self-evident a given as it was during the earlier post-colonial years, and where, it is suggested, it needs to redefine and come to terms with its 'Indian-ness'. Similarly, the emergent European political framework essentially started from a secular framework, with notable primacy being given to notions and instruments for market homogeneity and planning. This process has extended over several decades and Europe has now reached a stage where its common institutions in and of themselves are believed to be insufficient to give it meaning and identity. Thus, it has likewise become engaged in a process of re-examining, defining and accommodating its 'European-ness'; hence a parallel search for cultural 'roots', Christianity, Renaissance, Enlightenment, the welfare state, or whatever.

These searches for and articulations of identity formation are both internally and externally oriented. Moreover, there is an important connection between them: any externally oriented or induced nationalist, proto-nationalist, or regional superpower assertion of distinctiveness can become the point of reference for internal self-definition (and vice versa). This implicitly or explicitly emphasizes distinction and difference from others, and initiates new interactions with identity articulations from regionally or culturally defined subaltern groups. It is common for centres of power and dominant strata to attempt to enhance their claims to hegemony through such searches for an internally and externally recognized identity. In Europe, this encourages an identification and special emphasis on 'common' roots which can help gloss over centuries of differences and violent conflict between religions (mainly between different branches of Christianity) and nationalities. The search will necessarily concentrate on additional, overarching layers of cultural identity, though with the possible inclusion of a seemingly liberal note of reference to pluralism. While such formulae are meant to provide a basis for accommodating cultural differences within an integrated Europe, the recent upsurge of nationalist sentiments in various parts of Europe tends to question the longer term feasibility of these projections. At the same time, it is increasingly evident that this wave of nationalist and regionalist 'pluralism' stands at variance with a diametrically different notion of 'cultural pluralism', that is, of accommodation and integration of large non-European immigrant populations. Most Western European countries have become multicultural in recent decades due to large-scale immigration from Africa, Asia and the Caribbean. Tension between these two different notions of multiculturalism is likely to remain a significant feature of socio-political processes in Europe during the next few decades.

In India, the secular framework is under pressure from divergent ethno-regional and religious elements, some quite chauvinistic, others representing reassertions of autonomy and identity. A good deal of this pressure has been unleashed as a result of the secular state's own manipulative encouragement and interference in communal competitiveness at earlier intervals (Kothari 1988b: Ch. 12). The question, however, is also one of the relative weight of the tendencies concerned: has the state's handling of these issues under previous governments been a *cause* or a *symptom* of the decline of the secular institutional legacy? In the latter case, how much room will there be under new governments for an eventual redefinition of the institutional legacy 'from within'? State identity, in the end, is either the expression of the primacy of dominant forces, or may rest on a relatively fragile consensus between rival forces agreed on having a neutral ground. But the central state in India in recent times has been increasingly on the defensive in these respects, and for some years has in fact been based on a coalition of the Hindutva-supported BJP with some regional parties. If, during earlier periods, the secular and 'relatively autonomous' grid in India was itself relatively dominant in relation to the various nationalities and communal groups, with the grid acquiring a more instrumental linking position between contending dominant forces, its scope and capacity in leading the task of redefining India's identity and destiny has accordingly been reduced. The initiative has instead begun to shift to other quarters and the grid may be pushed involuntarily into having to cope with Hinduization of one version or another, with consequent strains on other religious communities.

While the emerging European state framework over the past decades has by and large been in its ascendancy in its position of relative power and identity formation vis-à-vis the national states, India's secular state system in contrast appears to have been on the defensive vis-à-vis the assertion of subaltern identities. Both tendencies, however, may lead towards the formulation of more narrowly defined singular identities in the years ahead. As argued earlier, such developments are likely to be reinforced by the increasingly pronounced role as regional superpowers which India and Europe are likely to play in the context of ongoing globalization. In the current regional and global context, each of the main centres of power continuously receive impulses to try and manifest themselves as singular entities, with corresponding all-embracing identities. Although such identities can hardly replace all existing regional, national or communal identifications, conceivably such shifts could have implications in terms of the relative inclusion and exclusion of different population segments, and in the end may put some of them under pressure.

One factor likely to have an impact on the outcome of the two contrasting trajectories concerns the extent of commitment and coherence of the respective ruling elites. At the European end, anything approaching a European political class distinct from national ruling groups has not yet crystallized, though it may conceivably emerge in future. A basic consensus and common outlook on strategy among leading categories from the various member-states, as had been at the basis of the European Union's initial success (Haas 1967), would be essential for the enlarged project to remain sustainable. The possibility of such a 'class' actually coming into existence may now partly depend on whether the European Union's market homogenization policies tend to induce any such common interests and outlooks, and also on whether or not stronger unity of action by various institutional interests behind the European Union will be prompted in the context of global power rivalries. Given the diverse interests of the states that have joined the European Union so far (plus the ones still expected to join), however, one may have to count as well on the possibility that national interests may come to play an increasingly important role in EU deliberations and strategies, thus detracting from rather than adding to emerging commonalities.

On the Indian end it appears that a political class with broadly shared perspectives, which was once characteristic for India's politics and development strategies, has been receding in recent decades. The relatively cohesive political class which had emerged in the nationalist struggle, though originating from diverse backgrounds, during the first few decades of independence clearly held sway over basic strategies of the Indian state. However, it appears it has been insufficiently capable of maintaining a common all-India outlook while at the same time nurturing a meaningful rapport with India's heterogeneous cultural traditions and dynamics. Subjected to the forces of fragmentation that have been increasingly marking Indian politics, this stratum has had to accommodate more partial, regional and communal representations at the centre, opening up an era with enhanced internal squabbles about the distribution of political goods. Also, heightening confrontations between religiously inspired groups and the keepers of the secular state have not been conducive towards maintaining a broadly shared consensus and interest at strategic policy-making levels.

Thus, there are significant variations in the kinds of factors at play with regard to the processes of state and identity formation in India and

Europe. Nonetheless, at surface level, debates in India and in Europe are not so dissimilar: notions of India, Indian identity and 'Indian-ness' are continuously being subjected to scrutiny and redefinition (and sometimes rejection), although from quite a different starting point than in Europe. Significantly, the question still often asked in Europe is what *should be* the basis of its cultural identity, or of 'European-ness', while in India the question seems to be what *is* the basis of Indian identity. But while the search for identity and definition of European-ness and Indian-ness may raise questions and concerns about its possible direction, the impetus towards such searches must be accepted as a logical corollary to processes of state formation and regeneration. It is important therefore to question what meaning is given to this search in both cases, and to keep an eye on who is defining it: *what* Europe and India may emerge, and *whose* Europe and India? Actually Europe and India's longer-term future might best be served if these searches would *not* come to any early closure but were to remain open-ended and retain a fair degree of movement and tension between different conceptions. As identities and identity symbols are essentially constructed and manipulated, it is important to understand and identify the forces at play in formulating and manipulating identities. A critical intellectual vigilance to safeguard basic democratic values, room for pluralism and a sense of cultural empathy is then a particularly essential input in these processes of regeneration and redefinition.

These intellectual inputs can be more effective if care is taken to avoid some false dichotomies which may arise. There are two such dichotomies which should be taken note of in particular. The first is a construed opposition between secularism and cultural authenticity in which secularism, understood as a kind of a-cultural or anti-cultural force, is accused of depriving popular groups of their basic expression of cultural identity, as often happens in India today. Secularism, if understood as providing room for cultural pluralism, does not do this; rather it represents a precondition for the expression and co-existence of cultural identities (Mohanty 1989: 1219–1220, Oomen 2004, Sen 2002). Second, a dichotomy which basically appears to have lost its fruitfulness and relevance is the Westernization versus indigenous culture construct, associating modernizing technological forces with the West and the recipient victims, per definition, with the East. This posed dichotomy appears less and less valid not only because so much of today's technological innovativeness and change originates from East Asia, but also because the European West itself is facing similar and parallel confrontations between technological modernizing pressures and the defence of cultural specificities. It is important to recognize the increasingly common issues at stake in this respect in both 'the East' and 'the West', arising in both contexts from the impacts of processes of technological change occurring on a global scale. Recognizing these commonalities is an essential step towards an adequate engagement with basic questions, and may help avoid getting involved in the wrong debate.

8
When is a State a State?
Exploring Puntland, Somalia

Introduction

As previous chapters have highlighted, with the pervasive incidence of African state crisis the number of states that in recent decades have been subject to severe internal conflict is impressive and sobering at once. Uganda, Somalia, Mozambique, Angola, DR Congo, Sierra Leone, Liberia, Ivory Coast, Rwanda, Burundi, Sudan, Ethiopia and Eritrea have all hit international headlines in this respect at one time or the other, yet they basically represent the most striking examples of what at times seemed to have become a continent-wide phenomenon of sorts. Unsurprisingly, academic as well as more popular accounts have thus often sketched near-apocalyptic pictures of the continent's political trajectory and lack of sustainable perspectives, some perhaps overly alarmist, others less so while nonetheless sharing a general sense of concern. Yet, even here there are reasons for qualification. For one thing, while most of these countries have been through, or are still in crisis, it is important to note that they appear to be located at very different points within the respective spirals of conflict, confrontation and recovery they are traversing. Whereas countries like DR Congo and Sudan are still in deep crisis, Uganda and Mozambique at the present time at least appear to have passed that stage and for some years have shown appreciable rehabilitation on various fronts. Relapses remain possible, though. Other cases, like Burundi or Ethiopia may yet get drawn into deepening crisis due to internal conflicts that have essentially remained unresolved.

If such temporal dimensions already call for differentiation when surveying the African political landscape, the range of issues associated with state crises also deserves closer attention. Key words that have come into vogue to describe African crisis situations include state failure and collapse, fragmentation, disintegration, criminalization, warlordism, ethnocide, genocide and a whole range of others. Insofar as each of these terms tends to point to different kinds of issues we will need to be attentive to significant variations as to what African state crises may actually entail. Though constituting part of a broader pattern of state malaise, each case has its own distinctive features, following its own fault-lines and potential for specific kinds of strife and solutions. Caution is therefore necessary not to project one-dimensional negative teleologies *à la* Robert Kaplan (1994).

Moreover, not all such processes point in one and the same direction, and not all are necessarily 'negative'. We may also come across upbeat references to matters like grassroots technologies, 'bottom up' administrative structures, resilient informal economies, cultural revival and more to depict the fluctuating conditions on the continent. Significantly in this connection, new, at times unprecedented forms of political engagement may be emerging, in which states can be seen acting like private bodies while private actors may arrogate state-like powers. Gravitation may occur towards non-state processes of politics and power, but also into new formative political processes. State collapse as such may be the end of a long and complex process, but may also mark a basic transformation, opening up a new page. As Eisenstadt reminded us, there is always a 'beyond collapse' (Eisenstadt 1988: 293). Thus, re-constitutive processes may follow patterns of disintegration, and new processes of state formation may be shaping up, possibly quite imperceptibly so, following a state collapse once anticipated as the end of all things.

One premise for this study has thus been that processes of state formation and processes of state decline and collapse thematically belong to a common field, even if in their actual dynamics they will follow opposite tracks. State formation may be followed by state decline, state degeneration and collapse by reconstruction and (re-)formation, and so forth. Within the overall grey zone constituted by these various tendencies, an area which as noted may feature some kind of 'twilight institutions' (Lund 2006), we should thus expect to encounter instances of state formation 'at work' as well as instances of decline, interspersed by prolonged intervals of stalemate and stagnation. In not a few instances novel manifestations of the exercise of power, political violence and political processes have occurred in a kind of semi-public, semi-private, non-state or stateless sphere (Doornbos 1994). At times, this may throw up the question as to whether and when it is appropriate to speak (again) of a 'state' with reference to new political entities emerging from amongst the vestiges of collapsed states, or conversely whether such designations are no longer valid. In turn this may raise further queries as to how we should try to get an understanding of this problematic and what will be the relevant questions to ask.

Taking one concrete example, this chapter explores this question with special reference to Puntland State, a new political entity that has been emerging in the Northeastern part of the former Somali Republic which collapsed in 1991. Indirectly the case may also shed some light on the ongoing attempts to re-establish a Somali state as a whole. As of 1998 Puntland had been taking various steps, constitutional and administrative, towards establishing statehood of its own, even if this was with the proviso that it should be viewed as a provisional building-bloc towards the eventual reconstitution of a united state system in Somalia. Whether or not the latter objective is going to be achieved, in late 2004 Puntland leader Abdullahi Yusuf became elected President of Somalia by a representative assembly meeting in exile in Nairobi, Kenya, and by early 2005 was preparing to set up his government in Somalia itself, the exact place as yet being left undecided. It was evident, however, that he was going to be received in a rather hostile environment, which in turn raised important and as yet unresolved questions about the chances of success of his venture. At the present stage, therefore, while it may be possible to reflect on certain aspects of state formation and statehood with respect to Puntland State, the same can only be done in the most tentative sense with reference to the more inclusive quest for Somali statehood. Still, the main purpose of this discussion is not necessarily to arrive at any final determination of Puntland's (or Somalia's) 'stateness', but rather to grapple with the conceptual apparatus we have available to explore the terrain. Basically this calls for reflection on the question as to 'when a state is a state', and the processes and crises that may give rise to them. In taking this up, this chapter draws largely on processes of policy deliberation and political change which have been taking place within Puntland and the wider Somali context.

Questions about 'stateness': the example of Chad

As a point of departure, a brief shift in focus may be helpful. Chad observer Rob Buijtenhuijs at one point during his career raised the question 'Is Chad still a state?' (Buijtenhuijs 1984). This was at a time when profound internal strife had led to the emergence of two rival centres and spheres of power in that country, each claiming ultimate control over the whole but unable to gain and enforce it. The question was obviously pertinent to Chad at the time, but its significance reached way beyond that specific case as it forced us to revisit our criteria of 'stateness'. Phrased as it first was in the Dutch language ('Is Tsjaad nog een Staat?'), which accords a nearly identical phonetic ring to the two key words, the question's import appeared all the more underscored.

Chad at the time, or rather, the two main contending forces fighting over it, lacked one of Max Weber's basic criteria for statehood – monopoly of control over the means of violence throughout the territory of the state. The two key parties involved were the Southern dominated 'national' government of President Tombalbaye, which in early 1979 had felt forced to evacuate itself to the South of the country, and the Islamic FROLINAT movement of President Goukouni Oueddei and his one-time Minister of Defence Hissein Habré, which dominated the North and took over the capital, N'djamena. Each of these took the position that they represented the rightful government of the country as it remained represented on the international map. For a time each group commanded undisputed power and control within its respective 'home' area, but hardly beyond. In 1980–81 the situation became complicated even further following a split between Goukouni and Habré. For some time this led to large parts of the North being *de facto* administered by Libya on behalf of Goukouni, while Habré maintained himself in power in the East (Buijtenhuijs 1984: 305–306; see also Paul Doornbos 1984: 312–322). Regarding its qualifications for the marks of statehood, therefore, Chad then indeed posed an important theoretical question – did it still constitute a single political entity, or had it fragmented into two or three?

Chad's condition at the time was still fairly exceptional within the African context. The Cold War during the 70s and 80s ensured that most governments then in power received the backing of one of the superpowers in keeping insurgents challenging the regime and the state at bay. State integrity, or its semblance, was thus more easily maintained. At a much later stage, however, it became evident that the break-up of Chad at the time had but constituted an early example of patterns of fragmentation which subsequently would become more common and pervasive on the continent. Naturally, in the wake of these tendencies, questions about the relative resilience or fragility of states, and about the state itself as a conceptual category, would gain increasing relevance.

Buijtenhuijs' initial question has retained its validity over the years. It invites further discussion about the nature of the conceptual borderline area between 'state' and 'statelessness', and the manner in which 'non-state' but 'state-like' political structures may come to function and fluctuate within this sphere, in 'decline' or in 'formation' as the case may be. Among the political formations presently arising in Africa, there are indeed state-like bodies or proto-states with only varying degrees of affinity to Max Weber's criteria for statehood, that is, a common people, territory, and a ruling body enjoying a monopoly over the means of legitimate violence. Also, within this grey area between state and statelessness, which in some sense could be hypothesized as marking a 'final stage of decolonization', fluctuations in both directions may well be anticipated. As a sequel to Buijtenhuijs's query as to whether a configuration such as Chad in 1980 could 'still' be called a state, with regard to other entities the question might therefore be raised whether one can 'already' justifiably speak of a state. One such entity is Puntland.

The Somali context

Three aspects of the Somali context, resulting from the collapse of the former Somali state framework, have broadly set the scene and determined the prospects for state reconstruction in Puntland and other regions. These have been the virtually complete absence of functioning government structures over more than a decade, the unresolved relations among the different parts of the former Somali state, and the legacy of problematic contacts with external agencies, notably UN agencies. In origin these three elements have been closely related, as they all derived from the disintegration of the former Somali state system and the international interventions that followed in its wake. In the searches initiated from various sides since then to get out of the impasse, the difficulty of disentangling these three aspects seemed only to further prolong the Somali crisis and stalemate. Re-establishing governmental structures has been largely treated as contingent upon the re-creation of national unity and reconciliation, and vice versa, while the element of foreign intervention and mediation in retrospect appears to have augmented rather than reduced the levels of complexity involved. For a better understanding of the Somali context and the prospects it offers, therefore, it will be useful to further consider the implications of each of these three aspects (cf. Doornbos and Bryden 1998).

As a background, while it is not possible here to recount the story of the collapse of the Somali state, a brief reflection on how this particular chain of events could have come about will be useful. As may be recalled, at the fall of the regime of Siyaad Barre in 1991, intense competition for the seat of power culminated in full-fledged civil war among several contending factions, which rapidly engulfed the larger part of the country and its various population divisions (Lyons and Samatar 1995). The twofold consequence of this generalized strife was the relatively unique instance of a more or less complete falling apart of the post-colonial political framework into several, largely clan-based, territorial entities, several of them ruled by so-called 'warlords', and the cease of normal government functions within each of these areas. In the Somali case, therefore, both the state as a territorial entity and the state as the functioning apparatus of government effectively ceased to exist. In terms of problem aspects, the international dimension, prompted by humanitarian intervention and by preoccupations as to how to relate to a political–geographical entity that had no agency to speak for it, and thus no voice in a world of states, soon came to be added to the other two. Nonetheless, in juridical terms, the Somali state in the international legal context continued to be upheld. In this perspective it was the government and the government structure that collapsed. That was why in 2001, at one of the earlier attempts to resurrect a Somali state, a Transitional Government installed in Mogadishu could be given a ready acceptance in international (UN) and regional (OAU, IGAD and Arab League) institutions. It soon became clear, however, that it could not live up to its promises to reunite the country and re-establish the state framework.

Collapse of state institutions

Concerning the first aspect of the Somali context, there is a seemingly academic, yet quite pertinent question that has mattered in connection with the collapse of Somalia's state institutions, not least so with an eye on the prospects for rebuilding state structures in Somalia: was it just coincidence that Somalia became the first instance in the post-Cold War era in which the state in both above senses ceased to exist, or was there some 'logic' to it? The question is relevant in the context of discussions on reconstruction, as answers to it may shed some light on the extent of 'fit' with their social basis that state structures must have to be viable.

Basically, when looking at the disintegration of state functions, there seem to be good reasons for arguing that the collapse of state institutions in Somalia was not pure coincidence, but that there was a certain predictability that such a chain of events might occur in Somalia 'first'.[1]

---

[1] The Chad example discussed above was different in that it concerned a split into at least two competing centres of power, each claiming, and claiming to be, 'the state'; Somalia's novelty was that, albeit by default, it henceforth has done without a state for well over a decade.

In contrast to most other countries in Africa, Somalia's experience with modern state formation had been a relatively limited one. By and large, the experience(s) with colonial statehood, notwithstanding the prolonged battles of resistance fought early in the century by Sayyid Mohamed Abdallah Hassan and his Dervish forces vis-à-vis the British, Italian and Ethiopian presence, had been considerably 'lighter' than in many other parts of the continent (Doornbos 1975, Sheik-Ali 1993). Large parts of the country, especially in the North, had for long enjoyed a kind of benign neglect during colonial times, if only to keep the costs of government down. Somalia's 'state formation' in preparation of independence, in 1960, had also been notably short and hasty (Doornbos 1993). Without asserting that colonial and post-colonial state structures had left pre-existing social and economic patterns and processes undisturbed, they by and large seemed to have become ingrained less into the Somali social fabric than had been the case in many other African contexts. This was reinforced by the pastoral nomadic mode of life and organization of a majority of the population. As an institutional body, the modern state apparatus more than elsewhere retained a culturally distinct, if not alien, quality vis-à-vis basic ongoing forms of social organization in Somalia. Thus, especially when during the later phases of Siyaad Barre's regime the latter made increasing use of the repressive powers invested in the highly centralized government, one effect this had was to underscore the sense of separateness and alienation which had continued to exist between the state and society. When eventually the regime was overthrown in 1991, the state structure which, to use Max Weber's phrase once again, had been so much equated with the monopoly over the means of violence, could all the more easily be thrown aside. As of that moment until the present time (2005), Somalia's experience has been that all aspirants to overall leadership have been denied the monopoly over the use of force required for a state to function.[2]

This background is relevant in view of its implications for state (re-)building designs. In the Somali case, having a 'state' historically has been a less self-evident proposition than it has been in many other contexts (Lewis 1980, Laitin and Samatar 1987). In various other situations,

---

[2] Whether new President Abdullahi Yusuf will be able to change that remains to be seen. In March 2005 the debates in the Somali parliament in exile as to where finally the new government was to be set up and whether or not an African Union peacekeeping force should accompany them reportedly ended in a chaotic riot, which does not augur well for tranquillity in the country.

past experience with state structures, at times going back to immemorial times, have often provided a ready-made basis and socio-cultural disposition onto which new political frameworks could be grafted. In contrast, the basic fragility that has characterized state–society relations in the Somali context has continued to cast its shadow over all efforts at state rebuilding. Non-state forms of political interaction and exercise of power which had been characteristic for the pre-colonial context – notably the clan system as a representational construct and certain forms of conflict resolution derived from the pastoralist mode of production – would continue to play important roles albeit in drastically changed settings. Their final significance is a matter of seemingly inexhaustible dialogue and debate: in the wake of Lewis's (1961) analysis many would view clanship as the basic explanatory variable in virtually all processes and conflicts in Somali politics, whereas others would instead point to the limitations of their relevance in appreciating the socio-economic and political conditions and issues of the early twenty-first century. In turn, this could lead to the paradox that 'traditional' institutions could become regarded as a key part of the solutions to the Somali predicament, and at the same time as one of the major obstacles to overcoming present-day problems. By and large, however, the fact that most Somalis over the past 15 years or so have somehow managed to do without state structures, appears to underscore a relative lack of self-evidence to the notion of statehood in the Somali context.

This is not to suggest that Somalis of many walks of life would not recognize a need for governmental functions of various kinds. On the contrary, the demand for these, as articulated at not a few occasions, at times has seemed surprisingly strong (Doornbos and Bryden 1998, Heinrich 1997, Höhne 2004). There is ample 'grassroots' recognition, for example, that traders need some minimum of regulation: urban-building activities, a basic ground-plan, social service provision, some overall co-ordination and so on. Other common state functions 'missed' by Somalis in the context of 'statelessness' have been the issuance of recognized travel documents, the establishment and regulation of financial institutions, a framework for international investment, protection of their coastal waters, and access to bilateral and international assistance. In various other regards, however, including international communication and trade, some schooling and health facilities, the Somalis appear to have done reasonably well over the past years without the benefit of state structures. Phone and internet services are surprisingly cheap and in recent years there has been a booming unofficial export and import trade (Little 2003). One implication of Somalia's enduring 'statelessness' and its significant historical precedents, however, is that renewed efforts at state reconstruction are likely again to encounter formidable obstacles, and may only succeed on the basis of extraordinary patience and sensitivity to local needs and preoccupations.

One key question in this connection is whether modern administrative and government structures can be devised which are consistent with ongoing social divisions, particularly in clan and kinship terms, and at the same time relevant to the occupational pursuits of the large numbers of Somalis engaged in a pastoral mode of existence. This is not to suggest that they must be *based* on kinship structures: though certain strands of Somali opinion might favour such an alternative, for many purposes and interests this would seem to be too restrictive. The search, however, may need to be for the kind of institutions that could coexist with clan-based organization and develop fruitful synergies with it, without seeking either to replace it or becoming fully absorbed by it. In fact, this represents a basic challenge that the Somali context poses to contemporary modes of thinking about institutional alternatives.

Fragmentation of the Somali state

The second dimension of the Somali state's disintegration concerned its falling apart into a number of largely clan-based entities, each with its own militia. In the Northeast, conditions of relative stability had prevailed over a prolonged period, until this tranquillity was ruptured by new internal strife that broke out in 2001. In other parts of the former Somalia, especially the central areas, ongoing hostility and violence between various clan-based factions and intra-sub-clan groups fighting for control for long remained recurrent features.

Indirectly, the wider picture of Somalia's fragmentation continued to have important effects for the state of affairs and prospects for rebuilding in the Northeast. Paradoxically, the collapse of the Somali state in 1991 had been triggered by the fierce competition for state power which had followed the demise of the previous regime. Different factions, led by warlords that had earlier joined forces in the struggle to overthrow the Siyaad Barre regime, now collided amongst themselves over the question of control over the state. This internal war first raged for several years, and if anything seemed aggravated by the UNOSOM intervention from 1992 till 1995, before it subsided to some extent and began to allow for a whole series of regional initiatives at mediation and reconciliation. Led successively by Kenya, Ethiopia, Egypt, Djibouti and then again Kenya, these initiatives have all been basically oriented towards trying to re-establish a united Somali state of one kind or another. The differences between these various departures were largely determined by the kind of leadership profiles and degree of centralization favoured by the mediating third parties involved. Despite the pervasive traumas incurred during the internal strife, the idea of a shared Somali identity that all the various clan-based groups would have in common, for a long time nurtured feelings among most groups that national reconcilation efforts should be given a chance. Only the Isaaq and Gadabursi in the Northwest, who at the fall of the Barre regime re-established (ex-British) Somaliland in the light of their frustrating experience with its unification with the formerly Italian Somalia that had been worked out at independence, stayed away from most talks convened to try and re-establish a united Somalia. That position, however, has caused Somaliland to become treated as a scapegoat by the other regions of the former Somali Republic for their own failure to reunite amongst themselves, being repeatedly blamed for blocking the re-integration of the rest of the former union after it had stepped out of that to revert to its own 'separate' status.

In the course of the years following the 1991 collapse, this picture began to change. As the prospects of internationally led reconciliation succeeding seemed to remain as dim as ever, in various parts of the former republic, most notably in the Northeast and later also in the Southwest, conviction grew that there would be no point in waiting for any general re-unification to come about. Instead, it was argued, that time may have come to put one's own house in order first, and to see about the relations with the rest of the former state at a later stage.

Failed interventions

The third relevant aspect of the Somali context has been that of the legacy of problematic relations with international organizations and the latter's limited presence in Somalia. A major legacy of misgivings and distrust dates from the days of the US-led UNOSOM operation. At that interval, ill-conceived attempts at humanitarian intervention in a situation of severe man-made famine caused international troops themselves to get hopelessly entangled into the webs of internal conflicts, in the end becoming a prime object of hatred and derision. Given the resulting heightened risk factors, international agencies such as UNDP, UNHCR, UNICEF, WFP, FAO, EU, ICRC and international NGOs have since then been running their operations largely from Nairobi, keeping only a few support staff in some of the main towns like Boosaaso and Kismayo.

Within the international community at large, the UNOSOM intervention was defended by the humanitarian argument that the UN system had a right if not an obligation to intervene in crisis situations in individual countries in the absence of a government capable of exercising sovereignty. At the time, however, the Somali crisis and its repercussions represented quite a novel situation in international law and international relations. As a matter of fact, international jurists might have had difficulty citing solid legal grounds for any such right to intervene, which involved attempts to put substitute government functions in place (Yannis 2002). Instead, the UN intervention could possibly better be viewed as the international system's 'natural' reflex to the emergence of blank spaces on the global political map – a prospect which many in the system would have difficulty getting used to. But if at bottom the Somali crisis should be read as one in which the populace had withdrawn the sovereignty it had bestowed upon the government when the latter no longer fulfilled its primary task of providing basic security (Brons 2001), then it would be unlikely that international intervention could constructively provide a substitute 'sovereignty'.

Has Puntland become a state?

Against the background of the lingering stalemate concerning possible re-constitution of the former Somali state framework, in the late 1990s a different idea began to gain ground in a few regions: the expectation that developing political and administrative institutions on a regional basis might be a meaningful alternative. In the Northeast, this position was prompted by a variety of considerations. The three administrative regions making up the Northeast, that is Bari, Nugal and North Mudug, had been sharing relative political tranquillity since 1991, although Mudug for some spell in 1992 had experienced severe clashes between rival clan forces vying for power within the region and its main town, Galkaayo. In the end the latter got subdivided into two clan-based sections, a Daarood-Majeerteen (North Mudug) and a Hawiye-Habar Gedir one, separated by an invisible 'green' line. Demographically, the area as a whole was relatively homogeneous, as most of the population belonged and belongs to the Majeerteen, the dominant Daarood sub-clan within the three regions. In addition, though, the Dulbahante and Warsengeli sub-clans straddling the borders with Somaliland share an over-arching Harti identity with the Majeerteen. Many Majeerteen who used to live in Mogadishu had fled to the Northeast during the serious strife of the early 90s, causing an unprecedented population increase in places like Boosaaso and other towns. Economically, also, there was a basic complementarity among the three regions, with the predominant economic activity consisting of livestock trade focused on the port of Boosaaso for export to the Gulf countries, followed by the production and export of frankincense and fisheries.[3] Incidentally, again, the fact that a majority of the population in the past was engaged in pastoralist activities had important implications – and limitations – for the reach of governance institutions, and may have that again in future. If government structures would be created in which pastoralist communities would only have a marginal role, the resulting state institutions in the long run are unlikely to remain very viable.

Lastly, it was felt and argued in the late 1990s that the regions of Bari, Nugal and North Mudug since 1991 had gained some positive experience in working together, generally under the political patronage of the Somali Salvation Democratic Front (SSDF), the main militia force within the Northeast. The SSDF, though divided into two major political wings, had come to play a unifying role especially after 1992, when its forces ousted a radical Islamist group which had made a short-lived attempt to assert its control over the strategic port of Boosaaso and gain power over the wider region. As of that time the SSDF had provided an 'un-official' political umbrella for various collaborative contacts between the three Northeastern regions. Basically the conclusion emerging from this by 1998 was that the Northeast fulfilled the main pre-conditions for creating its own state framework, though one that could form a component block of a future reunited Somalia. A name for it, with appropriate historical antecedents, was readily conceived: Puntland (Kitchen 1993).

As a prelude to state formation processes specific to Puntland, deliberations on priorities for reconstruction and development had been taking place for some time in different parts of the Northeast at the initiative of the Life and Peace Institute (Uppsala) and the UNRISD *War-torn Societies Project* (Geneva) (Doornbos and Bryden 1998, Heinrich 1997). The aim of these projects had been to assist community representatives to identify policy priorities for social, economic and political reconstruction and rehabilitation. The lively discussions this entailed were significant in quite a fundamental respect. In the situation of 'statelessness' in which the various regions found themselves, questions of a 'what first' order naturally commanded great attention. When starting from scratch

---

[3] In recent years, however, the embargo on Somali livestock for alleged Rift Valley Fever infection by Gulf countries has had devastating effects on Puntland's economy and that of Somalia in general.

towards state reconstruction, where does one begin? With basic security first, to establish a framework for social and economic development, or with key developmental activities first, from which security might emanate indirectly? But then, how should this security be understood: as human security in terms of personal and collective well-being and reciprocal care, as some of the few women representatives tried to put forward? Or alternatively as physical security, to be given concrete expression through the recruitment of police forces to handle issues of law and order? But again how can security be established and maintained if there is not first an agreed upon legal framework and a body of legal instruments to work from? And, last but not least, while proper security forces and other administrative cadres will need to be paid from some local tax basis as yet to be established, how can such taxation capacity be installed without having instruments of law and order in place? These and other related questions are of course of profound philosophical import, though they usually remain confined to the virtual realities of textbook discussion. It is extremely rare to find them debated in concrete non-state situations. It is even more striking to witness this happening with the keen sense of awareness of their implications given the uncertainties and choices people were facing, as was the case in Northeast Somalia around 1998 (Doornbos and Bryden 1998).

Nonetheless, an important qualifier that should be noted is that the 'stateless' condition against the background of which these deliberations took place was one which was not unknown in the Somali region. Historically, statelessness had meant that other institutions (clans and lineages as well as accepted procedures for the reconciliation of conflicts) performed tasks that elsewhere would be associated with political processes in or around 'government' and 'the state'. Absence of state structures in such situations thus is not necessarily as dramatic as would be the case in contexts that had known well-established state institutions, nor would the re-introduction of state structures necessarily signal unqualified positive development here.

In 1998, one important factor enhancing interest in the deliberations taking place in what was then to become Puntland, emanated from significant changes taking place within the wider political context of the Northeast. As mentioned, local outlooks on political rebuilding strategies had begun to shift away from the idea that national reconciliation should be attained first and should then determine the shape of subsidiary institutional arrangements. Instead, in the light of the frustrations with the proceedings of the Sodere Somali peace process hosted by Ethiopia in Sodere from late 1996 till late 1997 and the subsequent

Egyptian-led reconciliation strategy in Cairo from late 1997 until early 1998, a conviction grew that the Northeast should put its own house in order first. Thus, in July 1998, after almost three months of deliberations, a community conference of the three regions of Northeast Somalia, together with some representatives from the neighbouring areas of Sanaag and Sool in Somaliland, declared the formation of a Puntland State as a sub-unit of a future federal or con-federal Somalia. A Constitution was adopted and a president and prime minister were appointed, though not without some initial hurdles as to who should be appointed to which post. As of that moment, Puntland State was a fact.

Despite strong initial popular support, however, the new government of Puntland's President Abdullahi Yusuf, the erstwhile SSDF militia leader, was soon facing internal opposition, especially after he decided to choose his own interpretation of the provisions for replacement rather than abide by the new constitutional arrangements or the rulings of the High Court trying to enforce these. His term expired in 2001 and he was voted out of office in line with Puntland's constitutional procedures. Abdullahi Yusuf himself was determined to stay on, however, claiming he was still the legitimate president, and accusing his opponents led by Jama Ali Jama of being supporters of Usuman bin Laden (Dorward 2003). His removal from office in June–July 2001 allegedly was effected with support from the fledgling transitional government that had arrived in Mogadishu, but he quickly made a comeback and recaptured power with the support of militias loyal to him as well as with Ethiopian and American backing. The Ethiopians sent troops and the Americans at the time blockaded Bosaaso in the name of preventing *Al Qaida* from securing a base in Somalia. As of that moment and until early 2003, internal strife and repeated massive violence with numerous casualties once again became characteristic for Puntland politics, somehow suggesting a sardonic correlation between the resurrection of formal government institutions and the resumption of struggles for power. In early 2003, a peace initiative led by the traditional leader Boqor Buurmadow brought the conflict between Abdullahi Yusuf and his main opponent Gen. Adde Muuse, who had continued the struggle after Jama Ali Jama had fled, to an end. Adde Muuse and his troops were partly incorporated into Puntland's military and political set-up, to the point that Adde Muuse even became the new Puntland president in January 2005. Nevertheless, political tensions about power sharing continued to prevail (Markus Höhne, personal communication).

Consistent with Puntland's 'building block' philosophy about state re-building in Somalia as a whole, the Puntland leadership participated in continued discussions between various constituent groups convened under international sponsorship in Nairobi. In 2004 a parliament was thus formed out of the various clan and regional constituencies represented and subsequently a president was elected by the parliament, who in turn was called upon to appoint a prime minister and a new cabinet. Surprising perhaps to observers not fully familiar with the intricacies of Somali politics, it was Col Abdullahi Yusuf who emerged as the winning candidate for the presidency. Evidently the sense of the election had been to opt for a strong man both vis-à-vis rival clan-based groups within Somalia and in confrontation with the Somaliland leadership which had persisted in its re-assertion of its independence. Also, it was with Somaliland that competing claims over the jurisdiction of the areas of Sanaag and Sool would still have to be sorted out, which thus aggravated the tense situation in which a resurrected Somali government would need to start its activities.

Is Puntland a state?: some preliminary observations

Puntland State has a population, a territory, and a constitutional–political framework theoretically holding a monopoly over the means of violence, which at its initiation seemed to enjoy the support of a majority of the population. It has also begun to develop a taxation capacity through the levies it raises from Boosaaso port. Nonetheless, some qualifications must be made with respect to each of these Weberian criteria for statehood. First, the renewed internal strife over the Puntland Presidency between Abdullahi Yusuf and his opponents could hardly be called conducive towards strengthening that political framework's legitimacy. Still, it does not necessarily follow that it will instead detract from it. Popular support no doubt 'helps', but (too) many state systems in history have been able to do without it. In the vein of the distinctions once formulated by Duverger (1963), people in Puntland conceivably might want to distinguish between the legitimacy of the political framework and that of the power-holders of the day, thus bestowing legitimacy to the framework but not to its incumbents, for example. On the other hand, it must be recognized that Puntland State since its inception has not had much time to prove and establish itself as a distinct political–juridical entity. Some local onlookers therefore may not make too much difference between the 'state' and its ruler (or even the SSDF). In the end, the question this boiled down to was whether Puntland State would be able to survive Col Abdullahi Yusuf's clinging on to power. A serious challenge to the survival of the idea of Puntland as regional state had indeed become the greed for power and lack of respect for the constitution as demonstrated by the colonel. Whether his subsequent election as President of Somalia has left his Puntland constituency with a stronger sense of trust in its own statehood remains to be seen.

As for the related Weberian criterion of Puntland State's monopoly over the means of violence, with Kalashnikovs available in virtually every household this seemed to be a rather theoretical proposition to begin with. The question in part hinged on the extent to which the government would retain a final say about the conditions under which these guns would be used. Given the re-emergence of internal violence and the fresh rifts within the political–constitutional order, it was in any case less certain that Puntland would still be able pass this particular test of statehood.

Prudent observers might thus have called for more time for Puntland to demonstrate its viability as a state in a number of respects before passing any final judgement. In contrast to the former Somali republic, which during its latter days no longer commanded the tacit acceptance for the exercise of popularly based sovereignty from a majority of its people, Puntland when it started seemed to have stronger cards to present itself as a legitimate alternative in this regard (Brons 2001). In the light of the renewed internal strife following the creation of Puntland State, for many people the question presumably became whether their identification with the idea of a Puntland state remained strong enough to survive their misgivings over the misuse of power.

With respect to the territorial dimension, the Puntland leadership did not make its case easier by claiming that parts of neighbouring Somaliland's territory – the districts of Sanaag and Sool inhabited by the Dulbahante and Warsangeli sub-clans – should be integrated with theirs. Puntland's claims over the areas of Sanaag and Sool have been seriously challenged by neighbouring Somaliland. The clash here is between taking *clan membership* as a basis for state formation, which has been Puntland's position, as opposed to recognizing *ex-colonial boundaries* as a point of departure, which has been Somaliland's line, and its *raison d'être*. Prevailing constitutionalist opinion is most unlikely to be ready for a shift from the latter to the former principle, however. While the candidature of both for getting recognition as a state – in Puntland's case 'internal' and for Somaliland 'external' – remain delicate issues, internationally it will not be easy to find a receptive ear for Puntland's position regarding the criteria for state boundaries. But then, unlike for Somaliland, international recognition has not been Puntland's priority. Instead, Puntland's push for recognition of its claims on Sanaag and

Sool may be interpreted as being motivated to sabotage Somaliland's attempts to go independent (Höhne 2004). One must expect Col Abdullahi Yusuf in his new role as Somali president to remain quite adamant on this particular position, and to continue to oppose Somaliland's strivings towards separate independent statehood within the ex-colonial boundaries. It is significant that he has now come into the position of getting the backing of the international community for his stand. For Somaliland, however, to accept the principle of clan-based authority would mean negating its very (claim to) existence as an ex-colonial state, even though in terms of clan population it happens to be largely Isaaq-dominated.

In the light of the stalemate, neither of these two positions allows room for a third and alternative option, namely to find out, by plebiscite or otherwise, what the people in question would want. Given the clan-based regionalization that occurred in the troubled Somali context of the 1990s, it is quite conceivable that a good number of people of Sanaag and Sool would now opt for joining Puntland (as their elders already did in 1998) out of fear of becoming a minority within Isaaq-dominated Somaliland (Höhne 2004). Significantly, in the multi-party elections held in Somaliland in April 2003, no voting took place in three districts of Sanaag and Sool 'for reasons of security' (De Wit and Rip 2003). For some time after 2000, following the installation of an earlier transitional government in Mogadishu and the threat this appeared to entail to both Puntland and Somaliland, the latter two had first seemed inclined to put their mutual differences over Sanaag and Sool on ice. Since then, however, there has been at least one occasion of violent strife over the matter between Somaliland and Puntland armed forces. Today, the issue remains as explosive as the respective 'state-building' premises are different, adding a highly unstable element to an already complex situation.

For more than one reason, therefore, whether Puntland is 'already' – or 'still' – a state is likely to remain a matter of debate for some time to come. By itself that could be said to reflect its embryonic condition. But it may be interesting to look at this issue from yet another angle, focused on a different dimension of state-building. First, it is noteworthy how much the question of the future of Sanaag and Sool, and indirectly the question of the relationships between Somaliland, Puntland and Somalia, appear to hinge on the primacy accorded to political identity in the context of state formation in this case. Unlike various other situations, where state building per se took precedence and reorientations of political identity might (or might not) follow, identity is here the unmistakable starting point for state building designs. By the same token, however, this may mask another difference. The kind of situations in which state building efforts come first, identity second, so to speak, are likely to reveal relatively more powerful cohorts of state builders being in command than is the case here. In contrast, the sensitivity presently displayed by the various parties concerned for the position of Sanaag and Sool rather seems reflective of a relative weakness and lack of capacity to 'act' of the various incipient state bodies representative for the different polities in the Northeast of the former Somalia. Nonetheless, the question causes a continuing stalemate and is likely to remain a sensitive point in the ongoing saga of political turmoil in the Somali region.

Just like in respect of whether Chad was 'still' a state in 1981, therefore, though for different reasons, whether Puntland is 'already' a state, or the 'stateness' of Puntland, cannot be unequivocally determined, depending as it does on the criteria and perspective with which the question is approached, and by whom. Conceivably, for example, many people in Puntland may still argue that they have a state of their own, notwithstanding the serious challenges from within to which it has been subject in recent years. Others within the former Somalia, however, might in any case deny Puntlanders the right to go it alone, or would not consider Puntland State to possess the legitimacy prerequisite for recognition as a state of whatever kind. Though only a theoretical issue at the moment, there is in any case strong a priori support for the latter position within the international system, which tends to be extremely reluctant to recognize any state boundaries except the 'given' ones. Somaliland's continued lack of international recognition, notwithstanding its much stronger historical credentials, is a significant signal in this regard. But then, it is by no means assured that the new efforts towards Somali reunification will succeed. If they fail, then Puntland once again may have to confront its future alone.

In conclusion: assessing 'stateness'

How would Max Weber have assessed Puntland's 'stateness'? The criteria by which we continue to judge this question in the twenty-first century are essentially the ones that Weber drew up about a century ago, which it should be remembered was a period that seemed particularly pre-occupied with hierarchy, territorial integrity and boundaries. Weber's criteria for 'stateness' then were essentially formal and analytical-descriptive. As they have stood the test of time, they have often been accorded a status of prescriptive evaluative yardsticks in contexts that are vastly different from nineteenth-century Europe. However, with Weber's unquestioned imagination and power of analysis, it seems plausible to presume that today he might have laid much greater stress on aspects of functionality of various kinds that political entities have (or have not) within their socio-political contexts. Notably, a contemporary criterion and test as to whether a political entity would qualify to be called a 'state' might stress the number, variety and weight of its policy decisions regulating different spheres of public activity, and the extent to which it appears in overall control over the management of resource conflicts within its domain. With some distance such an approach would appear akin to the criteria Karl Deutsch once proposed for analysing governments as communication and decision-making centres (Deutsch 1966).[4] In such a perspective, 'stateness' could primarily be understood as referring to the extent to which the state institutions concerned are effectively engaged in policy-making and decision-making concerning processes of social and economic management. Whether, based on that criterion, Puntland would pass the test of 'stateness' again would require closer examination and cannot be assumed a priori. In turn this would call for an adequate methodology, which at the present time is lacking. Nonetheless, it would be that kind of examination which might tell us whether, or to what extent, a particular politico-institutional entity is demonstrating or acquiring substantive functional as opposed to purely formal features of a state. Theoretically, 'stateness' in this regard can leave aside the question of ultimate sovereignty, or juxtapose it with other criteria, which in the case of Puntland is relevant as its declared intention has been to construct a state as a provisional building-block towards future Somali re-unification. In principle this could highlight the possible paradox of a central Somali state invested with sovereignty while lacking stateness in substantive terms, together with a Puntland state lacking sovereignty but demonstrating an appreciable measure of stateness in functional and substantive terms.

A further potentially useful aspect of such a way of assessing 'stateness' would be that in principle it is applicable in reversible situations, and for analysing trade-offs between processes of state ascendancy and decline. It has often been observed, for example, that as the European Union

---

[4] Interestingly, Deutsch warned that a communication overload or a decision overload could conceivably lead to the breakdown of states and governments (Deutsch 1996: 162), a problem Puntland or various other African state systems are unlikely to face.

grows in terms of the weight of decision-making impacting on social and economic processes throughout the member countries, the role and influence of individual member-state governments tends to recede. Processes of (expanding) state formation may thus go together with, and be reflected in, parallel processes of state shrinking or relative decline at another level. Likewise, an interesting contrast could become applicable in regard to the respective Puntland and Somali contexts: *if* Puntland were to maintain a relative significance in terms of the extent of public policy-making taking place within its domain, then the weight of the Somali 'state' context might accordingly remain reduced, and vice versa. Clearly, this is now only a tentative theoretical proposition. But trying to apply it may help identify whether we can talk of an emerging state, or 'stateness', in given situations.

Adding such a dimension to other, more familiar yardsticks might further illuminate the patterns and tendencies concerned. Notably, in conceptualizing the state, and 'stateness', Max Weber conceivably might have recognized that in Africa and other regions outside Europe, territoriality today should be treated less categorically and 'fixed', at times appearing to peter out on the margins, than was the case in Europe during his time. Today's realities include frequent instances of increased fluidity in these respects, even though international law as yet has few if any ways of accommodating this diversity. Thinking in terms of 'core states', that is, state systems with a relatively enduring presence in the centre of their juridical–political domain but with only a nominal 'presence' in their periphery, may better match such different realities and add a realistic complement to our ways of conceptualizing the state.

In conclusion, the question as to whether Puntland can presently be labelled a state may well remain of some continuing theoretical interest. But enquiring into its status, and that of comparable entities elsewhere, will be more illuminating if the analysis goes beyond satisfying formal taxonomic curiosities and will open windows towards a better understanding of formative processes taking place in Africa and other regions. Basically, therefore, the question whether and when a state is a state might best be complemented, and operationalized, by asking how we can recognize degrees of 'stateness', and trying to determine the relevant dynamics in that respect.

9
Conclusions: Whither the State?

The previous chapters have highlighted current inroads of global forces on the state, paying particular attention to the processes of state restructuring and collapse affecting countries in the South. Related to the discussion about 'failed' or 'failing' states, though departing from a reverse perspective, the focus has been on how globalization impacts on states and state structures in the South, and on the latter's varying capacities to maintain themselves amidst new challenges and uncertainties. In thus looking at globalization, state restructuring and collapse from a unified perspective, the concern in this study has been to explore a field of political transformation and analysis which appears of crucial importance to an understanding of the contemporary context.

One perception underlying the study has been that processes of state formation, state decline and state restructuring represent a never-ending continuum, even though the scale at which this is happening has markedly varied over time. Historically, in many instances the dynamics concerned have manifested themselves indirectly, in the aftermath of drastic interventions like wars and other conflicts or through numerous incremental modifications prompted by longer-term social and economic transformations. State formation in some cases may thus be discovered only in retrospect and long after it has taken effect. Similarly, a spiral of state decline culminating in state collapse may not be visible until after the fact. And patterns of state restructuring at times may need to be identified through close observation of numerous partial revisions and adjustments of policy and state frameworks over some period of time.

This study has brought together various key aspects of these recurrent processes, with a focus on the dynamics of conflict and disintegration, the emergence of state and non-state entities, and the interplay between identity and power in the past and present. Main themes addressed have been the political and institutional repercussions of globalization, patterns of externally guided state formation and state restructuring, the role of the 'good governance' discourse, and trajectories of state collapse and re-starts. Within this context attention has also been devoted to the politics of statelessness, to manifestations of identity and power, and of ethnic conflict triggered or fanned by these impacts.

The study has sought to place current trends within a broader historical perspective, starting out with an attempt to link a renewed intellectual curiosity in the conditions of early state formation to growing concerns about the prospects of contemporary war-torn societies and the collapse of state systems. Common to such situations, which are vastly different in time and space, are questions concerning the political relevance of cultural identities, particularly in the case of states that are not nations and of nations that are not states. Besides, there appear to be instances, in the past as well as present, of recurrent emulation patterns and domino effects in state formation as well as in disintegration processes. 'Pull' as much as 'push' factors may be noted on either end of the state formation–collapse nexus. The larger question thus arising is what parallels, conceptual links or common lessons may be drawn from such contrasted situations. Though final answers can hardly be expected in this regard, the dynamics of state collapse and state resurgence in the contemporary situation appear to underscore fundamental puzzles about the past as well as the future of social and political organization.

Following the introductory discussion on dynamics of state formation and collapse, the study engaged in a further exploration of the contemporary connections between the dynamics of globalization and the changing role and position of the state. Among other things, this discussion touched upon the ongoing debate about the future of the state and the prospects for global civil society and democracy. Special attention was paid to regional variations with respect to the capacity of state systems to withstand or adjust to the forces of globalization, market forces but also donor directives. In the light of this, the changing appreciations of the role of the state have been illustrated further through a look at the fate of the African state, which as of the years of independence first enjoyed the (externally sanctioned) status of 'prime mover' in all development efforts and designs, but later came to be widely regarded as development's major obstacle, relegated to an increasingly marginalized role and existence. The analysis highlighted the exalted expectations that had initially been raised about the potential of African states to act as agents of modernization and development, which were followed by widespread disillusionment with their performance and a wave of international re-appraisals that resulted in the policies of structural adjustment and calls for 'good governance'. African state systems henceforth were subjected to the impacts of a different range of global forces, at times threatening their very continuity and survival. They experienced a drastic 'de-statification' of sorts, leaving several of them exposed to further erosion and disintegration, but also often to re-statification of violence and replication of military structures in civil society. In the light of these transformations the question what has happened to the once prominent notion of the 'relative autonomy of the state' is pertinent. Global forces continue to make pervasive inroads – economic, political and cultural – on the idea of 'state autonomy'. They have also led to significant shifts in the nature and levels of autonomy in various contexts, such as when autonomy is granted to institutional bodies placed outside the regular government structure but with direct authority over certain policy areas and close links with international agencies operating within the same domain. In turn this has reinforced significant transformations taking place within the institutional 'grey area' between the state and non-state spheres. In the light of the shrunken accountability of the national state for numerous concerns within its formal domain, a revisit to the notion of relative state autonomy helps to illuminate some of the key changes that have taken place.

This reappraisal was followed by a discussion and intellectual history of the concept of 'good governance' as a policy metaphor. First designed to offer a normative umbrella for the launching of political conditionalities focused on the restructuring of state systems of aid recipient countries, this was subsequently restyled as a selection principle of aid 'deserving' countries. Of course the 'good governance' discourse, which now already has had its days for well over a decade, has had an enormous spread into numerous fora. Together with the concept's rise in popularity there has been a proliferation of meanings associated with the term 'good governance', some of them quite contrasted, and even contradictory. As a policy metaphor, good governance certainly did not as such advocate the overthrow of entire state systems in order to have them replaced by some different preferred set-up, like what has been happening in Iraq and in a way in Afghanistan. Nonetheless, it has been instrumental in preparing the minds of various actors in the global arena to the idea that the forms, styles and purposes of governance in various Third World states constituted an obstacle to proper liberal–democratic development, and might be considered a suitable target (military or otherwise) for overhaul and reform. Significantly, proponents of 'good governance' usually had an eye mainly for the intrinsic qualities of the governance models they would wish to transplant. They had little or nothing to say or suggest as to how they would propose linking their preferred government mechanisms to existing patterns or to prevailing socio-cultural norms and practices. The latter would characteristically be treated as irrelevant and ignored, in principle to be replaced by modern, robust and neo-liberal, that is, 'market-friendly' institutions. While the present text has obviously not been about Iraq, it has addressed some of the global 'state restructuring' thinking prior to Iraq as implied in the 'good governance' discourse, and may invite further reflection on 'regime change' and its implications in the wake of American interventionism.

Related themes, amply highlighted in the study, have included those of state collapse and the 'propensity for collapse' in the face of global forces impacting on weaker state systems. While the chances of state collapse appear to have been on the increase due to the lessening resilience of state structures and state–society linkages in many cases, instances of state collapse do not necessarily follow single tracks of causation. Instead, what appears called for is a more nuanced scrutiny which can differentiate between factors leading to collapse in specific instances, and a re-consideration, in the light of such scrutiny, of responses and possible external actor involvement. The study thus considered the complex web of conditioning and facilitating factors that may or may not set in motion a chain reaction leading to state collapse, examining the extent to which any emerging patterns can be identified. In this connection, it also looked more closely at the response side to incidences of state collapse, specifically external responses. Whilst external actors, notably the 'donor community', have been trying to better prepare themselves for the eventualities of crises of governance and state collapse in various countries, it remains to be seen to what extent there is a 'fit' between the determinants and dynamics of state collapse and the responses and solutions for restoration which are being offered.

Changing realities of the role of the state have also been reflected in the changing dynamics of identity and the politics of pluralism, which have been taken up with specific reference to the African context as well as through a comparison of Indian and European patterns of state and identity formation. Here as in other discussions of identity one key issue has been whether ethnic identity should be viewed as an autonomous propeller of political action, or whether its manifestations should be understood as reflecting and following conflict and change in other, structural respects. On balance, the present text has come down on the latter side. In Africa at the present time multi-partyism and decentralization are strong currents prompting a new twist to manifestations of ethnic identity and to new forms of interplay between identity and power. Variables of identity and power have also been key to an understanding of the dynamics occurring at a mega scale in India and Europe. Here the processes concerned have differed from each other in several important respects, though several of the issues put forward in the two cases are formulated in remarkably similar ways, such as the concerns among various constituent groups that distinctive cultural identities risk obliteration as a result of global homogenizing forces.

The study finally re-examined the links between state collapse and the resurgence of new state forms, through exploring questions of 'state-ness' with particular reference to Puntland State. This regional state entity has since 1998 emerged from what was the Northeastern Region of the former Somali Republic. It is an interesting case through which to explore the question of when a state can be called a state. Drawing on processes of policy deliberation and political change within Puntland and the wider Somali context, the purpose of the enquiry was not so much to arrive at any final determination of Puntland's (or Somalia's) 'state-ness' – which as yet may best be defined as embryonic. However, it called for grappling with the conceptual apparatus available to explore the terrain, an enquiry which also appears relevant to some other situations in Africa, such as DR Congo, and elsewhere. While noting that with respect to the standard Weberian criteria for statehood the status of Puntland State would raise important qualifications, the study tentatively put forward some alternative ways of evaluating 'state-ness', including assessing the density of public policy decision-making within a state's institutional domain. With so many variables impinging upon the nature, structure and autonomy of the state, we may require different ways of assessing the resilience and robustness of states, that is, their relative degree of 'state-ness', from those used in Weber's time. By and large, conventional formal definitions of the state are of limited usefulness in this regard. Conceivably, if an alternative approach as suggested were applied in some contemporary state contexts, this might bear some surprising results.

Retrospect and prospect

It will have been noted that this study's scope has been rather wide-ranging and has had few anchor-points. The discussion has moved back and forth between instances of ancient state formation and the present, and from European precursors in statehood and crisis to contemporary African and Asian state configurations, while reflecting on the interplay between state power and political identity in widely different contexts. Moreover, several recurrent elements in this discussion, especially the idea of the state itself, have been used to refer to a variety of different incarnations, including entities as contrasted as some micro-political formations on the one hand and the ascendant giant European Union on the other. Basically this relatively loose use of the notion of state has been deliberate, as it would be difficult to discuss transitional configurations from incipient to full-fledged 'modern' states – and back, if applicable – if the entities concerned are expected to have already met the standard Weberian criteria for statehood. Besides, in the relevant literature on early states it is not uncommon to speak of state forms with less than the full set of paraphernalia one takes for granted when referring to well-established states. Still, for most instances the point of departure has been that of a state system of sorts having at its exclusive disposal an institutional apparatus, however embryonic, to help prepare, implement and enforce its policy decisions within a given territory and among a set of identifiable inhabitants.

If a wide-ranging flight over a diverse political and historical landscape has its inherent limitations, it also has its own insights to offer. Elementary as it may appear at first sight, it remains remarkable and fundamentally important that in many situations far apart in terms of history, geography and culture, power-holders keen to lay down and extend their rule have time and again found recourse to basically similar kinds of strategies and organizational techniques to further their objectives. At many different junctures they have displayed reliance on feudal or bureaucratic lines of command (often with a gradual shift from the former to the latter); fostered political loyalty and obedience not just by the use or threat of superior power but by trying to cultivate collective identities, as through language policies and state religions; sought to impose taxation monopolies so as to gain some autonomy of action for their state, and demanded recognition and sovereignty in exchange for providing security. Evidently, humankind has developed only a relatively limited range of basic structural forms and idioms for the maintenance of power, even though their specific manifestations may show an infinite range and variety of different instruments.

For all the resulting variability, the focus in this book nonetheless has been continuously on 'change', specifically on *change of state forms*. Again, however, 'change' in this regard has assumed many different dimensions and directions, such as transition, transformation or various other equivalents that can be found in Roget's *Thesaurus*. Frequent use of terms like 'dynamics' and 'processes', occasionally even 'flux', has further underscored the transformational character of the core subject-matter dealt with. Even as a central characterization, therefore, 'change' needs further elucidation and specification as to what meanings it is supposed to convey in different instances: 'change' as processes of state formation and decline, as transformations from one kind of state to another, as formative processes by way of emulation of state forms, or 'change' in terms of state restructuring at the behest of larger global directives. But it is also these different characterizations which can help us see what contrasting kinds of tracks have been involved in the change of state forms over time, all the way from changes inherent in the dynamics of growth and decline to those predetermined by global actors and designs. An essential qualitative difference that suggests itself in this regard is the one between scenarios of changing state forms from *within*, as in processes of state formation by emulation, and those of *externally* influenced or driven state restructuring, as appear to have become more prevalent in recent times. If this observation is correct, it has a good deal to say about the nature of political organization of the contemporary world.

Evidently, states are not static but subject to continuous change, gaining new roles while losing others. Functions of different states increasingly intertwine within the grey areas of innumerable over-arching institutions and complex treaty relationships, if not within ambitious projects along the lines of the EU model. Thus the contours of where one state begins and ends increasingly lose sharpness, making it more and more difficult to delineate individual states. Conceivably, if in the final analysis constituting a state, or 'state-ness', could be measured on the basis of the amalgam and significance of key decision-making and strategic policy initiatives a state body undertakes, one might well find that some state systems are gaining in 'state-ness' in this respect whereas not a few others are in decline. Conceivably, the European Union as well as the case of Puntland discussed here, though representing state propositions at vastly different scales, might both be located on an ascending track in this sense. But within a future-oriented perspective state-ness also needs to be conceptualized with regard to the global institutional complexes which encompass and transform existing states, by and large causing a relative decline of state-ness, and by implication of state autonomy. In some instances the locus of power and governance may then shift to other less directly identifiable institutional spheres. In the end one may ask in various instances what role will there still be for the state, however defined? The question *Who Governs?*, once provocatively raised by Robert Dahl as an entry point in an altogether different kind of context with diffuse boundaries for governance (Dahl 1961), now appears fitting in situations where weak state bodies lack the capacity and tools to prepare and monitor much needed policy interventions while, around the corner, staff of multilateral bodies are busily engaged in multifaceted policy preparations and negotiations with partner organizations ostensibly for the benefit of the respective host government.

In the present era we may witness several of the tendencies described here as concurrent waves, coinciding and occasionally leading on to new interactive dynamics: micro state formation of sorts in the margin of the extension of superpower hegemony, collapse and attempts at state resurgence as in some African cases, global designs for state restructuring prompting ethnic revivals, emergent European state forms paralleled at some levels by a growing sense of common identity, at another by resurging national and regional identities to resist the homogenization perceived to be an essential part of it. All these trends feed on, and in turn give rise to, recurrent attempts to reinterpret the past so as to fit the present, as well as to efforts to give institutional identities a semblance of continuity with the past – invariably with particular preferred readings of past history. Together the plurality of all these currents offer an impressive, at times bewildering mix of ongoing tendencies and counter-tendencies, in principle shaping and reshaping state contours as they have done since time immemorial.

It has been very evident that the experience with state forms and the manner in which they develop and discharge their roles has been mixed and uneven in many constellations. Among them, national states and states aspiring to become 'national' have appeared especially prone to conflict and fragmentation, not per definition, but as an outflow of the contradictory aspirations that have been bestowed upon them in many cases. In recent times the record of 'national' states, with exceptions, thus has been pretty dismal and can hardly serve as a model of inspiration. These experiences instead invite reconsideration of the proposition of the post-national state. The idea of state per se, in its most essential core, seems necessary and inevitable towards the organization of collective activities at different levels. While with all its mixed success so far the European Union represents an attempt at creating some kind of post-national state, various traumatic and insoluble conflict situations in Africa such as in the larger Horn increasingly call for consideration of some kind of post-national arrangement or another. Whether in the end any of these would lead to more meaningful alternatives than what we have now is impossible to say. The only thing certain is that the idea of the nation-state does not offer the solution.

We have also noted that one key dynamic factor within this overall dynamic field is the range of global forces – institutional, political and economic – which are presently impacting on states and state structures in all corners of the world. Closely related are the active interventionism and apparent neo-imperialist ambitions for the sake of preserving 'world order' displayed by today's remaining superpower. By their very nature, the latter ambitions may be placed alongside those of a sobering row of precursor imperialist designs, illustrated by empire building from Roman to Ottoman, colonial and Soviet times, among others. Striving towards expansion of the realm of power has always been intrinsic to the idea of empire, and constitutes a key facet of their collective histories. One crucial difference pointing to a qualitative change compared to most previous imperialisms, however, lies in the a priori unrestricted global scale and agenda of the present drive. Today's global imperialism, among other things, seeks to enhance its influence by exercising control over strategic multilateral global institutions based in Washington and elsewhere.

The concentration of power and scale of operations of today's version of imperialism is simply unprecedented historically. It is crucial to look at the implications this has for the kind of coping strategies which people in different parts of the world are trying to develop, and to see what linkages, organizational alternatives and global perspectives they seek to construct. Global power configurations will continuously shift and take on new dimensions and patterns. Empires generally have proved inherently fragile, and in the end may fade away or collapse.

The current danger of imperial ovrestretch does not remain restricted to the single remaining superpower. Parallel to that, the world's main development institutions must beware of issuing ever more elaborate policy prescriptions to state systems across the globe. It is not just that, in the end, any such system of new style Indirect Rule is unlikely to remain sustainable. Above all, state systems in the South must regain the autonomy of action they require to be able to effectively act as seats of policy initiation and co-ordination.

Bibliography

Abrahamsen, Rita, 2000, *Disciplining Democracy: Development Discourse and Good Governance in Africa*, London/New York: Zed Books.

Ahrens, Joachim, 1999, 'Towards a Post-Washington Consensus: The Importance of Governance Structures in Less Developed Countries and Economies in Transition', in Niels Hermes and Wiemer Salveda, eds, *State, Society and Development: Lessons for Africa?*, CDS Report No. 7, University of Groningen.

Alavi, H., 1972, 'The State in Post-Colonial Societies: Pakistan and Bangladesh', *New Left Review*, 74: 59–81.

——, 1989, 'Nationhood and the Nationalities in Pakistan', *Economic and Political Weekly*, 8 July, 1527–1534.

Anderson, Benedict, 1983, *Imagined Communities: Reflections on the Origin and Spread of Nationalism*, London: Verso.

Applegate, Celia, 1990, *A Nation of Provincials: The German Idea of Heimat*, Berkeley/Los Angeles: University of California Press.

Arora, Guljit, K., 2004, *Globalisation and Reorganising Indian States: Retrospect and Prospects*, New Delhi: Bookwell.

Azarya, Victor, 1988, 'Re-ordering State–Society Relations: Incorporation and Disengagement', in Donald Rothchild and Naomi Chazan, eds, *The Precarious Balance: State and Society in Africa*, Boulder/London: Westview Press.

Bastian, Sunil and Robin Luckham, eds, 2003, *Can Democracy be Designed? The Politics of Institutional Choice in Conflict-torn Societies*, London: Zed Books.

Baumann, P., 1998, '*Panchayati Raj* and Watershed Management in India: Constraints and Opportunities', ODI Working Paper No. 114, London: Overseas Development Institute.

Baxi, Upendra and Bhikhu Parekh, eds, 1995, *Crisis and Change in Contemporary India*, New Delhi/Thousands Oaks/London: Sage Publications.

Bayart, J -F., 1986, 'Civil Society in Africa', in P. Chabal, ed., *Political Domination in Africa: Reflection on the Limits of Power*, Cambridge: Cambridge University Press.

——, 1989, *L'Etat en Afrique*, Paris: Fayard.

——, 1993, *The State in Africa: The Politics of the Belly*, London: Longman.

Bayart, Jean-François, Stephen Ellis and Béatrice Hibou, eds, 1999, *Criminalization of the African State*, London: James Currey.

Behrend, H., 1991, 'Is Alice Lakwenya a Witch?', in Holger Bernt Hansen and Michael Twaddle, eds, *Changing Uganda: The Dilemmas of Structural Adjustment and Revolutionary Change*, London: James Currey.

Berdal, Mats and David Malone, eds, 2000, *Greed and Grievance: Economic Agendas in Civil Wars*, Boulder/London: Lynne Rienner Publishers.

Berting, Jan, 1997, 'European Social Transformations and European Culture', in Martin Doornbos and Sudipta Kaviraj, eds, *Dynamics of State Formation: India and Europe Compared*, New Delhi/London: Sage Publications.

Berting, Jan and Hans van de Braak, 1988, 'L'identité culturelle de la "Grande Europe": Mythe ou réalité?', CRE-Action, 2: 49–65.

Bowra, C. M., 1967, *Primitive Song*, London: Weidenfeld and Nicolson.

Boyce, James, 1996, *Economic Policy for Building Peace: The Lessons of El Salvador*, Boulder/London: Lynne Rienner Publishers.

Bratton, M., 1989, 'The Politics of Government NGO Relations in Africa', *World Development*, 17/4: 569–587.

Breman, Jan, 1977, 'Het nieuwe regime in Azie; de overgang van de weke naar de harde staat', *Internationale Spectator*, 31/3: 137–151.

Brenner, N., 1999, 'Globalisation as Reterritorialisation: The Rescaling of Urban Governance in the European Union', *Urban Studies*, 36: 431–451.

Brett, E. A., 1991, 'The Resistance Council System and Local Administration in Uganda: A Background', in H. Bernt Hansen and M. Twaddle, eds, *Changing Uganda: The Dilemmas of Structural Adjustment and Revolutionary Change*, London: James Currey.

Brons, Maria, 2001, *Society, Security, Sovereignty and the State: Somalia, from Statelessness to Statelessness?*, Utrecht: International Books.

Bruyning, L. F., 1991, 'De Europese gedachte: gebruik en misbruik van een idee', in W. A. F. Camphuis and C. G. J. Wildeboer Schut, eds, *Europese Eenwording in Historisch Perspectief*, Zaltbommel: Europese Bibliotheek.

Buijtenhuijs, Robert, 1984, 'Is Tsjaad nog een Staat?', in Wim van Binsbergen and Gerti Hesseling, eds, *Aspecten van Staat en Maatschappij in Afrika: Recent Dutch and Belgian Research on the African State*, Research Report No. 22, Leiden: African Studies Centre.

Buzan, B., 1991, *People, States and Fear: The National Security Problem in International Relations*, Sussex: Wheatsheaf Books.

Campbell, Bonnie, ed., 2005, *Qu'allons-nous faire des pauvres?*, Paris: L'Harmattan.

Canetti, Elias, 1973, *Crowds and Power*, Harmondsworth: Penguin Books.

Carneiro, Robert L., 1987, 'Cross-currents in the Theory of State Formation', *American Ethnologist*, 14: 756–770.

Castells, M., 1996, *The Rise of the Network Society. The Information Age: Economy, Society and Culture*, vol. 1, Oxford: Blackwell.

——, 1997, *The Power of Identity. The Information Age: Economy, Society and Culture*, vol. 2, Oxford: Blackwell.

——, 2000, *End of Millenium, Second edition, The Information Age: Economy, Society and Culture*, vol. 3, Oxford: Blackwell.

Chabal, P., 1986, 'Introduction: Thinking about Politics in Africa', in P. Chabal, ed., *Political Domination in Africa: Reflection on the Limits of Power*, Cambridge: Cambridge University Press.

Chakravarty, Sukhamoy, 1987, *Development Planning: The Indian Experience*, Oxford: Clarendon Press.

Chatterjee, Partha, 1994, *The Nation and Its Fragments: Colonial and Postcolonial Histories*, Delhi: Oxford University Press.

Chossudovsky, Michel, 1999, 'Human Security and Economic Genocide in Rwanda', in C. Thomas and P. Wilkins, eds, *Globalization, Human Security and the African Experience*, Boulder/London: Lynne Rienner Publishers.

Claessen, H. J. M., 1993, 'Ongezocht en Onbedoeld? Over het Ontstaan van de (Vroege) Staat', *Antropologische Verkenningen*, 12/4:1–9.

——, 2000, *Structural Change: Evolution and Evolutionism in Cultural Anthropology*, Leiden: CNWS.

Claessen H. J. M. and Peter Skalnik, eds, 1978, *The Early State*, The Hague: Mouton.

Cliffe, L., 1977, ' "Penetration" and Rural Development in the East African Context', in L. Cliffe, J. S. Coleman and M. Doornbos, eds, *Government and Rural Development in Africa: Essays on Political Penetration*, The Hague: Martinus Nijhoff.

——, 1987, 'The Debate on African Peasantries', *Development and Change*, 18/4: 625–635.

Cliffe, L. and John Saul, eds, 1972, *Socialism in Tanzania*, vols 1 and 2, Dar es Salaam: East African Publishing House.

Cliffe, L. and Robin Luckham, 2000, 'What Happens to the State in Conflict?: Political Analysis as a Tool for Planning Humanitarian Assistance', *Disasters*, 24/4: 291–313.

Cliffe, L., J. S. Coleman and M. Doornbos, eds, 1977, *Government and Rural Development in Africa: Essays on Political Penetration*, The Hague: Martinus Nijhoff.

Coleman, J. S., 1977, 'The Concept of Political Penetration', in L. Cliffe, J. S. Coleman and M. Doornbos, eds, *Government and Rural Development in Africa: Essays on Political Penetration*, The Hague: Martinus Nijhoff.

Collier, Paul, 1999, 'Doing Well Out of War', Working Paper. Washington DC: World Bank.

——, 2001, 'Rebellen zijn Gewoon Criminelen' ('Rebels are simply criminals') (Interview), *Internationale Samenwerking*, 04: 22–25.

Conable, Barber B., 1992, 'Opening Remarks', in World Bank, *Proceedings of the World Bank Annual Conference on Development Economics 1991*, Washington DC: World Bank.

Corbridge, Stuart and John Harriss, 2000, *Reinventing India: Liberalization, Hindu Nationalism and Popular Democracy*, Cambridge: Polity Press.

Cowgill, G. L., 1988, 'Onward and Upward with Collapse', in N. Yoffee and G. L. Cowgill, eds, *The Collapse of Ancient States and Civilisations*, Tuscon: The University of Arizona Press.

Dahl, Robert, 1961, *Who Governs?: Democracy and Power in an American City*, New Haven/London: Yale University Press.

Das, Arvind N., 1992, *India Invented: A Nation in the Making*, New Delhi: Manohar.

Daube, D., 1963, *The Exodus Pattern in the Bible*, All Souls Studies, London: Faber and Faber.

——, 1972, *Civil Disobedience in Antiquity*, Edinburgh: Edinburgh University Press.

De Gaay Fortman, Bas, 2000, 'Dilemmas of Transition: The Case of Albania', in Fatos Tarifa and Max Spoor, eds, *The First Decade and After: Albania's Transition and Consolidation in the Context of Southeast Europe*, The Hague: CESTRAD/ Institute of Social Studies.

Degnbol-Martinussen, John, 2001, *Policies, Institutions and Industrial Development: Coping with Liberalization and International Competition in India*, London: Sage.

Deutsch, Karl, W., 1966, *The Nerves of Government: Models of Political Communication and Control*, Second edition, New York: The Free Press of Glencoe.

De Wit, Annemieke and Riemke Rip, 2003, 'Voting for Democracy: Presidential Elections in Somaliland April 2003', Alkmaar: Alkmaars Steunpunt Vluchtelingen.

Dharma, P. L., 2003, 'Identities versus Identities', *Third Concept*, November: 46–50.

Dijkzeul, Dennis, 2003, 'Programs and the Problems of Participation', in Dennis Dijkzeul and Yves Beigbeder, eds, *Rethinking International Organizations: Pathology and Promise*, New York/Oxford: Berghahn Books.

——, 2004, 'Old Optimism and New Threats', in Dennis Dijkzeul, ed., *Between Force and Mercy: Military Action and Humanitarian Aid*, Bochumer Schriften zur Friedenssicherung und zum Humanitären Völkerrecht 50, Berlin: Berliner Wissenschafts-Verlag.

Disasters, 2000, Special Issue on 'Complex Political Emergencies: Grasping Contexts, Seizing Oppurtunities', 24/4.

Doornbos, Martin, 1970, 'Kumanyana and Rwenzururu: Two Responses to Ethnic Inequality', in R. I. Rotberg and A. A. Mazrui, eds, *Protest and Power in Black Africa*, New York: Oxford University Press.

——, 1972, 'Some Conceptual Problems Concerning Ethnicity in Integration Analysis', *Civilizations*, 22/2: 263–283.

——, 1974, 'A Note on Time Horizons and Interpretations of African Political Change', *The African Review*, 4/4: 557–564.

——, 1975, 'The Shehu and the Mullah: The Jihads of Usuman Dan Fodio and Mohammed Abdallah Hassan in Comparative Perspective', *Genève-Afrique*, 14/20.

——, 1977, 'Recurring Penetration Strategies in East Africa', in L. Cliffe, J. S. Coleman and M. Doornbos, eds, *Government and Rural Development in East Africa: Essays on Political Penetration*, The Hague: Martinus Nijhoff.

——, 1990, 'The African State in Academic Debate: Retrospect and Prospect', *Journal of Modern African Studies*, 28/2: 179–198.

——, 1993, 'Pasture and Polis: The Roots of Political Marginalization of Somali Pastoralism', in John Markakis, ed., *Conflict and the Decline of Pastoralism in the Horn of Africa*, Basingstoke/London: Macmillan.

——, 1994, 'State Formation and Collapse: Reflections on Identity and Power', in Martin van Bakel, Renée Hagesteijn and Pieter van de Velde, eds, *Pivot Politics: Changing Cultural Identies in Early State Formation Processes*, Amsterdam: Het Spinhuis.

——, 1995, 'State Formation Processes under External Supervision: Reflections on "Good Governance" ', in Olav Stokke, ed., *Aid and Political Conditionality*, EADI Book Series 16, London: Frank Cass.

——, 2000, 'African Multipartyism and the Quest for Democratic Alternatives: Ugandan Elections, Past and Present', in Jan Abbink and Gerti Hesseling, eds, *Elections and Election Observation in Sub-Saharan Africa*, London: Macmillan.

——, 2000, *Institutionalizing Development Policies and Resource Strategies in Eastern Africa and India: Developing Winners and Losers*, Basingstoke/London: Macmillan.

——, 2000, 'When is a State a State?: Exploring Puntland', in Piet Konings, Wim van Binsbergen and Gerti Hesseling, eds, *Trajectoires de libération en Afrique contemporaine*, Paris: Karthala.

——, 2001, *The Ankole Kingship Controversy: Regalia Galore Revisited*, Kampala: Fountain Publishers.

——, 2002, 'Somalia: Alternative Scenarios for Political Reconstruction', *African Affairs*, 101: 93–107.

——, 2003, ' "Good Governance": The Metamorphosis of a Policy Metaphor', *Journal of International Affairs*, 57/1.

Doornbos, Martin, 2005, 'Transizione e legittimitanegli Stati africani, con parti-colare riferimento a Somalia e Uganda', in Anna Maria Gentili e Mario Zamponi, eds, *Stato, democrazia e legittimità: Le transizioni politiche in Africa, America Latina, Balcani, Medio Oriente*, Rome: Carocci editore.

Doornbos, Martin and Matt Bryden, 1998, 'WSP (War-torn Societies Project) in Somalia', Geneva: UNRISD/WSP.

Doornbos, Martin and Sudipta Kaviraj, eds, 1997, *Dynamics of State Formation: India and Europe Compared*, New Delhi/London/Thousands Oaks: Sage Publications.

Doornbos, Martin and J. Markakis, 1991, 'The Crisis of Pastoralism and the Role of the State', in J. Stone, ed., *Pastoral Economics in Africa and Long Term Responses to Drought*, Aberdeen: Aberdeen University African Studies Group.

——, 1994, 'Society and State in Crisis: What Went Wrong in Somalia?', in M. A. Mohamed Salih and Lennart Wohlgemuth, eds, *Crisis Management and the Politics of Reconciliation in Somalia*, Uppsala: Nordiska Afrikainstitutet.

Doornbos, Martin and K. N. Nair, eds, 1990, *Resources, Institutions and Strategies: Operation Flood and Indian Dairying*, New Delhi: Sage Publications.

Doornbos, Martin, Wim van Binsbergen and Gerti Hesseling, 1984, 'Constitutional Form and Ideological Content: The Preambles of French-Language Constitutions in Africa', in Wim van Binsbergen and Gerti Hesseling, eds, *Aspecten van Staat en Maatschappij in Afrika, Recent Dutch and Belgian Research on the African State*, Research Report No. 22, Leiden: African Studies Centre.

Doornbos, Paul, 1984, 'Enkele Opmerkingen over Tsjaad en Noord-Oost Afrika', in Wim van Binsbergen and Gerti Hesseling, eds, *Aspecten van Staat en Maatschappij in Afrika: Recent Dutch and Belgian Research on the African State*, Research Report No. 22, Leiden: African Studies Centre.

Dorward, David, 2003, 'Insights from a Trip Through Puntland: Civil Society in a "Quango-state" ', *Australasian Review of African Studies*, 25/1: 38–51.

Dower, Nigel, 2003, *An Introduction to Global Citizenship*, Edinburgh: Edinburgh University Press.

Drechsler, Wolfgang, 2005, 'The Re-emergence of "Weberian" Public Administration after the Fall of New Public Management: The Central and Eastern European Perspective', *Halduskultuur*, Tallinn: Tallinn University of Technology/Institute of Humanities and Social Sciences.

Duverger, Maurice, 1963, *Political Parties*, New York: Science Editions, John Wiley.

Dwivedi, Ranjit, 2001, 'Environmental Movements in the Global South: Issues of Livelihood and Beyond', *International Sociology*, 16/1: 11–31.

Eisenstadt, S., 1988, 'Beyond Collapse', in N. Yoffee and George L. Cowgill, eds, *The Collapse of Ancient States and Civilisations*, Tucson: University of Arizona Press.

Ellis, Stephen, 2001, 'War in West Africa', *The Fletcher Journal of World Affairs*, 25/2: 33–39.

Ellis, Stephen and Gerrie ter Haar, 2004, *Worlds of Power: Religious Thought and Political Practice in Africa*, London: Hurst & Company.

El Zain, M., 2006, *Environmental Scarcity, Hydro-politics and the Nile: The Pivotal Position of the Sudan*, PhD Dissertation, The Hague: Institute of Social Studies.

Eriksen, Stein Sundstol, 2001, 'The State We're In: Recent Contributions to the Debate on State–Society Relations in Africa', *Forum for Development Studies*, 28/2: 289–307.

Foreman, Shepard, Steward Patrick and Dirk Salomons, 2000, *Recovering from Conflict: Strategy for an International Response*, New York: Center on International Cooperation, New York University.

Fortes, M. and E. E. Evans-Pritchard, eds, 1940, *African Political Systems*, Oxford: Oxford University Press.

Galbraith, J. K., 1978, *The Affluent Society*, Second edition, Harmondsworth: Penguin Books.

Geertz, C., 1963, 'The Integrative Revolution: Primordial Sentiments and Civil Politics in the New States', in C. Geertz, ed., *Old Societies and New States: The Quest for Modernity in Asia and Africa*, New York/London: The Free Press.

Geschiere, P., 1982, *Village Communities and the State: Changing Relations among the Maka of Southeastern Cameroon since the Colonial Conquest*, London/Boston, MA: Kegan Paul International.

Gibbon, E., 1952, *The Decline and Fall of the Roman Empire*, New York: The Viking Press.

Gibbon, Peter, 1993, 'The World Bank and the New Politics of Aid', in Georg Sørensen, ed., *Political Conditionality*, London: Frank Cass.

Gordon, David, C., 1989, *Images of the West*, Savage, MD: Rowman & Littlefield Publishers.

Green, R. H., 1981, 'Magendo in the Political Economy of Uganda: Pathology, Parallel System or Dominant Submode of Production?', *Discussion Paper 64*, Institute of Development Studies, Brighton: University of Sussex.

Gregory, Derek, 2004, *The Colonial Present: Afghanistan, Palestine, Iraq*, Oxford: Blackwell Publishing.

Haas, Ernst, B., 1967, 'The Uniting of Europe and the Uniting of Latin America', *Journal of Common Market Studies*, 5/4: 315–343.

Habermas, Jürgen, 2001, 'Why Europe Needs a Constitution', *New Left Review*, 11, September–October: 1–16.

Hagmann, Tobias, 'War Against Terrorism?', unpublished manuscript, 12 December 2004.

Hardt, Michael and Antonio Negri, 2000, *Empire*, Cambridge, Massachusets: Harvard University Press.

Harris, Marvin, 1978, *Cannibals and Kings: The Origin of Cultures*, Glasgow: Fontana.

Harrison, Graham, 1999, 'Clean-ups, Conditionality and Adjustment: Why Institutions Matter in Mozambique', *Review of African Political Economy*, 26/81: 323–334.

——, 2001, 'Post-Conditionality Politics and Administrative Reform: Reflections on the Cases of Uganda and Tanzania', *Development and Change*, 32/4: 657–679.

Heinrich, Wolfgang, 1997, *Building the Peace: Experiences of Collaborative Peacebuilding in Somalia 1993–1996*, Uppsala: Life and Peace Institute.

Held, David, 1992, 'Democracy: From City-States to a Cosmopolitan Order?', *Political Studies*, Special Issue on Prospects for Democracy, 40: 10–39.

——, 1995, *Democracy and the Global Order: From the Modern State to Global Governance*, Cambridge: Polity Press.

Helman, Gerald B. and Steven R. Ratner, 1992–93, 'Saving Failed States', *Foreign Policy*, 89: 3–20.

Herbst, Jeffrey, 1996, 'Responding to State Failure in Africa', *International Security* 21/3: 120–144.

Hettne, B. H., 1991, 'Ethnicity and Development: An Elusive Relationship', paper presented at Nordic Conference for South Asian Studies: Ethnicity, Identity and Development in South Asia, Denmark, 11–13 October 1991.

Hinton, Peter, 1979, 'The Karen, Millennialism, and the Politics of Accommodation to Lowland States', in Charles F. Keyes, ed., *Ethnic Adaptation and Identity: The Karen on the Thai Frontier with Burma*, Philadelphia: Institute for the Study of Human Issues.

Hirst, Paul, 2001, *War and Power in the 21st Century*, Cambridge: Polity Press.

Hirst, Paul and Grahame Thompson, 1999, *Globalization in Question: The International Economy and the Possibilities of Governance*, Cambridge: Polity Press.

Hobsbawm, Eric and Terrence Ranger, eds, 1983, *The Invention of Tradition*, Cambridge: Cambridge University Press.

Hofer, Katharina, 2002, 'Das Movement in Uganda: Afrikanischer Sonderweg oder Irrweg?', *SWP-Studies*, S 40, Berlin: Stiftung Wissenschaft und Politik.

Höhne, Markus, V., 2004, 'Political Identity and the State: Reflections on Emerging State Structures and Conflict in Northern Somalia', paper presented at the *Somali Studies Association Conference*, Aalborg, 2004.

Hopkins, Terrence, K. and Immanuel Wallerstein, 1970, 'The Comparative Study of National Societies', in Amitai Etzioni and Fredric L. Dubow, eds, *Comparative Perspectives: Theories and Methods*, Boston: Little, Brown and Company.

Horne, Donald, 1986, *The Public Culture: The Triumph of Industrialism*, London: Pluto Press.

Hout, Wil, 2004, 'Political Regimes and Development Assistance: The Political Economy of Aid Selectivity', *Critical Asian Studies*, 36/4: 591–613.

Hyden, G., 1980, *Beyond Ujamaa in Tanzania: Underdevelopment and an Uncaptured Peasantry*, London: Heinemann.

——, 1983, *No Shortcuts to Progress: African Development Management in Perspective*, London: Heinemann.

——, 1986, 'The Anomaly of the African Peasantry', *Development and Change*, 17/4: 677–705.

——, 1987, 'Final Rejoinder', *Development and Change*, 18/4: 661–667.

Hyden, Göran and Michael Bratton, eds, 1992, *Governance and Politics in Africa*, Boulder, Co: Rienner.

Jackson, Robert, H., 1990, *Quasi-States: Sovereignty, International Relations and the Third World*, Cambridge: Cambridge University Press.

Jackson, Robert, H. and Carl G. Rosberg, 1982, 'Why Africa's Weak States Persist: the Empirical and the Juridical in Statehood', *World Politics*, 35/1: 1–24.

Jacquin-Berdal, Dominique and Martin Plaut, eds, 2005, *Unfinished Business: Ethiopia and Eritrea at War*, Lawrenceville, NJ/Asmara: Red Sea Press.

John, Peter, 2000, 'The Europeanisation of Sub-national Governance', *Urban Studies*, 37/5–6: 877–894.

Journal of Peace Research, 2004, Special Issue on Civil War in Developing Countries, vol. 39/4.

Junne, Gerd and Willemijn Verkoren, eds, 2005, *Post-conflict Development: Meeting New Challenges*, Boulder/London: Lynne Rienner Publishers.

Juergensmeyer, Mark, 1994, *Religious Nationalism Confronts the Secular State*, Delhi: Oxford University Press.

Kak, Subhash, 2005, 'Sunil Khilnani's *The Idea of India*', India Travelog Bookshelf, http://www.iw.sify.com/travel/bookshelf/book16-khilnani.html, accessed 21 June 2005.

Kanbur, Ravi and Todd Sandler, 1999, *The Future of Development Assistance: Common Pools and International Public Goods*, Economic Development Policy

Essay No. 25, Washington, DC: Overseas Development Council; Baltimore, MD: Johns Hopkins University Press.

Kaplan, R. D., 1994, 'The Coming Anarchy: How Scarcity, Crime, Overpopulation and Disease are Rapidly Destroying the Social Fabric of Our Planet', *Atlantic Monthly*, February, 44–76.

Kasfir, N., 1984, 'State, *Magendo* and Class Formation in Uganda', in N. Kasfir, ed., *State and Class in Africa*, London: Frank Cass.

——, 1986, 'Are African Peasants Self-Sufficient?', *Development and Change*, 17/2: 335–357.

——, 1989, 'The Uganda Elections of 1989: Populism and Democratisation', International Conference on Uganda: Structural Adjustment and Revolutionary Change, Roskilde, Denmark, 20–23 September.

Kaviraj, Sudipta, 1989, 'On the Construction of Colonial Power: Structure, Discourse, Hegemony', IDPAD Occasional Paper 2.

——, 1995, 'Religion, Politics and Modernity', in Upendra Baxi and Bhiku Parekh, eds, *Crisis and Change in Contemporary India*, New Delhi/Thousands Oaks/London: Sage Publications.

——, 1997, 'The Modern State in India', in Martin Doornbos and Sudipta Kaviraj, eds, *Dynamics of State Formation: India and Europe Compared*, New Delhi/London: Sage Publications.

Keane, John, 1998, *Civil Society: Old Images, New Visions*, Cambridge: Polity.

——, 2003, *Global Civil Society?*, Cambridge: Cambridge University Press.

Khilnani, Sunil, 1999, *The Idea of India*, Second edition, Harmondsworth: Penguin Books.

Kitchen, K., 1993, 'The Land of Punt', in T. Shaw, P. Sinclair, B. Andah and A. Okpoko, eds, *The Archaeology of Africa: Food, Metals and Towns*, London: Routledge.

Konings, P., 1986, 'The State and the Defence Committees in the Ghanaian Revolution, 1981–1984', in W. van Binsbergen, F. Reyntjes and G. Hesseling, eds, *State and Local Community in Africa*, Brussels: Centre d'Etudes et de Documentation Africaine (CEDAF).

Kooiman, Jan, ed., 1993, *Modern Governance: New Government-Society Interactions*, London/Newbury Park/New Delhi: Sage Publications.

Kothari, Rajni, 1988a, *State Against Democracy: In Search of Humane Governance*, New Delhi: Ajanta Publications.

——, 1988b, *Rethinking Development: In Search of Humane Alternatives*, New Delhi: Ajanta Publications.

Krader, Lawrence, 1968, *Formation of the State*, Englewood Cliffs, NJ: Prentice Hall.

Kumar, Ravinder, 1997, *State Formation in India: Retrospect and Prospect*, in Martin Doornbos and Sudipta Kaviraj, eds, *Dynamics of State Formation: India and Europe Compared*, New Delhi/London: Sage Publications.

Laitin, David, D. and Said S. Samatar, 1987, *Somalia: Nation in Search of a State*, Boulder, CO: Westview Press.

Landell-Mills, Pierre and Ismail Serageldin, 1991, 'Governance and the External Factor', Staff Paper, World Bank Annual Conference on Development Economics 1991, and in World Bank, 1992, *Proceedings of the World Bank Annual Conference on Development Economics 1991*, Washington DC: World Bank.

Landsberger, Henry, A., 1968, 'The Role of Peasant Movements and Revolts in Development: An Analytical Framework', *Bulletin of the International Institute for Labour Studies*, 4: 8–85.

Leach, Edmund, 1960, 'The Frontiers of "Burma" ', *Comparative Studies in Society and History*, 3/1: 49–68.

Leftwich, Adrian, 1994, 'Governance, The State and the Politics of Development', *Development and Change*, 25/2: 363–86.

Lemarchand, R., 1988, 'The State, the Parallel Economy and the Changing Structure of Patronage Systems', in D. Rothchild and N. Chazan, eds, *The Precarious Balance: State and Society in Africa*, Boulder/London: Westview Press.

Lensink, Robert and Howard White, 2001, 'Are there Negative Returns to Aid?', in Niels Hermes and Robert Lensink, eds, *Changing the Conditions for Development Aid: A New Paradigm?*, London: Frank Cass.

Lewis, I. M., 1961, *A Pastoral Democracy: A Study of Pastoralism and Politics among the Northern Somali of the Horn of Africa*, London: Oxford University Press.

——, 1980, *A Modern History of Somalia: Nation and State in the Horn of Africa*, London: Longman Group.

Leys, C., 1975, *Underdevelopment in Kenya: the Political Economy of Neo-Colonialism, 1964–1971*, London: Heinemann.

——, 1976, 'The "Overdeveloped" Post Colonial State: A Re-evaluation', *Review of African Political Economy*, 5, January–April, 39–48.

Lieven, Dominic, 2000, *Empire: The Russian Empire and Its Rivals*, New Haven/London: Yale University Press.

Lijphart, Arend, 1985, *Power-Sharing in South Africa*, Policy Papers in International Affairs No. 24, Berkeley: University of California/Institute of International Studies.

Little, Peter, D., 2003, *Somalia: Economy Without State*, Oxford: James Currey.

Liu, Xinru, 1988, *Ancient India and Ancient China: Trade and Religious Exchanges AD 1–600*, Delhi: Oxford University Press.

Livingstone, Ian and Roger Charlton, 2001, 'Financing Decentralized Development in a Low-Income Country: Raising Revenue for Local Government in Uganda', *Development and Change*, 32/1: 77–100.

Lonsdale, John, 1981, 'States and Social Processes in Africa: A Historiographical Survey', *African Studies Review*, 24 (2/3): 139–225.

——, 1986, 'Political Accountability in African History', in Patrick Chabal, ed., *Political Domination in Africa*, Cambridge: Cambridge University Press.

LSE Centre for the Study of Global Governance, 2003, Seminar on 'Legal Imperialism: The New Heart of Darkness?', http://www.lse.ac.uk/Depts/global/Yearbook/legalimperialismseminar.htm, accessed 5 April 2004.

Lund, Christian, 2001, 'Precarious Democratization and Local Dynamics in Niger: Micro-politics in Zinder', *Development and Change*, 32/5: 845–69.

——, 2006, 'Twilight Institutions, Public Authority and Political Culture in Local Contexts', *Development and Change*.

Lyons, Terrence and Ahmed I. Samatar, 1995, *Somalia: State Collapse, Multilateral Intervention, and Strategies for Political Reconstruction*, Washington D.C.: The Brookings Institution.

Malik, Yogendra K. and V. B. Singh, 1994, *Hindu Nationalists in India: The Rise of the Bharatiya Janata Party*, New Delhi: Vistaar Publications.

Mamdani, M., 1983, 'The Nationality Question in a Neo-Colony: An Historical Perspective', *Mawazo*, 5/1: 36–54.

——, 1988, 'NRA/NRM: Two Years in Power', Public Lecture, Kampala: Makerere University, March.

Mamdani, M., T. Mkandawire and Wamba-dia-Wamba, 1988, 'Mouvements Sociaux, Mutations Sociales et Lutte pour la Démocratie en Afrique', *CODESRIA Working Paper 1*, CODESRIA: Dakar.

Markakis, J., 1987, *National and Class Conflicts in the Horn of Africa*, Cambridge: Cambridge University Press.

Martin, Denis-Constant, 1992, 'The Cultural Dimensions of Governance', in World Bank, 1992, *Proceedings of the World Bank Annual Conference on Development Economics 1991*, Washington DC: World Bank.

Martinussen, John, 1998a, 'The Limitations of the World Bank's Conception of the State and the Implications for Institutional Development Strategies', *IDS Bulletin*, 29/2: 67–74.

——, 1998b, 'Challenges and Opportunities in Danish Development Co-operation', in Bertel Heurlin and Hans Mouritzen, eds, *Danish Foreign Policy Yearbook 1998*, Copenhagen: Danish Institute of International Affairs.

Mazrui, A. A., 1967, 'Tanzaphilia: A Diagnosis', *Transition*, 6/31: 20–26.

——, 1989, 'Privatization versus the Market: Cultural Contradictions in Structural Adjustment', International Conference on Uganda: Structural Adjustment and Revolutionary Change, Roskilde, Denmark, 20–23 September.

——, 1995, 'The African State as a Political Refugee: Institutional Collapse and Human Displacement', *International Journal of Refugee Law*, 7: 21–36.

Mehler, Andreas and Claude Ribaux, 2000, *Crisis Prevention and Conflict Management in Technical Cooperation: An Overview of the National and International Debate*, Wiesbaden: Universum Verlagsanstalt/Deutsche Gesellschaft für Technische Zusammenarbeit (GTZ).

Meillassoux, E., 1977, *Terrains et Théories*, Paris: Editions Anthropos.

Meynen, Wicky and Martin Doornbos, 2004, 'Decentralising Natural Resource Management: A Recipe for Sustainability and Equity?', *European Journal of Development Research*, 16/1: 235–254.

Mill, John Stuart, 1970, 'Two Methods of Comparison', from *A System of Logic*, New York: Harper and Row Publishers, 1888, reproduced in Amitai Etzioni and Fredric L. Dubow, eds, *Comparative Perspectives: Theories and Methods*, Boston: Little, Brown and Company.

Milliken, Jennifer, ed., 2003, *State Failure, Collapse and Reconstruction*, Oxford: Blackwell Publishers.

Minister voor Ontwikkelingssamenwerking, 2003, *Aan Elkaar Verplicht: Ontwikkelingssamenwerking op weg naar 2015*, The Hague.

Mitchell, James and Graham Leicester, 1999, *Scotland, Britain and Europe: Diplomacy and Devolution*, Edinburgh: The Scottish Council Foundation.

Mkandawire, Thandika, 2004, 'Can Africa Have Developmental States?', in Simon Bromley, Maureen Mackintosh, William Brown and Marc Wuyts, eds, *Making the International: Economic Interdependence and Political Order*, London: Pluto Press.

Mohanty, Manoranjan, 1989, 'Secularism: Hegemonic and Democratic', *Economic and Political Weekly*, 3 June, 1219–20.

Moore, David, 2000, 'Levelling the Playing Fields and Embedding Illusions: "Post-Conflict" Discourse and Neo-liberal "Development" in War-torn Africa', *Review of African Political Economy* 27/83:11–28.

Moore, Jonathan, 1996, *The UN and Complex Emergencies*, Geneva: UNRISD/WSP.

Moore, Mick, 1999, 'Taxation and Political Development', in John Degnbol-Martinussen, ed., 'External and Internal Constraints on Policy Making: How Autonomous are the States?', *Occasional Paper No. 20*, International Development Studies, Roskilde University.

Morss, E. R., 1984, 'Institutional Destruction Resulting from Donor and Project Proliferation in Sub-Saharan African Countries', *World Development*, 12/4: 465–470.

Motyl, Alexander J., ed., 1992, *Thinking Theoretically about Soviet Nationalities: History and Comparison in the Study of the USSR*, New York: Columbia University Press.

Mudimbe, V. S., 1988, *The Invention of Africa: Gnosis, Philosophy and the Order of Knowledge*, London: James Currey.

Mugaju, Justus and J. Oloka-Onyango, eds, 2000, *No-Party Democracy in Uganda: Myths and Realities*, Kampala: Fountain Publishers.

Myrdal, Gunnar, 1968, *Asian Drama: An Inquiry into the Poverty of Nations*, Harmondsworth: Penguin Books.

Nandy, A., 1987, *Traditions, Tyranny and Utopias: Essays in the Politics of Awareness*, Delhi: Oxford University Press.

Netherlands Ministry of Foreign Affairs, 2000, *Afrika Notitie*, The Hague.

Newman, Peter, 2000, 'Changing Patterns of Regional Governance in the EU', *Urban Studies*, 37/5–6: 895–908.

Ninsin, K. A., 1988, 'Three Levels of State Reordering: The Structural Aspects', in D. Rothchild and N. Chazan, eds, *The Precarious Balance: State and Society in Africa*, Boulder, CO/London: Westview Press.

Nordhaug, Kristen, 2002, 'Globalisation and the State: Theoretical Paradigms', *European Journal of Development Research*, 14/1: 5–27.

O'Gorman, E., 1961, *The Invention of America: An Inquiry into the Historical Nature of the New World and the Meaning of Its History*, Bloomington: University of Indiana Press.

Ohmae, Kenichi, 1995, *The End of the Nation State: The Rise of Regional Economies*, London: Harper Collins.

Oomen, T. K., 2004, *Nation, Civil Society and Social Movements: Essays in Political Sociology*, New Delhi/Thousands Oaks/London: Sage Publications.

Oyugi, W. O., E. S. Atieno Odhiambo, M. Chege and A. K. Gitonga, eds, 1988, *Democratic Theory and Practice in Africa*, London: James Currey/Portsmouth, NH: Heinemann.

Pfaff, William, 1995, 'A New Colonialism? Europe Must Go Back into Africa', *Foreign Affairs* 74/1: 2–6.

Pohjolainen Yap, Katri, 2001, *Uprooting the Weeds: Power, Ethnicity and Violence in the Matabeleland Conflict 1980–1987*, PhD Dissertation, University of Amsterdam.

Prazauskas, Algis, 1991, 'Ethnic Conflicts in the Context of Democratizing Political Systems', *Theory and Society*, 20: 581–602.

Pronk, Jan, P., 2001, 'Aid as a Catalyst', *Development and Change*, 32/4: 611–29.

Ranger, T., 1983, 'The Invention of Tradition in Colonial Africa', in E. Hobsbawm and T. Ranger, eds, *The Invention of Tradition*, Cambridge: Cambridge University Press.

Ravenhill, J., 1988, 'Adjustment with Growth: A Fragile Consensus', *The Journal of Modern African Studies*, 26/2:179–210.

Ray, D. I., 1986, *Ghana: Politics, Economics and Society*, London: Frances Pinter.

Reno, William, 1998, *Warlord Politics and African States*, Boulder: Lynne Rienner.

Reno, William, 2000a, 'Shadow States and the Political Economy of Civil Wars', in Mats Berdal and David Malone, eds, *Greed and Grievance: Economic Agendas in Civil Wars*, Boulder: Lynne Rienner.

Reno, William, 2000b, 'War, Debt, and the Role of Pretending in Uganda's International Relations', *Occasional Paper*, University of Copenhagen: Centre of African Studies.

Ribot, Jesse, C., 2002, 'African Decentralization: Local Actors, Powers and Accountability', UNRISD Programme on Democracy, Governance and Human Rights Paper No. 8, Geneva: UNRISD.

Richards, Paul, 1996, *Fighting for the Rainforest: War, Youth and Resources in Sierra Leone*, Oxford: James Currey.

Robertson, A. F., 1978, *Community of Strangers: A Journal of Discovery in Uganda*, London: Scolar Press.

Robertson, Robbie, 2003, *The Three Waves of Globalization: A History of a Developing Global Consciousness*, London: Zed Books.

Rolandsen, Oystein, H., 2005, *Guerilla Government: Political Changes in the Southern Sudan during the 1990s*, Uppsala: Nordiska Afrikainstitutet.

Roscoe, John, 1923, *The Banayankole*, Cambridge: Cambridge University Press.

Rothchild, D. and N. Chazan, eds, 1988, *The Precarious Balance: State and Society in Africa*, Boulder and London: Westview Press.

Rubin, Barnett, R., 2002, *The Fragmentation of Afghanistan: State Formation and Collapse in the International System*, Second edition, New Haven: Yale University Press.

Ruigrok, Inge, 2004, 'Negotiating Governance: Politics, Decentralisation and Cultural Ideology in Post-war Angola', PhD project, Free University, Amsterdam.

Said, Edward, W., 1978, *Orientalism*, London: Routledge & Kegan Paul.

Saith, A., 1985, 'Primitive Accumulation, Agrarian Reform and Socialist Transitions: An Argument', in A. Saith, ed., *The Agrarian Question in Socialist Transformation*, London: Frank Cass.

Salih, M. A. Mohamed, 1999, *Environmental Politics and Liberation in Contemporary Africa*, Dordrecht/Boston/London: Kluwer Academic Publishers.

Saul, J. S., 1972, 'Class and Penetration in Tanzania', in L. Cliffe and J. S. Saul, eds, *Socialism in Tanzania*, vol. 1, Nairobi: East African Publishing House.

Schaeffer, Robert, K., 1999, *Severed States: Dilemmas of Democracy in a Divided World*, Lanham, MD: Rowman and Littlefield Publishers.

Schech, Susanne and Jane Haggis, 2000, *Culture and Development: A Critical Introduction*, Oxford: Blackwell Publishers.

Scholte, Jan Aart, 1998, 'The International Monetary Fund and Civil Society: An Underdeveloped Dialogue', *ISS Working Paper* 272, The Hague: Institute of Social Studies.

Scott, James, C., 1998, *Seeing Like a State: How Certain Schemes to Improve the Human Condition Have Failed*, New Haven/London: Yale University Press.

Seddon, D., 1989, 'Riot and Rebellion in North Africa: Political Responses to Economic Crisis in Tunisia, Morocco and Sudan', in B. Berberoglu, ed., *Power and Stability in the Middle East*, London: Zed Press.

Sen, Amartya, 2002, 'The Predicament of Identity', *Biblio: A Review of Books*, March–April: 45–50.

Service, Elman R., 1975, *Origins of the State and Civilisation*, New York: Norton.

Sharma, Jyotirmaya, 2003, *Hindutva: Exploring the Idea of Hindu Nationalism*, New Delhi: Viking/Penguin Books.

Shaw, T. M., 1986, 'Ethnicity as the Resilient Paradigm for Africa: From the 1960s to the 1980s', *Development and Change*, 17/4: 587–605.

Sheik-Ali, Abdi, 1993, *Divine Madness: Mohammed Abdille Hassan (1856–1920)*, London: Zed Books.

Shivji, I. G., 1975, *Class Struggles in Tanzania*, Dar es Salaam: Tanzania Publishing House.

Shumway, Nicolas, 1991, *The Invention of Argentina*, Berkeley/Los Angeles: University of California Press.

Siedentop, Larry, 2001, *Democracy in Europe*, Harmondsworth: Penguin Books.

Simonse, Simon, 1992, *Kings of Disaster: Dualism, Centralism and the Scapegoat King in South-eastern Sudan*, Leiden: Brill.

Singh, Manmohan, address at University of Oxford upon receiving an Honorary Doctorate in Civil Law, 8 July 2005.

Skocpol, Theda, 1979, *States and Social Relations: A Comparative Analysis of France, Russia and China*, Cambridge: Cambridge University Press.

Slaughter, Anne-Marie, 2005, *A New World Order*, Princeton, NJ: Princeton University Press.

Smith, Anthony, D., 1986, *The Ethnic Origins of Nations*, Oxford: Blackwell.

Smith, William and Adrian Wood, 1984, 'Patterns of Agricultural Development and Foreign Aid to Zambia', *Development and Change*, 15/3: 405–434.

Sogge, David, 2005, 'African Civil Domains: Realities and Mirages', in Caroline Suransky, Ireen Dubel and Henk Manschot, eds, *Global Civil Society, World Citizenship and Education*, Amsterdam: SWP Publishers.

Sørensen, Georg, ed., 1993, *Political Conditionality*, London: Frank Cass.

Sørensen, Georg, 1995, 'Conditionality, Democracy and Development', in Olav Stokke, ed., *Aid and Political Conditionality*, London: Frank Cass.

Stacey, Tom, 2003, *Tribe: The Hidden History of the Mountains of the Moon – An Autobiographical Study*, London: Stacey International.

Stavenhagen, R., 1991, 'The Ethnic Question: Some Theoretical Issues', Geneva: UNRISD.

Stern, Theodore, 1968, '*Ariya* and the Golden Book: A Millenarian Buddhist Sect among the Karen', *Journal of Asian Studies*, 27/2: 297–328.

Stiglitz, Joseph, 2002, *Globalization and Its Discontents*, London: Penguin Books.

Stokke, Olav, ed., 1995, *Aid and Political Conditionality*, EADI Book Series 16, London: Frank Cass.

Storey, Andy, 2001, 'Structural Adjustment, State Power and Genocide: The World Bank and Rwanda', *Review of African Political Economy* 28/89: 365–386.

Strange, Suzan, 1996, *The Retreat of the State*, Cambridge: Cambridge University Press.

Stremlau, John, 1998, *People in Peril: Human Rights, Humanitarian Action, and Preventing Deadly Conflict*, New York: Carnegie Corporation.

Swamy, Subramanian, 2003, *Economic Reforms and Performance: China and India in Comparative Perspective*, Delhi: Konark Publishers.

Tainter, J., 1988, *The Collapse of Complex Societies*, Cambridge: Cambridge University Press.

Tarifa, Fatos and Max Spoor, eds, 2000, *The First Decade and After: Albania's Transition and Consolidation in the Context of Southeast Europe*, The Hague: CESTRAD/ Institute of Social Studies.

Ter Haar, Gerrie, 2000, 'Rats, Cockroaches and People Like Us: Views of Humanity and Human Rights', Inaugural Address, Institute of Social Studies, The Hague.

Terray, E., 1972, *Marxism and 'Primitive' Societies: Two Studies*, New York: Monthly Review Press.

Thapar, Romila, 2003, 'History as Politics', reproduced from the Professor Athat Ali Memorial lecture at the Aligarh Muslim University on 8 February 2003, titled 'History and Contemporary Politics in India', *indiatogether.org.*

Thoden van Velzen, H. U. E., 1977, 'Staff, Kulaks and Peasants: A Study of a Political Field', in L. Cliffe, J. S. Coleman and M. Doornbos, eds, *Government and Rural Development in East Africa: Essays on Political Penetration*, The Hague: Martinus Nijhoff.

Tilly, Charles, 1990, *Coercion, Capital and European States, AD 990–1990*, Oxford: Blackwell.

Törnquist, Olle, 1999, *Politics and Development: A Critical Introduction*, London, Thousand Oaks, New Delhi: Sage Publications.

Touraine, Alain, 1981, *The Voice and the Eye: An Analysis of Movements*, Cambridge: Cambridge University Press.

Tripp, Charles, 2002, *A History of Iraq*, Cambridge: Cambridge University Press.

Twaddle, M., 1985, 'Decolonization in British Africa: A New Historiographical Debate?', *Occasional Paper 1*, Centre for African Studies, University of Copenhagen.

Uganda Government, 2000, *Uganda Participatory Poverty Assessment Report: Learning from the Poor*, Kampala: Ministry of Finance, Planning and Economic Development.

Utting, P., ed., 1994, *Between Hope and Insecurity: The Social Consequences of the Cambodian Peace Process*, Geneva: UNRISD.

Uvin, Peter, 1993, ' "Do as I Say, Not as I Do": The Limits of Political Conditionality', in Georg Sørensen, ed., *Political Conditionality*, London: Frank Cass.

Van Binsbergen, Wim and Gerti Hesseling, eds, 1984, *Aspecten van Staat en Maatschappij in Afrika: Recent Dutch and Belgian Research on the African State*, Research Report No. 22, Leiden: African Studies Centre.

Van der Hoeven, Rolph, 1999, '*Assessing Aid* and Global Governance', in Niels Hermes and Robert Lensink, eds, *Changing the Conditions for Development Aid: A New Paradigm?*, London: Frank Cass.

Van Kersbergen, Kees and Frans van Waarden, 2001, 'Shifts in Governance: Problems of Legitimacy and Accountability', The Hague: MagW, Social Science Research Council.

Vaughan-Whitehead, D., 1999, *Albania in Crisis: The Predictable Fall of the Shining Star*, Cheltenham: Edward Elgar.

Verwimp, Philip, 2003, 'An Economic Profile of Peasant Perpetrators of Genocide: Micro-level Evidence from Rwanda', Economic Research Seminar Paper, 23 October 2003, The Hague: Institute of Social Studies.

Villain Gandossi, C., 1990, 'Le concept de l'Europe dans le processus de la CSCE: Une approach interdisciplinaire', in K. Bochmann, C. Villain Gandossi, K. Bochmaner, M. Metzeltin and C. Schäffner, eds, *Le Concept d'Europe dans le Processus de la CSCE*, Tübingen: Günther Narr.

Wade, Robert, 1996, 'Globalization and Its Limits: The Continuing Economic Importance of Nations and Regions', in S. Berger and R. Dore, eds, *Convergence or Diversity? National Models of Production and Distribution in a Global Economy*, Ithaca, NY: Cornell University Press.

Wallerstein, I., 1974, *The Modern World System*, vol. 1, London: Academic Press.

Waterbury, J., 2002, *The Nile Basin: National Determinants of Collective Action*, New Haven: Yale University Press.

Waterman, Peter, 2002, 'Reflections on the 2nd World Social Forum in Porto Allegre: What's Left Internationally?', *ISS Working Paper* 362, The Hague: Institute of Social Studies.

——, 2003, 'Place, Space and the Reinvention of Social Emancipation on a Global Scale: Second Thoughts on the Third World Social Forum', *ISS Working Paper* 378, The Hague: Institute of Social Studies.

Weiss, Linda, 1998, *The Myth of the Powerless State: Governing the Economy in a Global Era*, Cambridge: Polity.

West, Deborah, L., 2005, 'Combating Terrorism in the Horn of Africa and Yemen', Program on Intrastate Conflict and Conflict Resolution, Belfer Center for Science and International Affairs, John F. Kennedy School of Government, Harvard University, Cambridge, Massachusets.

Wetenschappelijke Raad voor het Regeringsbeleid (WRR), 2001, *Ontwikkelingsbeleid en Goed Bestuur*, Rapporten aan de Regering No. 58, The Hague: Sdu Uitgevers.

Williams, G., 1987, 'Primitive Accumulation: The Way to Progress?', *Development and Change*, 18/4: 637–659.

World Bank, 1992, *Proceedings of the World Bank Annual Conference on Development Economics 1991*, Washington DC: World Bank.

——, 1997, *World Development Report*, Oxford: Oxford University Press.

——, 1998, *Assessing Aid: What Works, What Doesn't and Why*, Washington DC: World Bank.

Wuyts, M., 1989, 'Economic Management and Adjustment in Mozambique', *Working Paper* 52, Institute of Social Studies, The Hague.

Yannis, Alexandros, 1997, 'State Collapse and Prospects for Political Reconstruction and Democratic Governance in Somalia', *African Yearbook of International Law*, 5: 23–47.

——, 1999, 'State Collapse and the United Nations: Universality at Risk?', *Brassey's Defence Yearbook*, 109: 174–99.

——, 2002, 'State Collapse and Its Implications for Peace-Building and Reconstruction, *Development and Change*, 33/5: 817–835.

Yoffee, N., 1988, 'Orienting Collapse', in N. Yoffee and George L. Cowgill, eds, *The Collapse of Ancient States and Civilisations*, Tucson: The University of Arizona Press.

Yoffee, N. and George L. Cowgill, eds, 1988, *The Collapse of Ancient States and Civilisations*, Tucson: The University of Arizona Press.

Yurlova, E. S., 1990, *Scheduled Castes in India*, New Delhi: Patriot Publishers.

Zartman, I. William, ed., 1995, *Collapsed States: The Disintegration and Restoration of Legitimate Authority*, Boulder: Lynne Rienner.

Index